NO HUMAN
INVOLVED

NO HUMAN INVOLVED

THE SERIAL MURDER OF BLACK WOMEN AND GIRLS AND THE DEADLY COST OF POLICE INDIFFERENCE

CHERYL L. NEELY

BEACON PRESS
BOSTON

BEACON PRESS
Boston, Massachusetts
www.beacon.org

Beacon Press books
are published under the auspices of
the Unitarian Universalist Association of Congregations.

28 27 26 25   8 7 6 5 4 3 2 1

This book is printed on acid-free paper that meets the uncoated paper
ANSI/NISO specifications for permanence as revised in 1992.

Text design and composition by Kim Arney

Library of Congress Cataloging-in-Publication Data

Names: Neely, Cheryl L., author.
Title: No human involved : the serial murder of Black women and girls
and the deadly cost of police indifference / Cheryl L. Neely.
Description: Boston : Beacon Press, [2025] |
Includes bibliographical references.
Identifiers: LCCN 2024023595 (print) | LCCN 2024023596 (ebook) |
ISBN 9780807004562 (hardcover) | ISBN 9780807004586 (ebook)
Subjects: LCSH: African American women—Violence against—Press
coverage—United States. | African American girls—Violence
against—Press coverage—United States. | Murder victims—United
States. | Police—United States—Attitudes. | Racism in
law enforcement—United States.
Classification: LCC HV6250.4.W65 N44 2025 (print) | LCC HV6250.4.W65
(ebook) | DDC 362.88082—dc23/eng/20240716
LC record available at https://lccn.loc.gov/2024023595
LC ebook record available at https://lccn.loc.gov/2024023596

And for every Michelle, there's a . . .
Gwendolyn . . .
An Andrea . . .
A Christine . . .
A Caren . . .
A Princess . . .
A Desiree . . .
An Alianna . . .
A woman or girl who dies at the hands of men.
Who see them as objects . . . or possessions.
Or prey.
And play God.
And, equally egregious,
Police fail to see as human.

—CHERYL NEELY

For Courtney Neeley

CONTENTS

PROLOGUE

O N THE EVENING of December 19, 2019, I received a text that I stared at in disbelief as the words sent a chill down my spine. "Hey Cheryl," the message began. "He pleaded guilty today. 50–100 years [in prison]. Sentencing is Jan. 8 . . . He had confessed to 7 murders." The sender of the message was Jodie Kenney, the cousin of my murdered friend and high school classmate. Sixteen-year-old Michelle Kimberly Jackson's life was brutally snuffed out when she was sexually assaulted and strangled in Detroit, Michigan, in January 1984. Her body had been found in an abandoned garage only steps from a wintry bus stop where she waited alone for a bus to school. Several weeks prior to the text, I attended the initial arraignment of Kennith Dupree, a now seventy-three-year-old unemployed sexual offender who had been incarcerated for a number of felonies over his lifespan, including rape. After listening to graphic testimony from detectives at the scene and the medical examiner's report, I was too traumatized to attend the court hearing in which he would plead guilty to my friend's rape and murder. For over thirty years, I periodically imagined what her last moments must have been like. The fear and all-consuming terror she must have felt in that cold dark space was a psychic death that no doubt preceded the physical one.

Now reading Jodie's text, I was sickened by news that illuminated a malevolent pattern I discovered while conducting research for my first book, which centered on the violent deaths of Black women being overlooked by both the media and the police. The book, *You're Dead, So What? Media, Police, and the Invisibility of Black Women as Victims of Homicide* (Michigan State University Press, 2015) was predicated on my PhD dissertation and examined how Black females were ignored by both media and law enforcement in contrast to their white counterparts. Michelle's death is one of many sex-related homicides that have plagued a misogynoiristic (a hatred of Black women) and patriarchal society where violence against Black women is an almost everyday occurrence. And yet her story is also a microcosm and reflection of a larger system of racial indifference and police corruption, as well as an overall disdain for women of color in America by the criminal justice system. The murders of Michelle and other Black girls and women—both cisgender and trans—shine a discomfiting light on the reality that Black lives simply do not matter in a country whose inception of the American Dream was literally built upon the plunder of Black bodies, and the sexual commodification of Black female reproduction to proliferate slave labor.

The creation of stereotypes that rendered Black females, irrespective of age, as unrapeable and, consequently, fodder for sexual predation, has led to an increased vulnerability for Black girls and women. Collectively, they make up approximately 7 percent of the US population, yet they comprised 36 percent of 2018 homicide victims in the US and thus were three times more likely to die by homicide compared to white females.[1] Nevertheless, their deaths are often ignored by mainstream media and are treated apathetically by law enforcement officials. And it is this disregard of, this irreverence for, Black women and girls by police, that exposes them to an even greater likelihood that they will remain disproportionately vulnerable to lethal violence.

To wit, an acutely disturbing element of Michelle's murder case (as well as of others) was that an innocent man, Eddie Joe Lloyd, spent seventeen years in prison after being forced into a false confession by Detroit homicide investigators. Therefore, while police allowed Lloyd to languish behind bars for a murder he did not commit, the real killer, Kennith Dupree, continued to prey upon other victims. Thirty-five years after killing Michelle Jackson, he confessed to the murders of seven additional women while being interrogated by cold case detectives. Where was the sworn duty of police officers to serve and protect *these* women from a cold-blooded murderer?

Sadly, in my research on Black female homicides, the pattern of repeated victimization is not unusual, as authorities routinely conduct subpar investigations of crimes against them. Pervasive in the cases of homicide I studied was a consistent complaint that police did not treat the killings as though they warranted a thorough and serious investigation, and, when victims were initially reported missing, police either dismissed their cases as that of runaways or assumed that the victim abused drugs or engaged in sex work.

There was the case of Romona Moore, a twenty-one-year-old Brooklyn college student kidnapped by two men described by the press as psychopaths and gang members who held her in a basement that they fashioned into a torture chamber, raping her repeatedly before bludgeoning her to death.[2] As police refused to initiate a search for Romona, despite her mother's desperate pleas, her killers senselessly murdered her, then dumped her body under an abandoned ice cream truck only blocks from her home. Two days later, they kidnapped and raped a fifteen-year-old girl, who managed to escape after the two men fell asleep. She had overheard them complain about the lack of coverage Romona Moore's disappearance received on the evening news and expressed the desire for notoriety after her body was found, saying, "We better make the news."[3]

There were the frustrated Black women in Los Angeles that confronted the LAPD for failing to warn the community about a predator who terrorized Black women for close to twenty years, and who even took a ten-year hiatus before resuming his killing spree. Lonnie Franklin Jr. killed at least nine Black women and a fifteen-year-old girl before he was finally apprehended and convicted for his crimes. Until his death in March 2020, he remained a suspect in the deaths of many additional victims, as more than one hundred photos of unidentified women were found in his home by police.

Even when I interviewed Jodie Kenney and Carlotta Jackson (Michelle's mother) in 2013, they informed me that when she filed a missing person report, police dismissed Carlotta's concern about her missing daughter as an overreaction, instead suggesting that her daughter had run away with a boyfriend that the family did not know about. Carlotta described her desperation to make the police understand the urgency of her daughter's disappearance. She offered to show them Michelle's report cards, hoping her honor student status would indicate that she was a responsible girl. But it was to no avail. Unfortunately, Carlotta's actions are not unusual. Research has shown that missing Black teens are often assumed to be runaways; therefore, parents are made to feel that they must prove that their children warrant an immediate search.[4] The frightened mother begged police to look for Michelle, especially considering that, that year, a series of rapes of schoolgirls had plagued Detroit. The police became so annoyed with Carlotta's requests to search for her missing daughter that one officer barked, "Look for her yourself if you don't think we are moving fast enough."[5] His callous retort left Carlotta with little hope of law enforcement locating Michelle. She and Jodie decided to search for her on their own the next morning. They tragically found her, deceased, her body brutalized, in a dilapidated garage.

When considering Michelle Jackson's case, one can argue that law enforcement's dereliction of duty is killing Black women.

As a sociologist who studies Black women as forgotten victims of violence, I feel it is important to note that this is emotionally difficult subject matter. The thrust of my previous book demonstrated that Black females are invisible as victims. The thesis of this text is to highlight the danger of this invisibility and, thus, to provide a humane depiction of an inhumane phenomenon. In order to do so, I must tell Michelle's story, as well as those of several others whose lives were not only cut short but who also received either delayed justice or no justice at all from the very institution designed to deliver it. More pointedly, it is an even greater tragedy that there exists a pervasive culture within law enforcement that is not compelled to prevent other Black girls and women from suffering the same fates. These stories are multitudinous, and most will never be told.

This book seeks to change that.

INTRODUCTION

O N MAY 5, 1962, an impassioned Malcolm X stood at a podium to officiate the funeral of Ronald Stokes, a Nation of Islam (NOI) member who was shot and killed by Los Angeles police while attempting to surrender during an altercation between law enforcement and members of an NOI mosque. Malcolm X was bitterly disappointed that Elijah Muhammad, the NOI's founder and leader, would not allow retaliation against the police and—contrary to Malcolm X's call for vengeance—ordered the grieving members to "stand down."[1] The Nation of Islam, a Black political and religious movement founded in 1930, urged a separate nation-state within the US for Black Americans, stressing economic independence and entrepreneurship.

As Malcolm surveyed the room, he began to speak, projecting his voice to emphasize the gravity of his message. In his powerful speech, he railed against anti-blackness and Black self-hatred, asking the more than two thousand funeral attendees, "Who taught you to hate the texture of your hair . . . the color of your skin . . . the shape of your nose and lips?" He urged not only the men in the audience to stand in defense of themselves, but also, most pointedly, the women of his race. The words he spoke that day exposed the tragic plight of Black women in America, whose intersectional identity culminates in a daily battle against both sexism and racism, with little escape from either:

> The most disrespected person in America is the Black woman. The most unprotected person in America is the Black woman. The most neglected person in America is the Black woman.[2]

While there are countless examples of America's lack of concern for the victimization of Black women, one case involving police violence against a Black woman exemplified the conundrum to a particularly shocking degree. In March 2020, twenty-six-year-old Breonna Taylor, a Black EMT, was shot and killed by police in her own home in Louisville, Kentucky. Police led a botched no-knock warrant on Breonna's home shortly after 12 a.m. while she slept in bed with her boyfriend, Kenneth Walker, who would insist that police did not announce themselves before using a battering ram to break down the front door. Walker fired a shot at the door in response to what he believed to be a home invasion, and police returned fire through it, hitting Taylor five times. She died within minutes from her injuries, while police frantically provided medical care to their wounded fellow officer, who had been shot in the leg, allegedly by the bullet fired from Walker's weapon. According to Walker, he watched Breonna "cough and struggle to breathe" for at least five minutes after the shooting, while police forbade her immediate medical intervention from the ambulance technicians who arrived on the scene.[3] Breonna received no medical assistance for a full twenty minutes after the shooting. None of the officers involved have been charged directly in her death. The only charge filed was brought against former detective Brett Hankison, for wanton endangerment, as he fired shots that entered a neighboring apartment. No one has been charged, considered responsible for, or indicted by a grand jury for the death of Breonna Taylor. While the drywall in the adjoining apartment received justice, Breonna Taylor received none. Incredulously, the initial police report noted that "no injuries" were sustained in the incident, dismissing the fact that Breonna was killed by five bullets *and* that one of the officers was shot. Black communities were left feeling outraged and frustrated at another example of Black lives having little to no value in American society.

Following the announcement that there would not be any direct charges for Taylor's death, it was reported that Daniel Cameron, the fifty-first attorney general of Kentucky and first Black person to serve in the position, withheld evidence from the grand jury that could have led to indictments against the officers. For many Black Americans, this was a bitter disappointment. Many assumed that Cameron's race and shared identity as a Black man would ensure justice, but, ultimately, his actions reflected his position as an agent for the criminal justice system—a system that is built to protect law enforcement first while upholding systemic racism.

Because of the close working relationship between their office and law enforcement, prosecutors are tasked with holding police officers accountable for unlawful acts while still relying on these same officers to provide the evidence required to successfully present criminal cases. As seen with Cameron, this tension can be further compounded when the case has to do with race and when the prosecutor's racial identity aligns with that of the victim, but the prosecutor chooses to remain professionally neutral, despite the racially discriminatory overtones in the case—a choice that, in this instance, was met with intense backlash and scrutiny, particularly from Black Americans.

Moreover, Cameron's handling of Breonna Taylor's murder appeared to frustrate some members of the grand jury. Shortly after the hearing, at least two of the jurors filed a lawsuit to release the audio recordings of the hearings to make the public fully aware of the evidence presented to them. Following the decision to only charge Detective Hankison with wanton endangerment, Daniel Cameron intimated that the decision to forgo charging all of the officers with Taylor's homicide was wholly the result of the grand jury's autonomy, and not because of an anemic presentation of evidence by prosecutors.[4] However, the audiotapes, which were released to the public by order of the court, revealed that jurors were told by Cameron that the officers were justified in shooting into Taylor's apartment. Cameron and other prosecutors did not instruct the jurors to review evidence as to whether or not charges should be brought against the officers in relation to her death. One juror told reporters that a few members asked repeatedly about evidence related directly to Taylor's shooting, yet none was presented.[5] The bulk of the testimony given and evidence shown to the grand jury supported the narrative of a justified police shooting. Breonna Taylor's life was not valued by the state of Kentucky, and Daniel Cameron's refusal to present a case for filing charges in relation to her death highlight an even deeper issue within the American justice system.

Malcolm X's pessimistic proverb about this nation's failure to protect the lives of Black women isn't mitigated even when the chief prosecutorial officer is a Black man.

The indifference to Black women as human beings worthy of defense and respect is not a new phenomenon. Enslaved Black women were bought, sold, raped, exploited, and, in many cases, violently killed since their arrival on the shores of Jamestown, Virginia in 1619. More than four hundred years later, Black women continue to remain unprotected. Simply put, there is not, nor has there ever been, a safe place in this nation for Black women. This is especially true within the purview of law enforcement: an institution whose very existence originates from slave patrol and apprehension.

This is shown in cases like that of Breonna Taylor, and so many other Black female victims of police brutality who are profiled in the vital book *Invisible No More* by civil rights attorney and scholar Andrea J. Ritchie. In it, Ritchie expertly recounts the shocking sexual and physical violence committed by police against Black women, including queer and gender nonconforming teens, that is rarely known. She specifically looks at how these young people are subjected to violence and even death at the hands of police.[6] The persistent narrative of Black criminality obfuscates law enforcement's ability to consider Black people as victims rather than perpetrators of violent crime.

Particularly in the case of Black women, there is the tendency to see them as criminals rather than victims in comparison to their white counterparts, even when they are killed by a serial offender.[7] This reality was further crystallized in the investigation of a series of murders of Black women in Los Angeles during the 1980s, when police officers used the acronym NHI to denigrate the victims of these horrifying homicides: an abbreviation for "No Human Involved" that is used as a classification in homicide cases comprising victims whom police view as having little to no value as human beings. The perpetrator of these crimes, Lonnie Franklin Jr., raped and murdered twelve Black women, including a fifteen-year-old girl, over the course of thirty years. It was believed by residents of the community that the killings were not solved for so long because police were indifferent to and dismissive of the victims.[8]

At the nucleus of this inhumane treatment is America's long and persistent history of refusing to *see* and *respect* the humanity of Black people. As Patrisse Khan-Cullors articulates in her powerfully poignant memoir, *When They Call You a Terrorist*, "Black people are the only humans in this nation ever legally designated, after all, as not human."[9] This begs the question that if people of African descent in the US are not human, what are they?

Not human, *but chattel slaves.*

Not human, *but a criminal threat.*

Not human, *but a perpetual tax burden.*

Not human, *but people whose lowest caste rank raises the status of every other group.*

In the eyes of the Los Angeles Police Department, these women were essentially nonpersons. They had been rendered disposable by the very organization that had the responsibility to not only find their killer but also to protect future victims from Franklin's reign of terror. Sadly, many cases of serial homicide with Black female victims have been treated in like fashion—ignored and dismissed by homicide investigators as the bodies piled up. When victims simply don't matter and are relegated to the invisible margins of a racist society, serial killers who prey on them go undetected and kill with impunity.[10] When my high school friend Michelle was murdered at sixteen years of age, police investigating her murder wrongly accused and convicted an innocent man. To them, it didn't matter that other young women and girls were at risk to suffer the same brutal violence at the hands of the man who killed her. They just wanted to close the case.

Following the Detroit police's decades of negligence, the real killer, Kennith Dupree, apprehended more than thirty years later, confessed to the murders of seven other victims. When police are indifferent to violence toward Black women, it is reasonable to expect that those responsible fail to be deterred in targeting them as prey.

Eldridge Cleaver, the appointed "minister of information" for the Black Panther Party in the late 1960s, admitted in his best-selling memoir, *Soul on Ice*, that he deliberately selected the bodies of Black women to "practice" sexual assault on before raping his most desired victims—white women: "I became a rapist. To refine my technique and modus operandi, I started out by practicing on black girls in the ghetto—in the black ghetto where dark and vicious deeds appear not as aberrations or deviations from the norm, but as part of the sufficiency of the Evil of a day. . . . I did this consciously, deliberately, willfully, methodically."[11]

Interestingly, Cleaver's memoir was lauded as a "groundbreaking classic," earning effusive praise and spawning numerous academic discussions and book reviews about white oppression and the call for Black resistance through revolution and social movements.[12] Yet, most notably, there was little to no outrage about his admitted (albeit later reformed) "career" as a sex offender whose malevolent hunt for white female rape victims was first predicated on the bodies of Black ones.

Law enforcement's failure to recognize the humanity of Black female victims of violence is even more egregiously evident when the victim is a Black trans woman. In stories on transgender violence, themes of police indifference and even blatant ridicule toward victims who report this violence are ubiquitous, culminating in a chilling refusal to help Black trans women who seek help from law enforcement.[13] Additionally, mainstream media compounds their invisibility by deadnaming and misgendering Black female trans victims, which obscures the actual number of murders.[14] In 2020 alone, at least forty-four Black trans women were murdered, and few arrests have been made.[15] Within the span of nine days, six Black trans women were murdered between June 25 and July 3, 2020—tragically, at the close of LGBTQ Pride Month.[16] With at least three of these unsolved killings taking place in the same community in Louisiana, some may wonder if these women were the victims of a single offender.

It is a startling fact that, disproportionately, Black trans women have the highest rate of violent and lethal victimization than any other group. According to the National Coalition of Anti-Violence Programs, a group dedicated to collecting data on violence against queer, trans, and gender nonconforming people, between 2010 and 2016 there were 111 murders of trans women in the US, and 72 percent of those victims were Black trans women.[17] Stated more succinctly by Mic, an online news website that tracks transgender hate crimes across the US, while the probability of becoming a homicide victim among the general population is 1 in 19,000, the probability of homicide for a Black trans woman is 1 in 2,600, resulting in them being 7.3 times more likely to die violently than any other group.[18] It is likely that the numbers are higher, but, again, transgender victims are often misgendered at death by police and media. In many cases, sexual and physical violence committed against Black trans women operates in the invisible margins of this community's existence and the overall societal disregard of the trans community's humanity.

Adding to increasing hostility toward trans women is the assault on the rights and protections of the trans community by conservative media and GOP-controlled state legislatures. Several states have considered legislation that denies transgender people even the basic semblance of privacy and safety when using public restrooms in accordance with their expressed gender identity. Instead, these legislators and some members of the public have expressed fear that trans people, particularly trans women, pose a sexual threat to cisgender women in public bathrooms, suggesting that a predatory male could disguise himself as trans to sexually prey on women.[19] In 2016, North Carolina was the only state to successfully pass a bill that targeted trans individuals by requiring that they use specific bathrooms that correspond with their sex assigned at birth or on their birth certificate. However, after receiving backlash and the potential loss of billions of dollars in revenue from boycotts by corporations and national sports teams (notwithstanding condemnation from a majority of the public), the bill was repealed.[20] Undaunted, other Republican-controlled state governments continue to consider bills that would restrict trans people's access to public restrooms.

In February 2021, the Iowa state legislature took up a bill that would ban transgender students from using school restrooms that did not match their sex assigned at birth.[21] The angst and paranoia sparked by the public restroom debate has no doubt contributed to the findings of a 2016 survey that revealed that at least 60 percent of trans people avoid using public restrooms for fear of harassment and violence.[22] Given the extraordinary risk of violence against Black trans women, such restrictions put these women in a particular position of vulnerability, especially in a public environment.

In the chapters ahead, I will lay bare the frightening connection between Black women's vulnerability to violent victimization by serial predators and the role police indifference plays in emboldening the men who target them. In doing so, I examine a number of serial homicide cases involving Black female victims. While it is disturbing to think that there are individuals who kill without consequence because they are confident that their victims have no humanity in the eyes of law enforcement, a number of serial killers have admitted that this is the case. Police refusal to care about Black female victims of homicide allows men to murder them and, subsequently, escape detection by police. The tragically sinister consequence of this is the repeated victimization of Black females by predators with murderous intent.

It's a vicious circle that continues to plague Black communities where vulnerable women are not only disregarded as victims but also, tragically, are viewed by some members of law enforcement as not human at all.

CHAPTER 1

BUT FIRST, MICHELLE

*The Cold Case Murder of My Friend
by a Confessed Serial Killer*

S IX-THIRTY A.M. IN DETROIT, Michigan, January 24, 1984, could be described by all who lived through it as a typically frigid time of day in the Midwest. It was the dead of winter. At that hour, the sky was still midnight black, and the only illumination came from the twinkling ice crystals embedded in snow, or from the occasional streetlight that actually worked, depending on what part of the city you lived in. With a decaying and crime-ridden metropolis where poverty gripped 30 percent of the population—the result of business disinvestment, paltry employment opportunities, white flight, and a controversial and embattled mayor at war with the surrounding suburbs—complaints by city residents about a lack of working light fixtures were commonplace.[1] Despite the temperature, reading at 3 degrees Fahrenheit, most Michiganders were accustomed to bracing for harsh winter weather, bundling up in layers to keep the sharp cut of coldness from reaching their skin. However, the cold that year wasn't the only chill in the air.

Fear riveted the city as unknown rapists stalked its streets, searching for preadolescent and teenaged girls who quickened to school past burned and abandoned structures across an icy landscape. By this time, forty-seven girls had been sexually assaulted since September 1983, the start of the school year. Detroit police strongly suspected that the crimes had been committed by a number of perpetrators, some opportunistically seeking the sexual plunder of young victims as a matter of convenience. "Copycat offenders" was the term touted by media to describe these faceless predators who hid under the cover of early morning darkness.

As Michelle Kimberly Jackson, age sixteen, an honor student at Detroit's Murray-Wright High School, rose from her bed and prepared to dress for school, she was probably more aware of the possible danger that day than in previous school years. In fact, in the days prior to January 24th, as Michelle and I waited for the bus home from school, we discussed our dread about the sexual assaults. The high school had taken to holding weekly assemblies to warn students about the dangers of walking to school alone and accepting rides from strangers. Additionally, female students throughout the city were admonished by teachers in the last hour of classes to stay safe, and flyers with safety tips were posted to the doors at the school's entrance and exits. It was an all-hands-on-deck effort to keep students safe.

Phillip Murray Senior High—named for the first president of the American Steelworkers' Union—opened in 1963 as an all-girls school, adjacent to an all-male school called Wilbur Wright Trade School (named for one of the famous Wright brothers and creators of modern aviation). The two schools merged into one coed campus in 1959 and thereafter became known as Murray-Wright Senior High School. By the time I entered as a freshman in 1980, the Wright building had been refashioned as a vocational training school, where students attended Murray High for academic classes in the morning and then walked two blocks to the Wright Trade School to take courses in cosmetology, woodshop, metalwork, tool and die, and electrical wiring. Michelle was one of many students at Murray (most people simply referred to it by its first name) who opted to take both academic and vocational training courses as part of her curriculum. Murray was located on the west side of Detroit, at the intersection of Warren Avenue and Rosa Parks Boulevard, just on the border of a slowly gentrifying community known as Woodbridge. The remaining neighborhoods surrounding the school reflected the ghostly aftermath of the 1967 rebellion, replete with vacant storefronts where businesses once thrived, and dilapidated homes that landlords had long since abandoned.[2]

Detroit has long struggled with its national reputation as a dangerous city. The ongoing rapes of schoolgirls reinforced the stigma and

sparked outrage among parents, who seized upon city council meetings to demand that police do more. Their anger was not abated by
the then chief of police William Hart's dismissive comments denying
the extent of the crisis and blaming media for framing the rapes as
an epidemic. "There is no crime wave," he said. "There is fear. People are scared as hell."[3]

Interestingly, Hart's denial stood in direct contradiction to comments he had made the month prior, telling reporters during a news
conference that the rapes had reached "epidemic proportions."[4] One
issue that parents saw as a contributing factor to the widespread attacks was the problem of abandoned buildings, which were multiply-
ing exponentially throughout the city. These dilapidated structures
were a primary location for most of the rapes. And, unfortunately,
these menacingly vacant structures could not be avoided, as they appeared on every street en route to our high school.

It was to enter this toxic and ominous environment that Michelle
Jackson left her home that fateful morning and traveled the short distance from where she lived to a lonely, isolated bus stop on Fenkell
Avenue to get to school. After dressing and packing her book bag,
she approached her cousin Jodie Kenney's bedroom door to awaken
her before leaving for school. One year prior, Michelle had moved
in with Jodie after her mother, Carlotta, had to relocate her family
suddenly to a neighborhood that was some distance from Michelle's
high school. Since Jodie lived closer to the school, it was decided that
Michelle would stay with her older cousin during the week and then
go home to her mother's on weekends.[5]

Jodie and Michelle had a close relationship, and Jodie, being the
first cousin of Michelle's mother, was more of an aunt to her. Since
moving in, Michelle often babysat Jodie's son while Jodie worked
during the day and attended college in the evening. According to
Jodie, because the schoolgirl rapes had the city in a frenzy, she said
she drove Michelle to school most mornings and expected that she
would catch the bus home with her friends and other students in the
afternoon. But on January 23, 1984, Jodie, Michelle, and a friend
enjoyed a late night at a Luther Vandross concert at Detroit's ornate
Masonic Temple, grooving to the velvet-voiced singer's greatest hits,

such as, "A House Is Not a Home," "Never Too Much," and "Bad Boy / Having a Party." As the two cousins swooned to the music in the packed auditorium, Jodie told Michelle that, given the lateness of the hour when they got home, Michelle would have to take the bus to Murray-Wright High in the morning.[6]

The next day, at 6:30 a.m., Jodie was still hard asleep when Michelle gently called out to her from the door of her darkened bedroom.

"Jodie . . . you up?" she asked.

As Jodie rose up on her elbows, she could see Michelle, dressed in her waist-length winter jacket, blue jeans, and boots, with the strap of her book bag over her shoulder, ready for school. "I always wanted to see what she was wearing to school," she explained to me later when I interviewed her for this book.

"You leaving out?" Jodie asked groggily. "Sorry about you catching the bus this morning." She yawned. "I'm so tired."

"No problem," Michelle answered. "I'll see you later this afternoon." She reminded Jodie that it was final exams week, and that, despite having a half-day at school and plans with her best friend, Charlotte, when class was dismissed, she would still be home in time to babysit Jodie's son. She then closed the door to Jodie's bedroom and left out the front door of the duplex, locking it behind her.

It would be the last time Jodie would see her young cousin alive.

A GOOD GIRL

Michelle Kimberly Jackson came into this world on a cloudy, 42-degree spring day on May 2, 1967, in Detroit. Ironically, Michelle made her earthly debut on the same day that Black Panther Party founders Huey Newton and Bobby Seale showed up at California's state capitol building in Sacramento along with forty others, armed with shotguns, rifles, and handguns to protest gun control legislation.[7] The events stood in stark contrast to the quiet and self-possessed girl Michelle embodied.

She was the eldest child of Carlotta Jackson, a single mother, who raised her along with Michelle's two younger brothers, Alexander (nicknamed Brady) and DeVon. She was my classmate and friend. At our high school, I was one grade ahead of her, and she and my now deceased younger sister, Suane, were closer in age and relationship. Even after forty years, what I recall most about Michelle was her enviable figure—slender yet curvy: the desired body for most Black girls growing up in Detroit in the 1980s. I used to joke with her while she and I waited for the bus together after school that she made me want to eat a can of biscuits twice a day. My tomboyish physique—hipless and tiny-breasted—garnered no attention from the hormone-raging teen boys who passed me in the noisy halls of Murray, but girls like Michelle were the topic of conversation among them.

She wore no makeup over her flawless complexion, wore a bouncy, feathered haircut with a flipped bang, and had large, bright eyes with a megawatt smile she'd easily offer both friends and strangers. Despite her obvious beauty, I remember a girl who carried her attractiveness with humility and grace.

During an interview, Jodie told me that Michelle's lack of boastfulness was the result of a grandmother who admonished her granddaughters to place an emphasis on internal beauty as opposed to outer appearance. "She would always ask us, 'Are you as pretty on the inside as you are on the outside?' Give her something to think about like personality. How you treat people, you know?"[8] Most of the time she was quiet and observant when my sisters and I waited at the bus stop with her, laughing effortlessly when a topic of conversation amused her, and leaning in conspiratorially when good gossip (usually from Suane) was being shared.

Michelle's closest friend since elementary school was Charlotte Grant. They attended the same middle school, Winterhalter, but then transferred to different high schools, separated for the first time in eight years. For a long time, they had lived next door to each other until a year before Michelle's death, when Carlotta had to find other housing. Charlotte describes her friend's young life as one filled with adult responsibilities. "She helped her mother with her two brothers," she said. "Michelle cooked, cleaned, went to the grocery store, and even did laundry. She was very responsible." Michelle's cousin Jodie Kenney's description of Michelle was similar. "Michelle was a very pleasant person," she recalled. "She wasn't drama . . . she wasn't a diva. She was very close to her cousins, too. She was very low-key, a pretty girl . . . so dependable to be the age she was . . . just so 'taking care of business.'" With only seven years in age difference, Jodie marveled at the maturity of her younger cousin and appreciated the help she provided to Jodie and her son when she moved in with her.

According to Charlotte, the two girls dreamed of attending college, with future plans of enrolling at Michigan State University.[9] Michelle planned to become an accountant, and Charlotte a teacher. Jodie told me of plans to take Michelle on a tour of Historically Black Colleges and Universities (HBCUs) the following summer in the hopes of providing her additional options.

Though Michelle spoke of a career in accounting or finance, Charlotte felt she had a greater calling. "If Michelle was living now, she would be some kind of humanitarian," she said, wistfully. "She loved people! She was almost a mother to Brady [Alexander] and DeVon, and she even mothered me. If she was living now, she would probably be one of those people in the soup kitchen for hours feeding people."

But, sadly, such was not meant to be. The world would never know Michelle Kimberly Jackson the accountant or the Wall Street financier, nor would they know the woman with a social worker's heart who was dedicated to caring for the poor and vulnerable. These dreams were snuffed out in a filthy and vacant garage on a cold winter's morning while Michelle's friends dressed for school and prepared to take final exams.

On the day of her murder, Michelle planned to watch Charlotte cheer at a varsity basketball game at a different high school, Central High. From Charlotte's recollection, her mother placed the front door key to their home in the mailbox on the morning of January 24, 1984, so that Michelle could let herself into Charlotte's house to wait for her to come home from school. They would travel back to the high school for the game. "She was supposed to meet me at my house because she had finals that week," she said, "but she also had a half day." When Charlotte returned home from school and Michelle wasn't there, she started making phone calls to mutual friends in search of her, but none had seen her that day. Disappointed but not yet troubled, she went to the game and cheered. After returning home and having not yet heard from Michelle, she finally phoned Jodie. "I told her that I was going to kick Michelle's butt for not showing up and making me late for the game." Jodie was confused. "She never showed up?! What do you mean, 'I haven't seen her'?"

At that point Jodie decided to call Carlotta, Michelle's mother, to inquire if she had heard from her daughter that day, explaining that Michelle did not show up at her best friend's house as planned. Carlotta said she had not seen or heard from Michelle, so Jodie began calling Michelle's cousins; again, none of them had seen or heard from her. She didn't want to panic Carlotta, but she had to tell her this. Worried, Carlotta told Jodie she would phone the school, while Jodie would reach out to Michelle's high school friends. After finding the girl's phone book in her bedroom, Jodie's anxiety increased as each call was met with a report of not having seen Michelle that day.

My sisters and I also received a call inquiring if we had seen Michelle. I was in my attic bedroom when my sister called up to me from the bottom of the stairs, asking me if I had seen Michelle in school. "She's missing," Suane said, worry coloring her tone. I sat up. "What do you mean . . . 'missing'?" My stomach dropped. I was all too aware of the sexual violence that stalked girls in Detroit that year. We all were. "She'll turn up," Suane reassured me. Even now, in retrospect, I believed that.

I could not have been more wrong.

More hours passed and, still, there was no word from Michelle. Carlotta and her sister decided it was time to go to the police station and file a missing person report. It was approximately 6 p.m., at least six hours since school ended. When Carlotta reported Michelle as missing to police, instead of receiving support and guidance from officers, she was met with questioning. "It was not nice . . . it wasn't nice," Jodie recalled. "They asked [Carlotta], 'How old is she? How well do you know her? She's probably just off with her boyfriend,' you know . . . " Her voice trailed off in frustration.

Unfortunately, in my own research, I have discovered this to be a common occurrence for Black parents with missing children, especially daughters. They routinely receive pushback from police who never seem to be convinced that the child's absence necessitates immediate action.

Michelle's mother protested that her daughter was a good girl, and that Michelle not coming home after school and not being where she was expected was completely out of character. One of the officers became increasingly annoyed that Carlotta expected a search to commence as soon as she filed the report and instead told the family to search for the missing teen on their own.

And that is exactly what Michelle's family did.

Feeling responsible for finding her young cousin, Jodie recalled that first sleepless night. "I don't keep my porch light on, but that night, I kept the porch light on just to make sure she gets home. You know, it's me thinking, 'What can I do?'" The concomitant feelings of helplessness, dread, and terror paralyzed Jodie, who lay awake that night, her mind racing with fervent prayers that the following day would return Michelle back to her family, safe and sound. And, still, something more indicting stalked her. There was the guilt . . . the self-blame that would plague her even more than thirty-six years later. There would be no absolution for it, no matter what any of her family said to her, or even my feeble attempts to exculpate her from it. She continues to blame herself for not taking her cousin to school the day she disappeared.

Before sunrise the next morning, at approximately 5 a.m., Jodie phoned Carlotta. "I'm going to look for her," she cried. "I just can't sit here and do nothing." The terrified mother, who also suffered through a sleepless night, implored Jodie to come and pick up both her and Michelle's aunt Wannie, Carlotta's sister. The three of them, along with Jodie's then-boyfriend Dexter, formed a search party of four and decided to go on foot, retracing Michelle's steps from Jodie's home to the bus stop. "We split up at one point," Jodie explained. "It was fresh snow on the ground. We walked two blocks and looked into backyards. There was an alley that runs on the backside of Fenkell Avenue businesses. Dexter and Carlotta went in a different direction and me and Wannie went right up the alley. The first business was fenced in . . . the next business was a cement garage. We walked in there and . . . " She couldn't finish her sentence. What she saw—what she found—was the body of her beloved cousin, sprawled on the dirty, garbage-strewn floor, naked from the waist down, with her long johns underwear wrapped tightly around her neck. Her lifeless eyes protruded from their sockets, staring straight ahead. Jodie and Wannie's screams led Carlotta and Dexter back in their direction, where each of the three had to restrain the devastated mother from falling on her daughter's body, to gather her in her arms and try in vain to love her back to life.

When police were called to the scene, including the now-embarrassed and contrite officer who had barked at Carlotta to look for Michelle herself, he offered the grieving mother a ride from the crime scene. To this day, Carlotta remains inconsolable and traumatized by her daughter's death. Forty years after Michelle's murder, there has been no erasing the horror of what her daughter endured.

One would think that police would want to find the person responsible for the brutality that ended the life of a teenage girl who was a pillar of support to both her mother and older cousin, a sustaining force for a best friend, a maternal figure to her younger brothers, and an honor student with dreams of college, but, unfortunately, that did not happen. Due to police corruption, an innocent man would soon become another victim in this tragedy, while the same predator that took Michelle's life continued to hunt for victims. Eddie Joe Lloyd, a thirty-seven-year-old father of a young daughter, and a man who had struggled with mental illness for most of his adult life, was coerced into falsely confessing to the murder of Michelle Jackson by Detroit police.

Amid the intensifying media scrutiny on the unabated sexual attacks on Detroit's children, police found in Eddie Joe Lloyd a convenient scapegoat. In total, the detective furnished Lloyd with twenty-seven details that were only known to police and of which Lloyd had no independent knowledge. According to the civil suit filed against the Detroit police by Lloyd's family, once Lloyd was successfully framed for the murder of the teen, "the officers deliberately failed to investigate other leads or suspects," and, as such, it was possible this failure had deadly consequences for the future victims of Jackson's *real* killer.[10]

Lloyd's trial lasted only three days, with the jury deliberating for approximately thirty minutes, reaching a verdict on May 2, 1985, that found Eddie Joe Lloyd guilty of first-degree felony murder and sexual assault. On August 26, 2002, more than seventeen years after his conviction, Lloyd was exonerated of all charges and released from prison with the help and advocacy of the Innocence Project, an organization founded in 1992 by lawyers Peter Neufeld and Barry Scheck to overturn wrongful convictions. Sadly, Lloyd died two years after his release from heart and vascular disease, a condition his family blamed on the stress he endured while incarcerated.[11]

It is astonishing that police would care so little about the gruesome murder of a teenage girl that they would use a false confession to convict an innocent man struggling with mental illness. With public pressure to find her killer, this was an obvious attempt to quell community outrage. Law enforcement's egregious behavior in this case not only reflects the lack of regard they had for the life of Eddie Joe Lloyd but also Michelle Jackson. Sadly, once Lloyd was released, in 2002, the case went cold, and police would not open an investigation into Michelle Jackson's homicide until 2019.

THE REAL KILLER IS CAUGHT, BUT OTHER VICTIMS PAY THE PRICE

At seventy-two years of age and with a height and weight of 5'5" and 140 pounds, Kennith James Dupree presents a disarming figure who would belie the actual threat he posed to the opposite sex. In person, it is difficult to imagine him being capable of the level of sadism the rape and murder of sixteen-year-old Michelle Kimberly Jackson had required. At first glance, Dupree's diminutive stature might not convey a threat. Yet, if one were to take notice of his countenance, perhaps they would see a demeanor reflective in his angry and stony eyes, bereft of sympathy, kindness, or mercy. He was thirty-eight years old when he assaulted and strangled Michelle, and no doubt stronger and more dangerous then.

On a crisp and cloudy morning in November 2019, thirty-five years after Michelle's murder, Kennith Dupree was arraigned in downtown Detroit on charges of felony murder and first-degree criminal sexual assault. I was invited to attend the hearing by Michelle's cousin Jodie, and despite my hesitation at coming face-to-face with Michelle's killer, I felt compelled to do so as her friend, as the author of this book, and as a supporter of her family. The prosecutor, Victoria Shackelford offered us the option to wait in the hall during the testimony, should we become upset during the proceedings. I decided to remain in the courtroom and listen to the facts of the case.

According to the testimony from the initial detectives on the scene, Jodie Kenney, and the medical examiner's report, Michelle's rape and murder was as horrific as we could have imagined. The autopsy revealed that her death was caused by strangulation, and that her brain had swollen resulting from the lack of oxygen. There was petechiae (hemorrhaging) of her eyes where capillaries had ruptured during the attack, and the hyoid bone in her neck was fractured. There was also evidence of vaginal and anal tearing and the presence of semen. And then there was the broken green Ale-8 soda glass bottle found in her rectum. It was a terrifying and agonizing way to die.

Kennith Dupree's confession to the rape and murder of Michelle Jackson was made to detective Isaac Tabb, a Black homicide investigator with the Detroit Police Department for more than thirty-five years.[12] Tabb read the confession in court as the killer sat emotionless, staring at the floor. In graphic detail, Dupree described how he used a knife to threaten Michelle and force her into a nearby abandoned structure, where he raped and then strangled her to stop her screams and cries for help. The detective told the court that when he asked Dupree why he chose Michelle as his victim, he answered, "I don't know. She was just there."

Dupree had a long history of violent sexual predation, so Michelle was not his first victim. In my interview with Detective Tabb, he said he seriously doubted Michelle Jackson was the accused killer's last. On September 28, 1971, a twenty-four-year-old Dupree appealed a rape conviction from a sexual assault he had committed in Detroit in 1970. According to the court docket, the victim testified that Dupree raped her at knifepoint, just as he used a knife in his sexual assault of Michelle. Police sources also confirmed that Dupree was convicted of four rapes prior to his rape-murder of Michelle Jackson. When

Michelle's murder occurred in 1984, given the extent of brutality in the case, it was highly unlikely that she would be his last victim.

When I spoke with Detective Tabb in April 2021, he repeatedly referred to Dupree as a serial killer. I asked him if Dupree confessed to killings beyond Michelle Jackson. He responded, "Yeah . . . he said he did about seven, but I think he did a lot more than that."[13] Tabb went on to say that Dupree took the detective and other investigators to the alleged scenes of other rape-murders he confessed to committing, including the strangulation of a female bus driver in Detroit. When I asked Detective Tabb if he was able to confirm the names of Dupree's other victims, he answered that Kennith Dupree said he was not able to recall the names of the women he allegedly raped and murdered.

Per investigative protocol, Detective Tabb explained that the information provided by Dupree was turned over to the FBI and the Violent Crime Task Force for follow-up. However, due to the ongoing investigation into Dupree's crimes, Detective Tabb could not confirm whether the killings Dupree confessed to had been substantiated by the FBI. Additionally, when I interviewed homicide detective Patricia Little and Wayne County prosecutor Victoria Shackelford, neither would answer my questions regarding Dupree possibly murdering other women, stating that they "could not comment on an ongoing investigation."[14]

Nonetheless, Dupree's confessions about other victims reveal a pattern in many cases involving Black women and girls as murder victims of unknown assailants—some of these killers feel emboldened to target victims that appear to have lesser value in the eyes of police. While Eddie Joe Lloyd languished in a prison cell for more than seventeen years for a crime he did not commit, it is likely that Kennith Dupree continued to prey on other victims. Dupree even expressed to Detective Tabb that he was aware of Lloyd's conviction, feeling both guilty and relieved that he had not been caught for the Jackson homicide.[15]

The Detroit homicide detectives seemed unconcerned that other young girls and women—Black females in particular—were in imminent danger from the man responsible for killing a teenage girl. What seemed to be paramount for police was that they *close* Michelle's homicide case rather than *solve* it. A further illustration of their indifference was the two-year delay in Dupree's arrest after he was identified through DNA that linked him to the Jackson rape-homicide. Neither Isaac Tabb, Patricia Little, nor Victoria Shackelford could explain why it took Detroit police two years to arrest Dupree after DNA analysis revealed him to be the killer of Michelle Jackson, a question also posed by the *Detroit News*.[16] Detective Tabb responded simply, "Somebody probably dropped the ball. The case probably just sat on someone's desk, and they forgot about it."[17] Unfortunately, such lethargy in police response does little to quell the belief by many members of the Black community that Black lives simply do not matter. In the case of my friend Michelle, her violent death rendered an anemic reaction from police, even when the offender had been identified.

More often than not, the families of missing, murdered, and victimized Black women are dissatisfied with police response. While conducting research for my first book, I noticed a pattern in which police were not sufficiently proactive in searching for missing Black girls and women. They often seemed reluctant to file an initial missing person report and would neglect to warn the community that a potential serial predator was targeting victims in their area. Even when some murders could be tied to a single offender, police were hesitant to attribute the crimes to a serial murderer. Doing so would necessitate additional manpower and resources from city, state, and federal governments to form a task force to find the suspect and prevent future murder victims.[18]

Had Detroit police valued the life of Michelle Kimberly Jackson, Eddie Joe Lloyd would not have lost eighteen years of his life to prison, the deaths of other potential victims would have been prevented, and the families of those victims would be spared the unbearable pain of losing a loved one. Unfortunately, the officers in this case modeled the systemic racism at the core of American policing, the effects of which are so engrained that Black officers often perpetuate the same implicit biases against members of their own race. Case in point: many of the officers involved in the coercion of Eddie Joe Lloyd for

Michelle Jackson's homicide were Black, yet it appears that neither her humanity as a victim nor the innocence of Eddie Joe Lloyd mattered to these officers.

And, tragically, Michelle's murder would not be the only one where police acted as though there was no human involved.

CHAPTER 2

PANIC IN ROXBURY

Serial Deaths in 1970s Boston

I N BOSTON, THE YEAR 1979 brought about the end of a tumultuous decade teeming with racial tension from school desegregation and racially shifting neighborhoods. For many Black people living in the historic city, Boston was not the idyllic, tree-lined metropolis with ancient brownstones and cobblestone streets seen as a beacon of cosmopolitan city life with the feel of a small town. Most Boston neighborhoods were deeply segregated, with angry white residents committing racial violence against Black people unfortunate enough to wander into the wrong area. This could be stumbling upon the ethnic enclaves of Irish and Italian working-class residents, daring to attend a Red Sox game at Fenway Park, or visiting a beach in South Boston to take a dip in the ocean.[1]

In addition to the threat of violence from both white residents and the mostly white police force, Black people living in the communities of Dorchester and Roxbury were facing the ominous threat of an onslaught of murders of Black women in their neighborhoods. On January 29, 1979, the dismembered bodies of fifteen-year-old Christine Ricketts and her seventeen-year-old best friend, Andrea Foye, were found in trash bags, wrapped in blankets, on a street near the Stride Rite shoe factory in Roxbury. The two teens had been strangled, and Foye sustained a severe injury to her mouth from what the medical examiner determined to be a forceful punch with a fist. The girls had been living in a hotel room with Ricketts's boyfriend, twenty-four-year-old Dennis Jamal Porter, who would later be convicted in the homicides of the young women.[2]

One troubling detail regarding police response in the case was their treatment of one of the victim's mothers. A few weeks prior to her death, Christine Ricketts's mother reported her daughter missing, but police refused to take the panicked woman's complaint seriously, instead assuming the teen "ran off with a pimp."[3] Christine's mother told the press she believed that the police's lack of immediate action was because they believed her daughter and Andrea Foye were high school dropouts who were now being trafficked by Dennis Jamal Porter as sex workers. It is not uncommon for Black girls to be hypersexualized and viewed as promiscuous and recalcitrant through the prism of a systemically racist society.[4] Unfortunately, police have often used these narratives to justify failing to initiate a missing person report (it is common to label missing Black girls "runaways") or delaying a search when they are reported missing by worried family members.[5] During the murder trial of the accused killer, prosecutors presented evidence that Porter instructed the two young women "on becoming prostitutes" and operated as their "pimp."[6] However, given their ages, the girls should have been viewed as victims of sex trafficking as opposed to possible sex workers or simply girls who put themselves in harm's way. Contemporary society has evolved in understanding sex work as work for many people and makes the distinction between it and the sexual exploitation of minors. The responsibility should always fall to the adult abusing their power in the situation. This differs from consenting adults who voluntarily engage in sex work as a means of income, survival, enjoyment, career, and so on.

Even so, no person has the right to take anyone's life because of their vocation.

Given the police and media's description of these young women as "prostitutes," I believe it is important to provide more information about their lives that recognizes their personhood and humanity. Unfortunately, in my research I had difficulty finding qualitative information regarding the personality characteristics of murdered Black girls and women in media stories about their deaths. With so little coverage of their murders at the time, there is little information available today about the lives of Christine and Andrea. However, I was able to locate an online site called the Estuary Projects Installation that was dedicated to honoring the murdered young Black women that described Christine as a shy and quiet teenager who once desired to become a social worker.[7] Likewise, Andrea was described as a "cheerful girl who spent her free time caring for ill grandparents."[8]

Dennis Jamal Porter, Christine's boyfriend at the time, was eventually convicted for both murders. However, considering the fact that Christine was underaged, one would think the prosecution would consider her an obvious victim of statutory rape, but Porter was not charged with this offense.

On January 30, 1979, barely twenty-four hours after Christine Ricketts and Andrea Foye were murdered, the body of Gwendolyn Yvette Stinson was found in a backyard not far from her home in Dorchester. She had been raped and strangled. She was fifteen years old, the youngest of ten children, her mother's favorite, and a gymnastics enthusiast. When Gwendolyn's mother reported her missing, police refused to initiate a search for the girl, prompting her mother to contact the press and beg for help.[9] A neighbor, forty-year-old James A. Brown, would be charged, tried, and later acquitted for the teen girl's slaying. The case would then go cold, with police ignoring the rising panic in Black Boston neighborhoods regarding the crimes.

Over the course of five months, from January through May 1979, eight more young women would tragically lose their lives, causing fear and frustration in Black communities. Black residents accused police of not taking the murders seriously nor providing protection to the vulnerable young Black women who lived there.

The first week in February 1979 would bring the victim count to four. Caren Prater, twenty-five, was an unemployed mother of a two-year-old daughter who often cared for her ailing grandfather. In a photo featured in the *Boston Globe*, Caren holds her then-infant daughter, smiling lovingly at the camera with her daughter's cheek pressed against her own. She was described as a devoted mother who was selflessly devoted to family.[10] On February 2, her body was found in Roxbury, only yards behind a local hospital, in a wooded area. She had been beaten and stabbed to death.

Despite the at least four brutal murders of young Black women, there was a lack of the ravenous media attention that typically follows such salacious news. The *Globe* provided a brief four-paragraph story with the headline "Two Bodies Found in Trash Bags" following the deaths of the first two victims, Christine Ricketts and Andrea Foye, but the story was buried on the paper's thirtieth page. Another short write-up announced the death of Gwendolyn Stinson on page 13: "Dorchester Girl Found Dead."[11] In spite of the paltry coverage of these multiple homicides, word quickly spread throughout the Black neighborhoods that young women were being murdered, and fear gripped Black women in Dorchester and Roxbury.

Residents had reason for concern. On February 21, 1979, less than three weeks after the death of Caren Prater, twenty-nine-year-old Daryal Ann Hargett, who had recently relocated from Williamston, North Carolina, was found dead in her apartment. She had been bound at the wrists, raped, and strangled. Daryal moved to Boston after graduating from Virginia Union University and was one of the first Black students to integrate her high school in Williamston. Friends described her as a quiet, well-liked social worker who sang in her church's choir.[12]

The body count continued.

On a 55-degree day, March 14, 1979, seventeen-year-old Desiree Denise Etheridge, a part-time student and neighbor of victim Gwendolyn Stinson, was found dead one hundred yards from the Ricketts and Foye murder scene. She had been bludgeoned to death with a tire iron and found partially nude, her body burned in an apparent attempt to destroy evidence of the crime. At this point, the lives of six young women had been taken, and the community felt the need to act. The growing fear, frustration, and outrage was laser focused on law enforcement, who pushed back against claims from Black residents that police were indifferent, callous, and slow to investigate the murders. These six young women met their demise with brutal violence, the first three victims being teenagers. Yet police downplayed the murders at first, ignoring the pleas from Christine Ricketts and Gwendolyn Stinson's mothers to initiate searches for their missing daughters and then justifying their inaction by suggesting the girls must be "prostitutes who fled with their pimps," insinuating that this somehow meant they deserved it.[13]

Within the next few weeks, the number of murdered young women increased to eleven.

On April 14, 1979, twenty-two-year-old Darlene Rogers was found dead in the Washington Park neighborhood that borders Roxbury. She was stabbed to death and was naked from the waist down, a victim of an apparent sexual assault.

On April 28, 1979, two weeks later, Darlene's death would be followed with the rape and murder of thirty-one-year-old Lois Hood Nesbitt, who was killed in her Roxbury apartment. She had been found with her hands bound behind her back and strangled with a radio cord. Her neighbor, Richard Strother, thirty-two, was arrested and tried for the homicide, but a jury acquitted him.[14]

On May 4, 1979, nineteen-year-old Valyric Holliday was stabbed to death in her apartment; her roommate, Eugene Conway, nineteen, was arrested after police claimed the victim named him as her attacker before she died from her injuries.

One day later on May 5, 1979, the naked and burned body of twenty-nine-year-old Sandra Boulware was found in a YMCA grass lot. Boulware had moved to Boston from Connecticut within the past year. She had been reported missing by her sister, who had not heard from Sandra for several days. A man named Osborne Sheppard, fifty-five, was arrested, charged, and convicted in her homicide. It was alleged that he and the victim had dated for a brief period prior to her murder.

The final murder in this troubling stream of killings was thirty-four-year-old Bobbie Jean Graham. Bobbie Jean was ambitious, with an entrepreneurial spirit, the owner of an insurance agency in the Back Bay area. Her battered body was found on May 7, 1979, in the rear alleyway of a building on Commonwealth Avenue, an upper-middle-class community of elegant brownstone apartment buildings and businesses. Bobbie Jean's live-in boyfriend, Delrue Lafayette Anderson, fled Boston the day after being interviewed by police and was arrested five years later in 1984 living under an assumed name in Seattle. He was tried and convicted in her death in February 1986.[15]

Bobbie Jean was also the only Black victim to be murdered outside the Black communities of Roxbury and Dorchester, and her death in a mostly white community would prove to be controversial when two years later a white woman died in the same Back Bay community. On March 14, 1981, a twenty-seven-year-old nurse, Deborah H. Smith, was raped and stabbed to death in her Commonwealth Avenue apartment. Boston police responded quickly with a vigorous investigation (unlike police response in Bobbie Jean's murder investigation) that included the formation of a fourteen-member task force to find the two assailants described by the victim before dying from her injuries.[16] Two days later, on March 16, 1981, two men were arrested. They were later tried and convicted in the rape-slaying.

Residents of the Roxbury community routinely spoke to media about their frustration that the Boston Police Department did not offer the same forceful response to the murders of Black women in the city as they did to the murder of Deborah H. Smith and to other rapes of white females during the same period in the mostly white Allston-Brighton community in Boston (more on this later). Boston in the 1970s was a city with a long and complicated history of police brutality and racism, a place where racial tensions festered as blatant differences in police action for Black victims became even clearer.

BOSTON'S UNEASY LEGACY OF RACIAL VIOLENCE AND POLICE BRUTALITY

Following the Massachusetts legislature's enactment of the 1965 Racial Imbalance Act, court-mandated desegregation of Boston public schools began in the 1970s. To ensure a "racial balance" throughout the public school system, Black students were bussed to white-neighborhood schools in South Boston, Charlestown, and Hyde Park, while the courts asked for select white students to simultaneously be bussed to schools in the primarily Black neighborhoods of Dorchester, Roxbury, Mattapan, and the South End.[17] This decision was met with hostility from many white residents. They didn't want Black children in their schools and scoffed at the idea of having their children attend the Black schools. Both white parents and children did not hesitate to express their resentment toward Black schoolchildren as the buses carrying them were pelted with stones, bricks, eggs, and, at times, racial epithets, as Black students cowered in their seats, terrified.

When the national media began reporting on the riotous behavior of the white parents who opposed the city's busing policy, others in the greater Boston area expressed shock that such behavior could exist in what is nostalgically regarded as the cradle of the American Revolution. Similar to the proverbial cliché that Atlanta, Georgia, was the "city too busy to hate," Boston believed itself to be the city that was immune from the riots that exploded throughout the country only a decade earlier from racial unrest and unrelenting police brutality in American ghettos. Many white Bostonians held the presumptuous belief that the city's relatively small population of Black residents (approximately 16 percent of the population in 1970[18]) seemed content with Boston's structural and systemic racial inequality.[19] For the most part, there were no upheavals nor violent protests even during the tumultuous struggle for civil rights and the subsequent assassinations of Medgar Evers, Malcolm X, Martin Luther King, and leaders of the Black power movements throughout the mid-to-late 1960s.[20]

Much of the racial violence was one-sided, with Black residents being attacked by white Bostonians and members of the predominantly white police force. Black people incessantly complained about the police brutality they experienced, and one such incident ultimately triggered the most notable riot in modern Boston history—the Roxbury Riot that spawned from the Mothers for Adequate Welfare sit-in of 1967. In June of that year, thirty protesters, mostly Black women receiving public assistance, staged a sit-in at the city's Grove Hill welfare office at Blue Hill Avenue. Some of the mothers even brought their young children with them to participate in the protest. They chained the front doors shut, locking themselves and the staff of the office inside, though, in later accounts, protesters insisted that staff could still exit from an unlocked rear door. Their demands to welfare officials consisted of ten items, which included: better treatment by caseworkers; having a representative on the policy board of directors; the removal of the program's director Daniel Cronin; and an appeals process to prevent their checks from being terminated based on what they described as "malicious gossip and lying officials!"[21]

Despite calling for his removal, the mothers also were insistent that the welfare director Daniel Cronin meet with them to discuss their grievances.

The protest lasted for two days and was mostly peaceful, with a crowd of supporters and family members gathered outside and conversing with the protesters through open windows. By the second day, Daniel Cronin showed up at the facility, but refused to speak with the women and balked at the suggestion that he climb through a window to enter the building and engage with them (the doors remained chained and locked). By that evening, city administrators' patience had worn thin, and a phalanx of one thousand police officers was called to the scene, some of whom had already been on-site, observing. According to witnesses, police forced their way into the building and began beating the women and some of the children, who were present with their mothers, with batons. These officers exercised little restraint in their use of violence on the bodies of poor Black mothers who simply did not believe that help from the government should come at the expense of human dignity.

As the melee unfolded, one of the protesters ran to an open window and yelled to the crowd, "They are beating your Black sisters in here!"[22] Another witness described to the press that police dragged the women across broken glass down the stairs and out of the building.[23] The crowd outside the welfare office reacted with violence and rushed the building to get inside and fight with police. The bedlam spilled onto the street and into the surrounding neighborhoods and, in the end, culminated in the destruction of property to the tune of $3.7 million in damages. This was especially evident on Blue Hill Avenue, a street that was densely populated with furniture stores, medical offices, shops, restaurants, and grocery stores. There were sixty-five reported injuries, including mothers and their children, and fifty arrests.[24]

Contemporary analysis of the events of 1967 centers on the racial hostility, suffocating poverty, indifference by Boston officials, and unrelenting police brutality that gives Boston its lingering reputation as one of the most racist northern cities in America.[25] Even today, Black people in Boston live almost exclusively in three neighborhoods—Dorchester (the largest of Boston's residential neighborhoods), Roxbury, and Mattapan—communities that historically lacked adequate housing, had high unemployment and high crime rates, and were where residents experienced frequent incidents of police brutality from the mostly white ethnic police force. Only a small portion of the Black population (less than 3 percent) migrated from southern states during the early twentieth century in an effort to escape Jim Crow discrimination and Ku Klux Klan terror.

Word spread quickly to would-be migrants that finding jobs and habitable abodes was extraordinarily difficult for Black Americans in the city of Boston, where open hostility from European immigrants was on full display and sanctioned by city officials.[26] As a result, the majority of Black residents in Boston by the mid-1960s arrived from the Caribbean territories of Jamaica, Dominican Republic, and Haiti, and the small West African country of Cape Verde.[27] Perhaps these new immigrants were oblivious to the systemic racism carried over from chattel slavery, but they would soon learn that having black skin had its price regardless of your place of origin.

The subarea of Dorchester borders the Roxbury neighborhood in Boston and is divided by Blue Hill Avenue, a four-mile-long street that cuts through the Dorchester, Roxbury, and Mattapan communities. Dorchester was once a largely Irish-Catholic and Jewish neighborhood, but, by the early 1960s, most whites had fled the area and moved farther south and, if income permitted, to outlying suburbs. For a time, Jews were the remaining white population in Dorchester, but they, too, began to move to suburban single-family-home communities outside the city, following their synagogues to greener (and less Black) acres.[28] Meanwhile, Irish and Polish ethnic groups made up 98 percent of the Boston police force and lived in the "sundown" sections of the city named Charlestown and South Boston—places where Black people dare not tread no matter the time of day.[29]

William Edwards, a sociology professor and visiting fellow at UMass-Boston, told a *Boston Globe* reporter in 1987 that his friends warned him about the city's racism before he left his teaching job at the University of California, Berkeley, and described Boston as "the Mississippi of the North."[30] Another Black sociologist at the same university explained that he told friends to "be very, very careful about where you live. Within my very soul I don't think there's any place in Boston free of racism . . . it's so pervasive."[31]

The overcrowded and impoverished conditions of the hyper-segregated Black neighborhoods contributed to increasing rates of crime and violence and burgeoning distrust between police and the Black residents and served as the catalyst for police commissioner Edmund McNamara's brief creation of an all-Black police force. The unit was referred to as the "Soul Patrol," whose primary mission was to decrease crime in the Black areas of Boston.[32] It was regarded as highly successful, as Black residents of Dorchester and Roxbury felt more trusting of Black officers and cooperated in crime investigations. As a result, "after-hour joints" (illegal drinking facilities) closed and at least four homicides were solved in quick succession.

Not everyone was celebratory of the unit's success.

Almost immediately, McNamara's attempt at creating an early example of community policing became a point of consternation among white law enforcement officers. The Boston police officer's union reacted with outrage at the creation of an all-Black unit, decrying the move as discriminatory and divisive. "We don't want this kind of thing in the police force," bemoaned Daniel J. Sweeney, the chairman of the Boston Police Patrolmen's Association. "White or Black doesn't matter. We're all police officers first."[33] This was an interesting comment, given the long history of Black Bostonians' complaints of police brutality, governmental mistrust among Black residents, and white cops' contention that Black people were resistant to providing information that would solve crimes in their own communities. Within a year, Commissioner McNamara yielded to pressure from the union and disbanded the unit. Resident grievances of police brutality increased, as did violent crime. Once again, white officers had free rein to terrorize Black communities with impunity.[34]

It would be these very officers who would be responsible for investigating the deaths of Black women when the series of brutal murders began in January 1979.

PANIC AND FRUSTRATION IN ROXBURY ENSUES

It did not take long for Black residents to notice that something ominous was happening as young Black women continued to be murdered. With the growing unease and lack of police intervention, a number of protests occurred in response. When Elizabeth Muse, the mother of Gwendolyn Stinson, was rebuffed by the police, she solicited assistance from newspapers and radio stations in finding her missing daughter. When Gwendolyn's body was found only a day after teenagers Christine Ricketts and Andrea Foye were discovered, Muse rallied residents in her Roxbury community to march to Boston mayor Kevin White's home and demand that police respond to the deaths of the three young victims.[35] This bold move caught the attention of Bill Owens, the first Black state senator from Massachusetts, known as a relentless champion for reparations for the consequences of slavery and systemic racism against Black Americans.

Owens reached out to the mothers of the four victims (by this time, Caren Prater had been murdered) and advocated for them to meet with the mayor. In a hastily arranged conference at a local elementary school between the grieving mothers, Senator Owens, and Mayor White, the mayor articulated what he felt was the solution to the problem, and it was *not* increased police presence, as the mothers demanded. Instead, he believed that the primary issue at hand was the need for increased community involvement among residents to tackle the ongoing crime wave of violence that plagued Black areas in Boston as a whole. In other words, the mayor lay blame for the murders (at this stage unsolved) on the proverbial cliché of Black-on-Black crime, thereby shifting to the community the responsibility that should be the onus of law enforcement. And, as if to underscore the insignificance of the lives of the dead teens, this meeting between Boston's most powerful government officials and a small group of grief-stricken Black mothers garnered little press; it was featured on page 5 of the *Herald American* and on page 15 of the *Boston Globe*.[36]

By the time Hargett, the fifth victim, was killed in February, the community had reached a boiling point, and the death of the sixth victim, Desiree Etheridge, sent them over the edge. On April 1, 1979, angered yet undaunted by the clear indifference of Boston's mayor, media, and police to the murders, community residents took it upon themselves to mobilize and march through the neighborhoods where the deaths occurred. Approximately 1,200 people participated in a two-mile rally from the community of South End to Roxbury, pausing briefly on Wellington Avenue in front of the apartment building where Hargett's body was found.[37] They also walked past the Stride Rite factory, the site where teenagers Christine Ricketts and Andrea Foye were discovered in trash bags, but did not pause at the location. Sarah Small, the aunt of Daryal Ann Hargett, warned the protesters that the company "didn't want us to stop in their parking lot for fear we might give them a bad image."[38] Apparently the company was more concerned about the impact the march would have on their profits and appearance than the brutal deaths of six young Black women.

There were several community groups, some recently organized in reaction to the murders, who participated in the march, including the Coalition for Women's Safety and the Combahee River Collective. There were also male speakers among the organizers who addressed the crowd. Their advice to the frightened women was simple and consisted of only two options to stay safe—sequester indoors or find a man to protect you—blithely ignoring the fact that it was men (and, in at least two of the murders, a romantic partner) who were suspected in the homicides.

This tone-deaf message, rife with sexism, incensed one member of the audience in particular.

Barbara Smith was at the time a thirty-three-year-old queer feminist community activist, and the cofounder of the Combahee River Collective. The group was formed as a Black feminist lesbian socialist organization whose name paid tribute to a raid on the Combahee River in South Carolina in 1853 that was guided by Harriet Tubman and led to the freeing of more than seven hundred slaves.[39] The women held meetings in the neighborhoods where the murders occurred, launching an aggressive community outreach effort to warn Black female residents that their lives were in danger and that someone was preying on Black women. Additionally, they provided self-defense classes and advice on self-protection, while also publishing a pamphlet whose cover was designed to encapsulate the trauma Black Bostonian women were experiencing with each murder. The title on the cover posed the question "8 Black Women: Why Did They Die?" and featured cartoon drawings of two Black women with anguished facial expressions. The number of deaths were crossed out as they multiplied, demonstrating how the bodies of Black females were piling up, and yet very little was being done by police to stop them. There would be four more victims added to the total within the year, bringing the number of murdered women to twelve, doubling from the initial death count of six when the pamphlet was first distributed. Most importantly, the question posed on the pamphlet demanded an answer to a question plaguing the segregated and impoverished community on the South End: Why were Black women being murdered?

Smith explained her motivation for the pamphlet when interviewed years later about the organization. "I said, 'I think we really have to do a pamphlet. We need to do something.' So, I started writing the pamphlet that night and I thought of the title . . . 'Six Black Women: Why Did They Die?' And I wrote it up."[40]

The activists' anger was fueled by what they perceived to be the lack of action from the police. With each report from a missing person's family, police kept refusing to search for the missing teens and women, dismissing the violence as part of a Black crime wave. It became well-known among the Roxbury and Dorchester communities that parents of several of the murdered teens sought police intervention when their daughters initially went missing and were met with insult. Grieving and frustrated, Elizabeth Muse, the mother of Gwendolyn Stinson, attended a community gathering and shouted in anger, "My daughter was not a prostitute!"[41] While this emotional proclamation received a standing ovation and raucous applause, it revealed the greater tragedy that murder victims with a history of sex work were not viewed as victims at all.

Unfortunately, for Black parents of missing people, it was not uncommon for them to be met with skepticism from the press. The media often takes its cue from law enforcement that a missing person is considered endangered and, thus, worthy of coverage.[42] Without police notifying the press of the need to highlight Gwendolyn's disappearance, it is highly unlikely that the press would provide significant attention to the case.

Yet while residents of Roxbury and Dorchester implored police to do more in their communities to protect young Black women from violence, in a more affluent and predominantly white community the occurrence of another type of violent crime wave garnered the rapt attention of both the Boston press and members of law enforcement. The media and police became laser focused on addressing the rapes of white women in the Allston-Brighton district of Boston but continued to ignore the homicides of Black women in Dorchester and Roxbury. The issue here isn't about which crime is more horrific, but rather to point out the imbalance in police response or lack thereof to the violence occurring in these segregated neighborhoods. Disheartened that the murders of Black women were scarcely mentioned in the press, and the few that were amounted to slightly more than a footnote, one frustrated Roxbury resident exclaimed, "Those white women were only raped!"[43]

TWO INVESTIGATIONS, ONE OBVIOUS DIFFERENCE

On November 18, 1978, two months before the start of the Roxbury murders, a series of six rapes and two attempted rapes began in the Allston-Brighton neighborhoods in Boston. Allston-Brighton are two separate neighborhoods that border each other and are often referred to as a hyphenated pair of communities. The neighborhoods in the 1970s were primarily a mix of mostly white student populations attending the surrounding colleges of Harvard University, Boston University, Boston College, and the Berklee School of Music, and newly arriving immigrant populations from Central America, Asia, and Russia, as well as a small number of Haitian refugees.[44]

The first rape happened in November, and the second occurred on Christmas Day, 1978, in the basement of the Longfellow Management Company in Brighton. By January 1979, several more rapes would take place, eight in total. Residents of the largely white community of Allston-Brighton angrily confronted the police, demanding that they find the assailant. A meeting was held between approximately seven hundred residents and law enforcement representatives in mid-January, and police were quick to mirror the outrage felt by the community regarding the sexual assaults. According to front-page articles in the *Boston Globe* and the *Herald American*, the police commissioner at the time, Joseph M. Jordan, emphatically reassured the residents, "We're going to get this guy!"[45]

Also present was Boston district attorney Newman Flanagan, who echoed Jordan's commitment to obtaining justice for the rape victims and sparing no mercy for the rapist. He promised that the individual would receive "no fine, no probation, and no suspended sentence." This pledge received immediate applause from meeting attendees. Contributing to the ire of the community about the rapes was local precinct detective Paul Rufo, who expressed to the frustrated residents his personal stake in finding the assailant. "It's my problem! It's my district . . . we want him as bad as you do!"[46] After the meeting, police distributed more than three hundred flyers throughout the city, detailing a description of the suspect based on the survivors' accounts and a drawing by a police sketch artist.[47] What amounted to an "all-hands-on-deck" commitment from law enforcement officials included the foot patrol of plainclothes officers to monitor neighborhood streets, and self-defense workshops to teach women to protect themselves from a would-be rapist. Not wanting to be left out of the effort to curb the rapes, the utility company Boston Edison installed extra streetlights around Commonwealth Avenue, the primary area of the sexual assaults.[48]

Bear in mind that the meeting between the mothers of the Roxbury murdered teens, Senator Owens, and Mayor White received little media coverage and resulted in the mayor summarily dismissing the concerns of Black residents and volleying the responsibility for addressing the killings back to the residents themselves. Furthermore, it was not lost on many in Boston's Black communities that the factor that seemed to galvanize the quest of law enforcement to find the perpetrator of the rapes was the alleged race of the offender. At least four of the victims identified the attacker as a Black male, five foot five, 160 pounds, bearded, with a pockmarked face, and a "Jamaican" accent.

Within weeks of the last reported rape, on February 1, 1979, Willie
Sanders, a thirty-nine-year-old married father of three, and a twenty-
two-year employee of the Longfellow Management Company, was
arrested and charged with four of the eight rapes (the victims in the
remaining four cases were unable to make a positive identification).
Longfellow managed two of the buildings where two of the rapes occurred. At the time of his arrest, Sanders had been married for fourteen years and had been employed at the company as a house painter
and was considered an exemplary employee.

Willie Sanders was also the company's *only* Black employee, and
it is for this reason that his attorney believed he was arrested and
charged with the assaults.[49]

While investigating the rapes, police asked the Longfellow Management Company for a list of all Black employees, and company officials provided them with the sole Black employee—Willie Sanders.
After questioning Sanders and taking a photograph of him, the picture was shown to each of the four victims who had provided a description of their attacker to the police. Despite Willie being at least
three inches taller than the rapist described to police, having no facial
hair, with smooth skin free of pockmarks, and being thirty pounds
lighter, the four victims provided a positive identification of Sanders.

During the trial, lawyers for Sanders pointed out that witness
identification was both faulty and unconstitutional, since police only
presented that singular photo to the traumatized women as the possible attacker in lieu of a standard police lineup. Another objection
raised by Sanders's attorneys was the timing of the man's arrest. Police called an emergency meeting with women in the Brighton community the night of February 1 to reassure residents of police efforts
to catch the rapist, as many in the community still complained that
police were not doing enough to stop the attacks. Willie Sanders was
arrested only hours after the meeting ended.

Lawyers argued that the arrest was timed to generate publicity and
to stoke the image of the "heroic" determination of police to make
good on their promise to find the offender.[50] Furthermore, serology
analysis would reveal that Willie Sanders was a non-secretor, meaning that his blood type would not be detected in semen evidence. This

factor alone should have eliminated him as a suspect in the rapes. Nevertheless, the Commonwealth of Massachusetts proceeded with the rape trial, despite the defense's objections and fury from the Black community members that Willie Sanders was an innocent scapegoat. At the conclusion of the controversial trial, a racially diverse jury found Willie Sanders not guilty on all counts of sexual assault.[51]

Meanwhile, arrests were slow to materialize in the murders of the eleven Black women and teen girls.

Women in the Roxbury community continued to hold rallies and marches in protest of what they viewed as an anemic response from police, particularly in comparison to the Allston-Brighton rape cases. The two feminist groups, Crisis and Combahee River Collective, organized a crowd of five hundred women in early May to march to the home of Mayor White to express their fear, rage, and discontent about the homicides, but White had conveniently left Boston for vacation that weekend.[52] Undeterred, the women stood in front of his home to observe a moment of silence in memory of the women who had been killed. Black women who participated in public protests felt under attack for expressing their anger. One of the organizers of Crisis refused to identify herself to reporters who were covering the march after she claimed she was attacked by two white men while trying to enter her apartment several weeks before. The woman claimed that she was called a "Black bitch" and struck by the men with a warning to "shut up" about the killings. She issued an ominous warning to the crowd of protesters: "Remember that what comes for me in the morning, will come to you at night!"[53]

Determined to not be counted among the increasing number of victims, many of the women felt the need to take matters into their own hands. From wearing whistles around their necks to carrying pocketknives, to staying indoors and venturing out only under the most pressing circumstances, Black female residents of Roxbury employed any means possible to protect themselves. One woman wistfully longed for Boston police to provide the same support for them as they did for the women in Allston-Brighton: "I wish police would give us the protective training classes they gave to the women in Brighton when they had a number of rapes over there."[54] Even she acknowledged to the reporter interviewing her that a whistle as a means of protection would be futile against a man determined to take a woman's life.

Complicating matters further was the proliferation of unfounded rumors, something almost certain to occur in a void of information and rampant distrust of police by the Black community. Discussions in barbershops, beauty salons, laundromats, and grocery stores echoed speculations of "carloads of Black youths or white youths" cruising through Boston's housing projects in search of unguarded female prey.[55] Police vehemently denied the truth of these stories and tried in vain to dismantle them, but to little avail.

As sociologist Patricia Hill Collins once noted, Black people (Black women in particular) oftentimes are the "outsiders within."[56] Their position of marginalization provides the vantage point of being able to observe unequal and unfair treatment of Black people in a predominantly white society compared to that received by whites. And, in the case of law enforcement, Black people are keenly aware that white people are treated with greater regard by police than members of Black communities.

In short, Black people notice when they are on the receiving end of discrimination.

Therefore, when speaking with reporters from the Black-owned newspaper the *Bay State Banner*—the only newspaper to provide consistent and almost daily coverage of the murders—female residents of Roxbury pointed out that police did not provide a foot patrol unit like they did in Brighton. "They need to get out of the car and walk around instead of hustling someone for having a marijuana cigarette," one resident offered. Another woman complained that more streetlights were needed in the neighborhood, just as the Boston Edison utility company so valiantly provided on Commonwealth Avenue in Brighton.[57] Commonwealth Avenue is a major street in Boston that runs through several predominantly white neighborhoods, including Back Bay and Kenmore Square, as well as Allston-Brighton.

Roxbury residents lived in fear as each passing week seemed to end with the brutal death of another young Black daughter, sister, mother, or friend. Despite the eventual development of a police task force to investigate the killings, and the slow trickle of arrests of suspects, many Black Bostonians held a more insidious view of the police response. From their purview, the officers appeared to avoid more cromulent methods of investigation to effectively solve the killings. The community was also suspicious when the responsibility of leading the investigation kept shifting between the police task force to the district attorney's office, and then back again to the task force.[58] Some police officials seemed displeased with the investigation and accused the DA of attempting to fortify future political aspirations on the backs of murdered Black women.

This criticism was one where both the police and Roxbury residents found consensus.

State senator Bill Owens expressed his concerns about the change in the investigation of the Roxbury murders in a statement that called for a press conference from officials to update the community about the case. He complained that the alteration in leading the examination of the murders was tantamount to playing a shell game of shifting responsibility between the district attorney's office and the police department, which ultimately "gives the community the impression of an unwillingness to press the investigations to a fruitful conclusion."[59] Owens also demanded that an additional four hundred police officers be added to the force to help with the investigations.

Either way, Roxbury residents only wanted to feel safe again. They continued to express frustration that women were still dying despite reassuring comments from police and the district attorney's office to calm their growing vexation. A particular point of controversy for the Black community regarding the murders was that the police continued framing the murders as unrelated and primarily the result of intimate partner violence. In the first four killings, Suffolk County district attorney Newman Flanagan opined that the murders of Foye, Ricketts, and Stinson had three different suspects (one man, Dennis Jamal Porter, was convicted in the killings of Ricketts and Foye), and that the motive in the murder of Caren Prater appeared to be rape. But he denied that a serial predator was involved in any of the killings.[60]

By the time the eleventh murder occurred, the attitude of police that the Black community was overreacting had not abated. A

Roxbury sergeant detective, Stephen Murphy, stated emphatically to *Boston Globe* reporters, "The thing we want to stress is that the murders are not the work of one individual. They all appear to be crimes of passion. In most of the cases, the victim knew the perpetrator. There is really nothing you can do to protect yourself from that type of crime unless you want to ostracize yourself from your family and friends."[61] Likewise, Sgt. Murphy's patience seemed to wear thin with reporters asking about the possibility that a serial killer could be involved in the homicides. "Look!" he said. "There's not one guy out there running around killing people. I can tell you that right now."[62]

Women in Roxbury were not convinced that enough was being done by police to protect them, and, despite the eventual establishment of a murder task force, complaints by the community continued. Contrary to the police's portrait of round-the-clock surveillance of the Roxbury community, the establishment of a hotline for tips, an accelerated response to distress calls, and a dedicated and focused task force, the residents told a different story. Again, there was frustration that police officers remained in their vehicles and drove through the streets of Roxbury as opposed to serving as a visible foot patrol unit; when residents called the hotline after midnight to report suspicious activity, no one answered the phone; many residents were unaware of the tip number to reach the task force; and there were a number of reports that when residents tried to flag down a patrol car, police did not stop.[63] And still police maintained that they were working diligently to solve the murders, while proffering that the vast majority were committed by spurned lovers or domestic partners.

The Combahee River Collective refuted this simplistic categorization of the murders as intimate partner or acquaintance violence, instead seeking a more accurate portrayal of "racialized and sexualized" violence against Black women. Whether the killings were committed by one assailant or several assailants, it cannot be denied that misogynoir and the possessive view of women as male property plays a role in the murders of women generally, and particularly for Black women. Moreover, there exists a denigration in the US of Black women's humanity by law enforcement officers in contrast to white women, whose bodies are paternalistically protected. In the cases of Roxbury and Dorchester, conspicuous police indifference and dismissal of the women's concerns contributed to a "free for all" climate of predation that seemed to embolden men in the community to kill Black women with little fear of consequence.

Antithetical to the Boston police's view of the assailants, my own research and review of information about the homicides counters the claim that each of the victims knew their killer and that the murders were an outgrowth of intimate partner violence. This argument proves to be problematic in a number of the cases. Encompassing a sociological view of the Roxbury murders would indicate that some of the killings were, in fact, related, and at least one serial predator appeared to be at work.

THE ROXBURY MURDERS INDICATE
AN OPEN SEASON ON BLACK WOMEN

In July 2020, I interviewed Thomas Hargrove, the founder of the Murder Accountability Project (MAP), a nonprofit organization that catalogs homicides throughout the United States. Hargrove refers to himself as a "murder archivist" who uses a mathematical algorithm to identify patterns in murders that would indicate serial predators, particularly in unsolved killings. To date, he asserts that MAP is the most comprehensive database of homicides in the United States, with more complete and accurate reporting of homicides than even the FBI's Uniform Crime Report, a database of serious crimes voluntarily reported by police agencies across the country. When I asked him about his method of identifying a serial killer among a series of homicides, he pointed to his algorithmic formula. "The algorithm looks for clusters of similar murders within a similar geography that has a very naturally low clearance rate," he explained.

Hargrove also pointed out that murders involving female victims who are bound and strangled with a ligature and sexually assaulted fit the modus operandi of a serial killer. In a shocking number of strangulation murders of Black women in the city of Chicago beginning in 2015, Thomas Hargrove worked collaboratively with Chicago police to identify patterns of serial murders (this will be examined further in chapter 6) and stressed that another key factor besides the method of killing the victim was the disposal of the victim's body. Was she dumped in an alley, a park, or a wooded area, or was she murdered in her home? Finding similarities in the murderer's method of ridding himself of the victim might also suggest a singular killer at play.

As a sociologist, I found this fascinating, since I was trained to look for patterns in any social phenomenon. To provide a closer look at the Roxbury homicides, I created a table with the victims' names, manner of death, and case disposition in an effort to determine if a pattern emerged among the killings. Below is the chart I constructed of the Roxbury murder victims.

FIGURE 2.1: *Roxbury Murder Victims Chart*

DATE	VICTIM	AGE	MANNER OF DEATH	ARRESTED/ CHARGED	CASE DISPOSITION
January 29, 1979	Christine Ricketts	15	Strangled, dismembered	Dennis Porter, convicted	Closed
January 29, 1979	Andrea Foye	17	Strangled, dismembered	Dennis Porter, convicted	Closed
January 30, 1979	Gwendolyn Y. Stinson	14	Raped, strangled	James A. Brown, acquitted	Unsolved
February 2, 1979	Caren Prater	25	Beaten, stabbed to death	Kenneth Spann, indicted by grand jury	Closed; no other public info available beyond appeal denied
February 21, 1979	Daryal Ann Hargett	29	Bound, raped, strangled with ligature	No arrest	Unsolved until 2011; DNA match to Richard Strother
March 14, 1979	Desiree Denise Etheridge	17	Bludgeoned, body set on fire	No arrest	Unsolved

DATE	VICTIM	AGE	MANNER OF DEATH	ARRESTED/ CHARGED	CASE DISPOSITION
April 14, 1979	Darlene Rogers	22	Raped, stabbed to death	No arrest	Unsolved
April 28, 1979	Lois Hood Nesbitt	31	Bound, raped, strangled with ligature	Richard Strother, acquitted	Unsolved until 2011; DNA match to Richard Strother
May 4, 1979	Valyric Holliday	19	Stabbed to death	Eugene Conway, convicted	Closed
May 5, 1979	Sandra Boulware	29	Raped, beaten to death, burned	Osborne Sheppard, convicted	Closed
May 7, 1979	Bobbie Jean Graham	34	Beaten to death	Delrue Lafayette Anderson, convicted	Closed
April 15, 1980	Cheryl Upshaw	29	Bound, raped, strangled with ligature	No arrest	Unsolved until 2011; DNA match to Richard Strother

You will notice that I included an additional victim from 1980 whose death occurred a year after the 1979 murders of Black women in Roxbury. Cheryl Upshaw, twenty-nine, similar to victims Daryal Hargett and Lois Hood Nesbit, was found in her apartment bound, raped, and strangled with a ligature. Each of the cases remained unsolved until 2011, when DNA analysis revealed that semen found on their bodies matched a man named Richard Strother, who died in 1998. Ironically, Strother was arrested, charged, and tried in Lois Hood Nesbitt's homicide, but was later acquitted by a jury. However, the 2011 DNA analysis confirmed he was in fact Lois's killer. Needless to say, there *was* a serial murderer stalking Black women in the Roxbury community, contrary to the Boston police's insistence that such was not the case. Eerily, there was another man by the name of

Ronald Strother, thirty, who was convicted in the 1970 rape and murders of two Roxbury women but was more infamous for the beating death of his eighteen-year-old cellmate, Ronald Brown, in 1972.[64]

Ronald Strother also lived in Boston and had a name very close to Richard Strother, and try as I might, I was unable to determine the relationship, if any, between the two men. If the two Strotherses are in fact related (possibly brothers, with Ronald being ten years older), both men were killers of women—serial killers at that—and posed a most terrifying reality for the Black women living in the Roxbury community. In my first book, *You're Dead, So What? Media, Police, and the Invisibility of Black Women as Victims of Homicide,* I chronicled my frustration and the challenges of trying to ascertain information about Black female murder victims via newspaper reports. Such was the case with Ronald Strother; there was no information available on his victims, Phyllis Galloway, twenty-three, and Regina Gayle, twenty, in the archives of Boston newspapers.

As it stands, three other homicides to this day remain unsolved; whoever killed Gwendolyn Stinson, Desiree Etheridge, and Darlene Rogers was never found. In the case of fourteen-year-old Stinson, her forty-year-old neighbor, James A. Brown, was tried and found not guilty by a jury. As in the case of Eddie Joe Lloyd (wrongfully convicted in the 1984 murder of my friend Michelle Jackson), Brown also had a history of mental illness and was frequently hospitalized at the infamous Bridgewater Psychiatric Hospital (Albert DeSalvo, the so-called Boston Strangler, was a patient at the institution in 1964). Is it possible that Boston police officials found Brown to be a convenient suspect in the Stinson homicide, especially when the Black community and the first Black state senator amplified their criticisms of the murder investigations? The teen girl was raped and strangled with a ligature. There is no evidence that she was murdered by a boyfriend or intimate acquaintance, and Boston police's classification of the homicides being perpetrated by lovers did not fit the Stinson slaying.

Again, seventeen-year-old Desiree Etheridge was a neighbor of Gwendolyn Stinson and was found one hundred yards from the location of the bodies of Andrea Foye and Christine Ricketts. Is it irrational that women in the community would find this coincidence suspicious? Furthermore, the teen was found partially nude, and the killer's attempt to burn her body made it difficult to rule out sexual assault. Another victim, Darlene Rogers, was found naked from the waist down and suspected of being a victim of rape. With her killing unsolved, how can police declare with certainty that she was *not* the victim of a serial predator? When murders remain unsolved, and all known acquaintances have been eliminated as suspects, is it judicious to rule out serial homicide?

One might question why the police are reluctant to classify a series of killings as serial murder, even when similar characteristics in killings are evident. I was curious about police reticence to identify serial murder and posed this question to Thomas Hargrove during our interview. He attributed the hesitancy to what he deemed a "logistical nightmare":

> The reality is that why would police set themselves up for that misery? If you announce a serial killer, you then are going to have increased demands for explanations from intense media, your local political supervisors are going to demand regular reports and ask, "How is the serial killer hunt going on? What progress have you made?" It's kind of nightmarish. There is a dreadful magic to the phrase "serial killer." We are just entranced by that phrase. And, so, police really try to avoid using it for perfectly understandable reasons.

Dissatisfied with that explanation, I countered that, despite their "nightmare" of a serial murder investigation, better the discomfort of police than potential victims and their families. This is not about what is convenient for police, but, rather, what is necessary to protect the lives of vulnerable women. Police have a duty to not only protect a community but also to warn it of danger, and Hargrove acknowledged that law enforcement is, in fact, duty-bound by law to do so. "The guidance from the Justice Department is to make a public warning when a serial killer has been detected and is believed to be killing to a particular pattern," he explained. "But that's actionable information, and they should warn potential next victims." He cautioned that failure to do so results in the creation of a "walking, talking testament that there is no sanction to murder."[65]

And, in the cases of murdered Black women in Boston, the failure of police to see their humanity, respect their fear, appreciate their vulnerability, and ensure their protection with the same fervency that police afforded white female victims exposed the women of Roxbury to the predatory instincts of male violence.

Whether they knew their killer . . . or not.

CHAPTER 3

TACO BELL TERROR

Serial Murders of Black Women in the Queen City

O N MONDAY, SEPTEMBER 25, 2016, a chaotic city council meeting was in session, the gallery filled with apoplectic, anguished Black residents from Charlotte, North Carolina. But, more than anger, there was palpable heartbreak at the shooting death of forty-three-year-old Keith Lamont Scott by Charlotte-Mecklenburg (CMPD) police less than a week before. Scott, a married father of seven children, was shot to death while sitting in his car, waiting for his son's school bus.[1] Officers involved in the incident claimed that when Scott saw them walking toward his vehicle, he emerged from the driver's side with a weapon in his hand. They also said they told him to drop the weapon and, when he refused, Brently Hinson, a Black police officer only hired by the CMPD in 2014, shot and killed Scott.

The problem with Officer Hinson's defense is that both dash and body camera video of police on the scene *and* eyewitness accounts with cell phone video taken by Scott's wife, Rakeyia, contradict his version of the events.[2] When police officials released video of the shooting, it is not clear Keith Scott had a gun in his hand. Another major point of contention in this case is that North Carolina is an open-carry state, and Scott being in possession of a gun would not have been an illegal act.[3] Yet Scott's consuming marijuana and having a gun in the car was deemed sufficient evidence to uphold Officer Hinson's "split second" determination that Scott was a threat, and therefore, the district attorney determined that the killing was justified.[4]

The anger felt by the Black residents of Charlotte regarding Scott's killing was compounded by a police shooting death of two other unarmed Black people several years before. On September 14, 2013, police shot and killed Jonathan Ferrell, a twenty-four-year-old former college football player after he, in an attempt to get help, knocked on resident doors following a car accident in the mostly white Brad-field Farms neighborhood on Charlotte's south side. A white woman claimed to have mistaken Ferrell for a burglar and called police, who, shortly after arriving on the scene, fired on Ferrell.[5]

On February 15, 2015, two years after the Ferrell shooting, Janisha Fonville, a twenty-year-old Black queer woman, was shot and killed by police in the apartment she shared with her girlfriend, Korneisha Banks.[6] Banks called police after Janisha, suffering from a mental health crisis, threatened suicide with a knife. Anthony Holzhauser, the officer who shot and killed Janisha Fonville, claimed that the young woman lunged at him with the knife, but Fonville's girlfriend, who was an eyewitness to Janisha's death, vehemently denied that Fonville was holding a knife in her hand when Officer Holzhauser shot her to death.[7] Once more, police officials and the district attorney accepted the officer's account of the events, and Holzhauser was not charged in Janisha Fonville's killing.

So, in September 2016, on a humid and overcast day, with mild temperatures in the low seventies, city officials felt the heat from Black citizens of Charlotte who packed the auditorium to express their collective frustration at what they believed to be yet another unjustified death of a Black person at the hands of the CMPD.

While many Black residents in attendance made comments that day, a speech from one of Charlotte's youngest Black residents went viral and struck at the core of the fear and hopelessness Black people throughout the United States experienced because of police violence. Nine-year-old Zianna Oliphant, wearing a rainbow-colored T-shirt, gingerly stepped to the podium, barely registering a height that would make her visible to most of the audience. In a strong voice trembling with emotion, tears streaming down her delicate chocolate-hued face, she beseeched the members of Charlotte's city council to make the killings of Black people by police stop. "We are Black people, and we shouldn't have to feel like this!" she exclaimed. "It's a shame that our fathers and mothers are killed, and we can't even see them anymore.

It's a shame that we have to go to their graveyard."[8] In that moment, little Zianna became the voice of an issue that no child at her age should ever be forced to reckon with: that police are not only responsible for the persistent killings of unarmed Black Americans but also indifferent to their lives, even in a progressive hub of the south known as the "Queen City."

The city of Charlotte, North Carolina (named for Queen Sophia Charlotte of Mecklenburg-Strelitz, the bride of King George III and believed to be the first Black queen of a European monarchy)[9] prides itself on its reputation of progressive politics and modernization in the heart of the Deep South.[10] As such, the city has a history of attempting to handle racial conflict without bloodshed. Charlotte's status as a racially progressive climate was due in part to its response to segregation and racial tension during the civil rights era of the 1960s. It was the first city to peacefully integrate its lunch counters at restaurants by forming a multicultural coalition of whites and Blacks agreeing to eat together in harmony.[11] Likewise, the city adopted a similar position on the issue of integrating their schools through busing.

In 1971, the Supreme Court decision in *Swann v. Charlotte-Mecklenburg Board of Education* unanimously upheld court-ordered busing to integrate public schools, and city leaders immediately implemented a plan to correct the racial imbalance in its public schools.[12] The city was nationally extolled as a successful example of integration as all Charlotte public schools received Black and white students at schools that were otherwise racially homogenous. However, in 1991, a white parent successfully sued the city of Charlotte, claiming that his daughter was not allowed to attend her school of choice due to "forced" racial integration, and the mandatory busing policy ended. Over time, schools in Charlotte became segregated again.[13]

Thus, while on the surface Charlotte appeared to engage in commendable efforts to address racial inequity on a number of fronts, the reality was that many Black people living in Charlotte were left behind to grapple with high rates of unemployment, poverty, and violent crime. In the year 1990, Charlotte's racial demographics were 66 percent white and 32 percent Black,[14] and most African Americans resided in the West End and east-side neighborhoods of Charlotte, referred to by city demographers as "the crescent," given its collared shape around the mostly white residential enclave of South Charlotte (nicknamed "the wedge").[15] In these neighborhoods, few of Charlotte's Black residents enjoyed the prosperity of the city's booming economy, and a vast majority worked low-paying service jobs in the fast-food industry.[16]

Moreover, one issue that has remained obstinately problematic is the deep distrust Black communities in Charlotte hold toward members of law enforcement. There exists a common paradox of Black residents in high-crime, impoverished neighborhoods both needing yet fearing police; they must contend with the threat of violence from criminals on the one hand, and police brutality on the other.

Like most Southern cities, the inception of policing began as slave patrols, commonly referred to as "town guards," whose mission was to control, surveil, and constrain enslaved Black people by enforcement of slave codes,[17] which were designed to prevent insurrection and violent slave rebellion.[18] Black men in Charlotte for more than ten years, from 1863 to 1877, made up 20 to 40 percent of police officers during that time. But, in 1877, during what has historically been referred to as "the Great Compromise," President Rutherford B. Hayes pulled federal troops out of the South, disrupting Reconstruction and leaving African Americans vulnerable to white resentment and extraordinarily brutal violence.[19] As a result, the police force in the city of Charlotte became completely white. Even as late as 1930, there were still no Blacks on the Charlotte police force.[20]

It wasn't until 1941 that the city of Charlotte hired three Black police officers, albeit without the official powers, weapon, and authority of their white counterparts.[21] Today, Black officers are 20 percent of Charlotte's police force, and Rodney Monroe was named Charlotte's first Black police chief in 2008; since his retirement in 2015, there has been no other.[22]

Police violence in a city like Charlotte, North Carolina, serves as a backdrop in understanding deep issues of distrust and friction between Black residents and police, as it does in most American cities. And it is this distrust that feeds the skepticism of Black residents that police actually care when Black people are victims of homicide and will effectively launch investigations needed to solve their murders. Therefore, public hearings where frustrated Black residents confronted city officials about police conduct in Charlotte were not unusual and became particularly volatile during the early 1990s, when a series of murders of young Black women rocked the city to its core.

Within the city's mostly Black West End and east-side areas, the beginning of this tumultuous decade ushered in a sweeping crack cocaine epidemic, skyrocketing homicide rates, and a shadowy serial predator who sexually assaulted and took the promising lives of ten young Black women who considered him a friend. And, yet again, many Black Charlotte residents would accuse police of callous indifference as it relates to Black lives mattering.

A TALE OF TERROR BEGINS

On May 27, 1992, thirty-three-year-old Sharon Nance was found murdered on a rural side road in East Charlotte.[23] A website reported that the attractive and petite single mother of a young son was employed as a "domestic worker" but little else about her life or details of her murder could be found in a search for news articles regarding her homicide.[24] Another website described Nance as a former convicted drug addict and sex worker who was beaten to death by her accused killer, Henry Louis Wallace, after demanding payment for sex, but I was unable to substantiate these particulars of her background via a search through other media or police sources.[25] This is not surprising, as I detailed in my first book about media's tendency to ignore the violent deaths of Black women in comparison to their white counterparts. Furthermore, given that her death occurred in the 1990s, at a time when the homicide rate increased substantially in Black communities throughout Charlotte (due in part to the burgeoning crack cocaine trade), Nance's murder, as one of many, most likely failed to register with local media.

However, less than a month later, twenty-year-old Caroline Love, an employee of the fast-food restaurant chain Bojangles, went missing after working an afternoon shift. According to her cousin Robert Ross, she purchased a roll of quarters from her manager to do laundry at her apartment. Ross told police he gave Caroline a ride home from work, watched her enter the lobby of her building, and drove away.[26] Caroline lived with a roommate, Sadie McNight, who later informed police she was not at home when Caroline was dropped off at the building and had not seen her since Caroline left for work earlier that day.

Kathy Love, Caroline's sister, became concerned when she did not hear from her for several days and after the manager at Bojangles informed Kathy that Caroline failed to show for work. Kathy Love and a man named Henry Louis Wallace—the boyfriend of Sadie McNight, Caroline's roommate—went to the police station to file a missing person report. There were indications of a possible struggle at the apartment; the sheets from Caroline Love's bed were missing, and the furniture in the apartment was out of place. Yet police filed the missing person report as that of a runaway and did not actively engage in a search to find her.[27]

Tragically, on March 13, 1994, two years after her disappearance, Caroline Love's body was found in a shallow grave. Henry Louis Wallace, the boyfriend of her roommate, confessed to raping and strangling her to death. The night Caroline entered her apartment, he was hiding in the bathroom after entering with a key he had stolen from McKnight. He later buried her body in a wooded area. He led police to the body of Caroline after confessing to her homicide.

Sharon Vance and Caroline Love would not be the only victims of Wallace, who, after being captured two years after the murders commenced, confessed in explicit detail to a series of rape-murders of at least ten young Black women in the East Charlotte neighborhood. Shawna Hawk, a pretty, small-framed, and studious twenty-year-old student who attended Central Piedmont Community College, worked at Taco Bell, and lived with her mother in a small two-bedroom home in East Charlotte. The youngest child and only daughter of her doting mother, Dee Sumpter, Shawna was studying to become a paralegal and worked part-time to fund her education and financially assist her mom. Ever the selfless and loving daughter, who was described as exceptionally close to her mother, Shawna even lied about her age in her early teens to work at McDonald's to help contribute to the household income.[28] Shawna was also known for her dependable personality; as part of her daily responsibilities, she often picked up her young godson from daycare after she arrived home from college classes. Therefore, when her mother returned home from work on the chilly afternoon of February 19, 1993, to find Shawna's purse and coat in the closet, but her car missing from the driveway, she immediately sensed that something was terribly wrong. Adding to her worry was a phone call she received that afternoon from the mother of the godson who told Sumpter that Shawna failed to pick the child up from daycare.

Sumpter immediately telephoned Shawna's boyfriend, who informed the worried mother he had neither seen nor heard from Shawna that day but offered to come to the house and help locate her. Shortly after arriving at Shawna's home, her boyfriend began searching through the house and entered a downstairs bathroom. To his horror, he found Shawna submerged underwater in the bathtub, lying in a fetal position, and began screaming. The shower curtain had been adjusted to hang on the outside of the tub to hide the young woman's body from view. The medical examiner would determine the cause of death was ligature strangulation.

The man who would be later convicted in her death was Henry Louis Wallace, who, incidentally, was her manager at Taco Bell and had hired her for the job. Wallace confessed to police that he went to Shawna's home under the guise of visiting her (they were coworkers, friends, and had dated briefly, according to him), but, after a short conversation, he began to physically assault the stunned young woman by hitting her in the head and dragging her into her bedroom. According to his confession, Wallace forced Shawna to undress, raped her, forced her to put her clothes on again, and then strangled her from behind in a chokehold until she became unresponsive. He then placed her body in a tub filled with water, attempting to destroy any physical evidence of the sexual assault.[29] Before leaving, Wallace admitted to police he stole fifty dollars in cash from Shawna's purse, took her car keys, and drove away with her vehicle. The car would not be located until several months after Shawna's murder. It was found abandoned in the parking lot of her college.[30]

Wallace's next victim was Audrey Spain, twenty-four, another Taco Bell employee and coworker of the killer. Audrey, the youngest daughter with four siblings, was adored by her family. In the limited articles on her death, her family described her as independent, outgoing, and excited about her new life in the city of Charlotte.[31] She had been dead two days before her body was found on June 25, 1993, after a maintenance man entered her apartment to conduct a welfare check. Audrey had recently moved to Charlotte from Bayboro, South Carolina, and had attended Horry-Georgetown Technical College. She found a job as a manager at Taco Bell and worked with Shawna Hawk, who was murdered by Henry Wallace a month prior to Audrey Spain's homicide. An autopsy would reveal that Audrey was raped and strangled to death with a bra and T-shirt. As in the murder of Shawna Hawk, Wallace stole Audrey's car and her ATM card to steal money from her bank account. He then returned to the apartment and wiped down surfaces to erase any fingerprints.

Two months later, on August 10, 1993, twenty-one-year-old Valencia Jumper, a senior at Johnson C. Smith University, was found dead in her apartment.[32] She was a friend of Henry Wallace's sister. Wallace was convicted of raping and then strangling Valencia with a towel he took from the victim's bathroom. In addition to being a college student nearing graduation, the industrious young woman worked two jobs to support herself. In his confession to police, Wallace revealed that he set fire to her body and apartment in an attempt to cover up his crimes. The medical examiner initially determined the cause of death to be thermal burns.[33] But after Wallace named Valencia Jumper as one of his victims, the medical examiner performed another autopsy and confirmed the brutal details of Wallace's confession.

On September 15, 1993, Wallace would strike again, raping and strangling to death twenty-year-old Michelle Stinson, a mother of two young sons who were at home during her murder. In addition to being strangled with a towel the killer left wrapped around her neck, Wallace stabbed Michelle four times in the back with a kitchen knife. Wallace confessed to police that he used a washcloth to wipe his prints from the knife and doorknob and, after exiting Stinson's apartment, threw the knife away in the backyard of the building. As in the cases of his other victims, Wallace knew Michelle, who opened her door to him at 11 p.m., under his pretense of a friendly visit.

Wallace would confess to four additional murders of young Black women in the following year. On February 20, 1994, Vanessa Little Mack, twenty-five, a medical worker who was employed by Carolinas Medical Center and a mother of two young daughters, was raped, beaten, and strangled with a pillowcase and a towel, which was left wrapped around her neck. She was found by her mother on her bed, unresponsive and bleeding from her ears, nose, and head. The youngest of her two children was at home during the killing but was not harmed.

Less than three weeks later, on March 9, 1994, Wallace raped and strangled twenty-year-old Betty Jean Baucom, an assistant manager at Bojangles restaurant and an acquaintance of the killer. She was found dead in her apartment, lying face down with the towel used to strangle her still wrapped around her neck. Autopsy reports noted additional injuries Betty Jean sustained in a valiant fight for her life.

Within hours on the same night of March 9, Wallace boldly returned to the same apartment building where he only hours earlier raped and strangled to death Betty Jean Baucom, determined to commit yet another homicide. According to his confession, Wallace told police that Brandi J. Henderson was his first intended victim of the night, but her boyfriend, Verness Lamar Woods, who lived with the eighteen-year-old mother of a ten-month-old son, Tyreece, had not yet left for work. Wallace disclosed that his plan was to rape, murder, and then rob Brandi and pawn valuables he stole from the couple's home to finance his crack cocaine addiction. However, when he showed up earlier to Brandi's apartment and saw that her boyfriend was there, he left and then went to Betty Jean Baucom's home instead. When he returned to Brandi's apartment, he found her home alone with her infant son and gained entry by pretending to have stopped by to visit her before leaving town.

Shortly after Brandi Henderson opened her door to Wallace, he attacked her. Wallace admitted that, while raping Brandi, she piteously begged to hold her son during the sexual assault to stop the frightened baby from crying and, more than likely, to evoke sympathy from the merciless killer to spare her life. According to his confession, Wallace callously retorted, with a smirk, "I don't think you want to do that considering what we about to do!"[34] After the rape, Wallace strangled both Brandi Henderson and her son with a towel; the infant survived, but Brandi did not. Brandi's boyfriend, Verness Woods, found Brandi and their son at the apartment later that evening and immediately began to resuscitate his son, who struggled to breathe. He also discovered that Wallace had stolen the couple's stereo and television, which the killer admitted he later sold for drug money. Both Betty Jean's and Brandi's bodies would be discovered by loved ones within hours on March 10, 1994, at the same apartment complex.

Police believed that Wallace's final victim in this disturbing series of rape-slayings was thirty-five-year-old Debra Slaughter on March 12, 1994. Like most of Wallace's victims, Debra was attractive and small in stature. The young woman lived alone, and it was her mother who found her dead on her kitchen floor after she let herself into the apartment with a spare key. Debra had been raped and then strangled with a towel and stabbed with a kitchen knife she kept in her purse for protection. Wallace confessed to police that, during the assault, Debra screamed repeatedly to alert neighbors, and that she fought for her life. Wallace also told police that he was aware that Debra Slaughter kept a knife in her purse, and, after he sexually assaulted her, he grabbed the purse, retrieved the knife, and stabbed her a reported twenty times in the stomach and chest.[35] The medical examiner ruled that both the stabbing and strangulation contributed to her death. Wallace also confessed to police that after he began to sexually assault Debra, he told his horrified victim that he was the person responsible for the murders of Brandi Henderson and Betty Jean Baucom only twenty-four hours before.[36]

In each of the homicides, Henry Wallace stole money and other valuables from the victims' apartments to purchase crack cocaine, and, in several cases, he stole the victims' vehicles to leave the crime scene. Yet police would argue the homicides appeared to have no connection to one another, since the killer employed several techniques to cover his tracks and confound homicide investigators. However, after the murders of Betty Jean Baucom, Brandi Henderson, and Debra

Slaughter, police zeroed in on Wallace and arrested him within hours of Debra Slaughter's homicide. Police interviewed family members of the murdered women, and each of the victims' families named Wallace as an acquaintance whom the victims would trust. In many of the cases, he was either an acquaintance or a former workplace supervisor to the victims. A criminal background search on Wallace revealed a troubling arrest record, including one for rape.[37] A warrant was issued for his arrest, and, within days, police apprehended him and took him into custody, where he confessed to ten unsolved homicides of young Black women in the city.

Yet, for most of the families and loved ones of Wallace's victims, his arrest would trigger more rage at police than relief from the community that a vicious and stealthy killer had finally been captured.

CRITICISM OF THE INVESTIGATION SPURS ACCUSATIONS OF RACIST POLICE INDIFFERENCE

By the time police arrested Henry Louis Wallace on March 14, 1994, ten young Black women, several of them mothers of small children, lost their lives at the hands of a man whom they regarded as a friend. All but two of the victims, Sharon Nance and Caroline Love, were found dead in their homes. All of them knew Wallace, and many were friends and coworkers of each other. Nonetheless, for almost two years, police failed time and again to make connections between the victims and their killer.

An anonymous letter sent to the editor of the *Winston-Salem Chronicle*, dated March 31, 1994, argued that there were early indications that characteristics of the murders fit a specific pattern that would point to a single killer being responsible.[38] Moreover, the writer contended that Wallace "placed snugly in the puzzle," and that, because the victims were Black and working-class women, police failed to aggressively investigate the murders. The letter highlighted the fact that police departments across the nation are largely white and male and, as such, have a history of racist behavior toward Black people. Police are also more likely to pursue Black men who victimize white people than they are to investigate violent crimes with Black victims, especially when the assailant is Black. Moreover, several academic studies assert that systemic racial bias in American policing within communities of color impacts law enforcement's ability to see its residents as victims as opposed to criminals.[39]

Media also began to question the slow response of police to the homicides. A *New York Times* article by journalist Peter Applebome, provocatively titled "2 Years, 10 Murders, and 1 Question," demanded to know why Wallace's murderous reign of terror took place over a two-year period without police concluding that the killings were linked to a single predator. Applebome mused: "In a kinder world, 10 black women would have not been strangled to death over the last two years in this shiny Piedmont boom town. In a simpler world, there would be a clear lesson about race and police neglect in the belated recognition that one man may have been behind it all."[40] Applebome also examined the contradiction between the anger felt by Black communities in Charlotte who angrily blamed police for failing to solve the murders due to racism *and* Black city officials rejecting accusations of biased policing to preserve the city's racially harmonious image.[41] Nevertheless, many family members of Wallace's victims remained unconvinced that police did everything in their power to protect the lives of young Black women in Charlotte.

On May 13, 2022, ABC aired a *20/20* broadcast about the killings titled "Lock the Door Behind You," a phrase George Burrell, the cousin of Brandi Henderson, said he overheard Brandi say to someone who visited her home on the night of her murder.[42] At the time, Burrell told interviewers, he had been speaking with Brandi on the telephone after she called him and asked him to visit her that evening. Additionally, Burrell claimed that the day after Wallace murdered Brandi and attempted to murder her baby, he visited a mutual friend of his and Brandi's in a neighboring apartment unit in Brandi's complex. Burrell said he saw Wallace sitting in the living room watching news coverage of Brandi Henderson's and Betty Jean Baucom's murders. Burrell said that, in a conversation with Wallace, the killer turned to him and said, "She [Brandi] was always alone with her baby. And she would tell you, 'Lock the door behind you.'" Burrell said he was shocked by Wallace's comment and realized for certain that Wallace was involved in the murder of his cousin. He told *20/20* reporters that he immediately reported his suspicion to police, but he was "blown off" by officers he spoke with.

"Lock the Door Behind You" crystallized errors police made in their clumsy handling of the investigation while focusing on media's criticism of homicide detectives' failure to make connections between the victims and the killer, and the anger and frustration felt by family members of the victims. The program also included historical footage of jailhouse interviews with Wallace by journalists after his conviction in January 1997. The episode provided a treasure trove of information that lay bare the investigators' paltry detective work to solve the murders, exposing them to virulent criticism by victims' families, the wider Black communities of Charlotte, and members of both local and national media.

And, as in many cases where Black victims appear to be ignored by law enforcement, the lack of action by police begets community activism from its residents. Much like the Black women activists of the Combahee River Collective in Boston and Margaret Prescod, the founder of the Black Coalition Fighting Back Serial Murders in Los Angeles, it was the unrelenting quest for justice by the mother of one of the victims that put pressure on police to finally solve the case. Dee Sumpter, the mother of Shawna Hawk (believed to be Wallace's third victim), channeled unspeakable grief and rage into activism and formed Mothers of Murdered Offspring (MOMO) in partnership with her daughter's godmother, Judy Williams, shortly after Shawna's death in 1993.[43] During her interview with *20/20* reporters in April 2022, she provided a straightforward explanation of why she started MOMO: "I just knew I had a daughter who was murdered. And it wasn't being investigated properly. I was appalled by that. Angered by it. And I was not going to stop until I found out who did this."

With each subsequent homicide, Sumpter contacted the press and criticized the police investigation. She stated several times in interviews over the years that she felt race played a role in the lack of results in finding the killer.[44] In 1993, consumed with desperation and anguish over the loss of Shawna, Sumpter even wrote a letter to the *Charlotte Observer* editorial page, where she directly addressed her daughter's killer, imploring him to turn himself in to police. Moreover, Sumpter believed that the person who murdered Shawna was responsible for the other yet-unsolved rape-strangulations, despite police's initial insistence that the killings were unrelated. And, in an ironic turn of events, on the very day that Sumpter's letter was published, there was a brief news story in the *Charlotte Observer* announcing the murder of Vanessa Little Mack, the seventh victim.

If one were to use only one of the cases to encapsulate the incredulity of what appeared to be a blatantly apathetic police response to the murders of young Black women in Charlotte, the homicide of Shawna Hawk presents the most illustrative example. I interviewed Sumpter in June of 2022 to verify information I'd found for this section of the book.

Resilient and soft-spoken, Dee Sumpter presents as a tower of strength, with a face that reveals the soul-crushing pain of losing her beloved daughter. With both memory and heartbreak intact despite the decades that have passed, Sumpter exudes the rage she felt the day she discovered her daughter's brutalized and broken body in the bathtub. She shared several details that left me stunned. She first told me that, immediately after phoning the police, homicide investigators did not arrive at the crime scene until the next day. Meanwhile, EMT and firefighters arrived almost instantly; however, they may have inadvertently destroyed evidence. "By the time I should say homicide got there, EMT had been through, the fire department had been through, the scene was grossly compromised," she explained.[45] Sumpter added that once the first responders saw that there was an active crime scene, they should have backed out of the bathroom immediately and called for police.

> The problem of the fact is on that night no one [police] even came into my home. No wonder it [the crime scene] came up clean. There was nothing there to investigate because their own municipalities had been in and they had destroyed levels of evidence that, had they upon the night EMT got the phone call, immediately said "Back it out, back it out! This is an active crime scene! We need to shut it down and then bring in the folks and conduct an investigation." None of that was done! None of that was done![46]

Further, Sumpter noted that twenty-four hours after Shawna had been murdered and her body was taken to a local hospital, a homicide detective arrived at her home to, she assumed, commence an investigation. Sumpter described being at first stunned and then apoplectic when detective Lisa Mangum, the assigned investigator, informed her that an investigation would not begin for several days due to the overwhelming number of homicides police were already investigating.

> To quote Lisa Mangum [CMPD homicide detective] who was as-signed the case that night, she walked in the next day, loudly pro-claimed to me, "You know I'm in an overloaded and overworked position right now. I am not going to be in here to investigate this case for at least four or five days." I looked at her and said, "Un-acceptable! No, ma'am! Not going to happen!"[47]

Sumpter said she then left her home, went directly to the police station, and demanded an investigation into her daughter's murder begin immediately, even angrily threatening the police chief.

> I went down to homicide; I won't repeat my language. It was foul but it got the point across because, again, I said to the acting chief of homicide, "If you don't get someone out to my house *today* to start an investigation on my daughter's homicide, you will be sorry!"[48]

According to Sumpter, several hours later Shawna's homicide was assigned to Gary McFadden, the only Black detective at that time in the homicide squad, and the person who would be named lead inves-tigator in the series of unsolved homicides shortly before Wallace's capture. Despite McFadden's promise to the grieving mother that he was committed to solving her daughter's death, Sumpter found her-self growing increasingly dissatisfied with the lack of action on the part of police, especially when the traumatized mother was expected to live in the home for several days before police processed the crime scene. She feared this would compromise an effective investigation to find Shawna's killer.

Another major frustration for the mother was police's inability to locate Shawna's stolen car for several months after her death. Sumpter stated that she provided a description of the vehicle and a photograph, but the car would not be found until much later, and not by police, but by the parking garage attendant at Central Piedmont Community College, the school Shawna attended and where she was last seen alive. The attendant telephoned Sumpter when he noticed the car parked awkwardly in the same spot week after week with a large oil spill beneath the body of the vehicle.

> And when I saw the car, again, I was livid. Because Gary McFadden, I called him and I called Lisa Mangum, and I forget the other detective, and I was literally walking back and forth until they, you know, pulled up and when they got out the car, I didn't even wait for them to close the doors of their car, I just started going off! I said, "Do you see this?!" I said, "How stupid do you have to be?!"

After confronting Detectives McFadden and Mangum at the scene where Shawna's car was located, she described how dumbfounded the officers seemed as she began to berate them. "And they are just standing there looking at me! The dumbest looks on their faces I had ever seen in my life," she said. And it was at this moment that the mother experienced a devastating epiphany. "That's when it really hit me then, Cheryl. I said, 'You guys, you're not even investigating! You are not even investigating!'"[49]

Despite vigorous denials and a full-throated defense by police officials that they put forth their best effort to solve the homicides, Dee Sumpter's accusation that there was no real investigation by homicide detectives is not without merit.

After meticulously combing through news articles, medical examiner reports, court documents, and interviews with police officials and family members of the victims, I laid out details of the murders and found myself at a similar conclusion. Not only was there inept investigative work in these homicides, but I, too, questioned whether a rigorous investigation took place at all. It is confounding that for two years investigators were unable to see links in the crimes that would indicate one person was responsible for the rape-murders of these ten young women.

One of the earliest clues would have been the commonality in employment at fast-food restaurants among the victims. Dee Sumpter also believed that these connections of the victims to each other and to Wallace should have given police some indication that these were related homicides. In a 1994 interview featured in "Lock the Door Behind You," she held up her hand in front of her eyes and said, "Everything was right here all along. It's been right here! And they've done everything [looking underneath her hand and from side to side to demonstrate searching] except look right here!" Years later, in 2022, she remained steadfast in that opinion. "Obvious! Obvious connections. There's that word again, connecting the dots. And, in my humble opinion, blatantly ignored!" During her interview with me, she disclosed that at no time did investigators ask her for a list of names of individuals Shawna would have trusted enough to allow entry into their home. An article about the Hawk homicide also revealed that police instead stayed laser focused on Shawna's boyfriend, Darryl Kirkpatrick, as a possible suspect, much to the irritation of Dee Sumpter, who at no time believed the young man murdered her daughter.[50]

Therefore, to reify the argument that police failed to launch a thorough investigation into the murders and at the very least conclude that there was more than enough evidence that a serial predator was responsible for the killings, I present point by point the facts of the case. I've created two flowcharts to illustrate connections between the victims, and their relationships to their killer, figures 3.1 and 3.2.

FACT 1: *Most of the victims were connected through friendships and/or employment.* As evident in figure 3.1, on the next page, connections exist between most of the victims that would defy any assumptions of coincidence. Only two of the victims, Sharon Nance and Vanessa Little Mack, appear to have no direct link to the other women whom Wallace murdered. However, as Cathy O'Hara, a former reporter for WSOC-TV in Charlotte noted in "Lock the Door Behind You," Vanessa's sister worked at the same Taco Bell where several of the victims had been employed. Shawna Hawk was both friends and coworkers

FIGURE 3.1: *Victimology Diagram of Victim-to-Victim Connection*

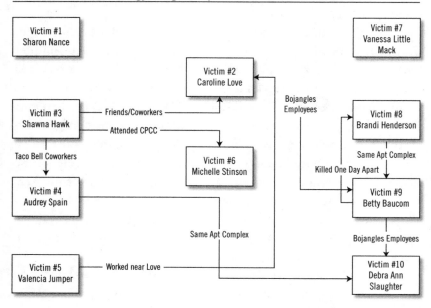

with Caroline Love (who also attended the same community college with Shawna) and Audrey Spain. In fact, in the *20/20* episode, Dee Sumpter said that after Caroline went missing in June 1992, Shawna expressed fear and concern for her friend—eight months before she, too, met her fate at the hands of Wallace. Coincidentally, Shawna also attended Central Piedmont Community College with victim Michelle Stinson. Caroline Love's place of employment, Bojangles restaurant (also the workplace of Betty Jean Baucom and Debra Slaughter), was in the same vicinity as Valencia Jumper's job at Food Lion. Additionally, Audrey Spain and Debra Slaughter both lived in the Glen Hollow apartment complex, although their murders occurred one year apart. Finally, Brandi Henderson and Betty Jean Baucom both lived in the Lakes apartment complex and were murdered within hours of each other. It wasn't until Brandi and Betty Jean's homicides (victims eight and nine) that police finally concluded there was a serial killer at play in the killings, according to assistant district attorney Marsha Goodenow. In an interview with *20/20*, Goodenow added that it was at this point that police finally used the term "serial killer" in reference to the murders.

With so many of the victims being associated with one another through employment, residence, or friendship, how could police miss such an obvious link? Ann Burgess is a renowned forensic profiler for the FBI's Behavioral Science Unit and a psychiatric nurse. Burgess expressed the opinion that Charlotte's homicide investigators failed to use a very basic and essential technique in studying murders with similar characteristics. "You've got to do the victimology first," she said in her interview with *20/20*, "because they would have realized that they knew each other in some capacity. And that would have been a way for them to zero in on Henry [Wallace]."

Crime investigators commonly use victimology to study the role of a victim either directly or indirectly in their victimization.[51] This often involves an examination of the associates or acquaintances of the victim, particularly if the victim is female. Disproportionately in cases involving homicides with female victims, the perpetrator is someone she knows.[52]

FACT 2: *There was no sign of forced entry into the victims' homes.* Again, victimology is key in this instance. Each one of these women opened their homes to the person who brutally raped and strangled them to death. In the investigations into the deaths of these ten victims, how often did police obtain a list of their male associates and conduct background checks to possibly identify their assailants? Had this very fundamental step been executed, they likely would not have missed Henry Wallace as the common denominator. In a 1987 study, criminologists John A. Humphrey and Stuart Palmer found that Black women were twice as likely to be murdered by a male friend or an acquaintance than white women, and ten times less likely to be murdered by a stranger than white female victims of homicide.[53] More recently, researchers Cara L. Frankenfeld and Timothy F. Leslie found the same to be true in their 2021 study on racial and ethnic characteristics of homicide victims across race.[54]

Had police been working from a list of male acquaintances for each of the ten victims, Wallace would have more than likely made every single list.

FACT 3: *All of the victims were strangled and sexually assaulted with the killer leaving a similar type of ligature wrapped around their necks.* Research on serial homicide indicates that for most serial killers with a predilection for sexual assault of female victims, strangulation tends to be their preferred method of killing.[55] In their defense, Charlotte police were quick to assert that they were overwhelmed by the number of homicides (129 homicides in 1993 alone) that occurred during the two years that Henry Wallace raped and killed his victims.[56] Gary McFadden, the Black homicide detective in charge of the investigation was placed into the position only hours before the first press conference. He blamed the crack cocaine epidemic for the escalation of violence in the Black communities within the city for the increase in Charlotte's homicide rate.[57]

However, the killings committed by Wallace did not fit the pattern of drug-related murders, which were typically linked to firearms, that were happening throughout the city. These were strangulations that followed sexual assaults. In at least three of the murders, Wallace left a towel wrapped around the victims' necks, reflecting a pattern.[58] In Wallace's detailed confession to police, he admitted to strangling Valencia Jumper, Michelle Stinson, Vanessa Little Mack, Brandi Henderson, Betty Jean Baucom, and Debra Slaughter with towels retrieved from their bathrooms. In the deaths of Vanessa, Betty Jean, Brandi, and Debra, their bodies were found with the towel still wrapped around their throats, yet police believed there was no connection between the killings.

FACT 4: *The murders occurred within five miles of each other, and, in at least two cases, in the same apartment complex or neighborhood.* Between June 1992 and March 1994, someone was targeting young Black women within a five-mile radius in the city's east-side neighborhoods. The killer struck twice within hours in the same apartment complex and murdered two victims one year apart in another complex. After the murders of Betty Jean Baucom and Brandi Henderson, police finally made the connection between the homicides and began to investigate the killings as serial murders.

And yet police action following the murders of Betty Jean and Brandi provoke more troubling questions. What emboldened Wallace to kill two women hours apart in the same location? In a news clip from 1994 featured in "Lock the Door Behind You," a reporter announces, "By daylight, detectives were back at the Lake Apartments with another murder on their hands." If police discovered a murder victim in one apartment the night before, the residence should have been an active crime scene, crawling with evidence technicians and homicide investigators. Some may question if police presence at the crime scene would have deterred Wallace from coming back to the apartment to not just kill again, but to then sit in a neighboring apartment to watch news footage of the killings with the victims' families, as George Burrell (Brandi Henderson's cousin) alleged? Why did police leave the premises after the first murder?

A lack of police presence at the crime scene was further confirmed by Dee Sumpter's complaint that police would not show up for several days before they could collect evidence and investigate her daughter's homicide. It is also likely that police did not secure the crime scene at the Lake Apartments complex, leaving Wallace with the opportunity to murder two women within a twenty-four-hour period. Bear in mind, there had been at least five other homicides of young Black women being raped and strangled in their residences with no evidence of forced entry, and two of those murders occurred within six months of each other. The final four killings occurred within an even shorter span of time. Vanessa Mack's murder took place on February 20, 1994—less than three weeks before Betty Jean and Brandi were killed on March 10, 1994. Two days later, Wallace murdered Debra Slaughter.

The strangled bodies of Black women were piling up, and police still made no link between the murders.

There is no doubt Charlotte police would be incensed at the mere suggestion that their lack of vigilance in the previous seven homicides indirectly gave permission to Wallace to target his last three victims: Betty Jean Baucom, Brandi Henderson, and Debra Slaughter. However, Wallace practically boasted as much in a 1994 jailhouse interview.

"The only time that police were concerned is when two murders occurred on the same day," the convicted serial killer glibly stated to FBI agents. "That's when all of a sudden they started seeing connections in things that happened twenty months ago."

FACT 5: *Each of the victims had personal property, cars, or money stolen from them by the killer.* Henry Wallace confessed to not only sexually assaulting and strangling his victims but also to robbing them of personal items and money to support his crack cocaine addiction. From his victims he took

- Caroline Love's roll of quarters she purchased to do laundry
- Shawna Hawk's car and fifty dollars in cash
- Audrey Spain's credit card, which he admitted to using to purchase gas
- Brandi Henderson's can of Pringles potato chips (later found empty in Betty Jean Baucom's stolen vehicle)
- Betty Jean Baucom's car
- and jewelry belonging to Valencia Jumper and Betty Jean Baucom, which he pawned at a local shop along with both women's television sets, VCRs, and stereos, which he sold for cash.

A video surveillance image captured Wallace unsuccessfully attempting to use the ATM card of Vanessa Little Mack, who deliberately gave him the wrong PIN. The footage was grainy, thus Wallace could not be easily identified, but what was evident in the video was a gold cross and hoop earring worn in one of his ears. This earring became a key identifier after Wallace's arrest, and his mug shot showed him wearing the same piece of jewelry. By coincidence, a different homicide detective entered the room where other detectives were looking at Wallace's mug shot and identified the earring from the ATM video. Imagine the possible delay in the killer's capture had he not happened upon other investigators who at the time were considering Wallace as a suspect. Why were detectives not collectively sharing information between the murder cases of unsolved strangulations?

Another important investigative question is whether police canvassed local pawn shops and made inquiries throughout the community to determine the identity of the person who sold these items for money. Could that have also led police to Wallace as a suspect in the homicides?

FACT 6: *Finally, each of the victims was connected to Henry Louis Wallace.* As can be observed in figure 3.2 below, Henry Louis Wallace was the common denominator among the victims. In some of the cases, he not only worked with several of the victims as manager of Taco Bell, but either he or his girlfriend, Sadie McKnight, were also regarded as friends by almost all of the young women. While it is highly unusual for serial killers to murder individuals with whom they have a personal relationship, again, Black women are more likely to be killed by male acquaintances than by strangers compared to their white counterparts.[59] Dee Sumpter denied that police requested a list of individuals who Shawna trusted enough to allow into their home, and,

FIGURE 3.2: *Victims' Connection to Henry Wallace*

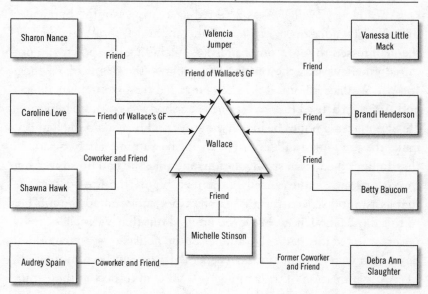

according to the *20/20* episode, this important investigative step was not initiated until the Baucom and Henderson homicides. It was at that point that Wallace emerged as a possible suspect in the killings and was apprehended within a week of the two killings—but not before he raped and strangled Debra Slaughter.

Once CMPD concluded that they were dealing with a serial killer, they contacted the FBI for assistance, and agents formulated a behavioral and psychological profile of the killer. Police conducted a thorough background check and found that Wallace had an arrest record. He had been previously charged with larceny and was also suspected in the unsolved rape-strangulation homicide of eighteen-year-old Tashanda Bethea, a young Black woman in Wallace's hometown of Barnwell, South Carolina. Tashanda disappeared in March 1990, and her body was found in a pond several weeks later, on April 1. Wallace was arrested and questioned in the young woman's disappearance but ultimately released. He left South Carolina shortly after being interrogated by police and relocated to the city of Charlotte. During his confession in the other homicides, he admitted to killing Tashanda Bethea, who, like his other victims, knew Wallace and considered him a friend.[60]

After Henry Wallace was arrested as a suspect in the homicides of Brandi Henderson, Betty Jean Baucom, and Debra Slaughter, he then confessed to seven other murders, including one police did not initially believe was the result of foul play—the death of Valencia Jumper. Wallace admitted that he first raped then strangled Valencia and, afterward, used rum to set fire to her body to cover up his crime. He also placed a pot of beans on the stove and turned up the flame to make the fire look accidental. The medical examiner later confirmed that Jumper died from strangulation, and that she had no soot in her throat or lungs, indicating that she died before the fire—a mistake that assistant district attorney Marsha Goodenow stated "haunts her to this day." Goodenow, however, pointed out that Valencia's family never accepted the medical examiner or the police's assessment of her death and were resolute in their belief that she had been murdered.

An examination of the actions by CMPD in respect to these murders demands an explanation, particularly because they claim that police did everything they could to vigorously investigate the murders from the first victim to the last, irrespective of the fact that the victims were young Black women from working-class communities.

However, the department's defenses were immediate, anemic, and deflective. The top brass of the CMPD was adamant in their denial that the victims' race contributed to what appears to be a lackluster investigation into the murders. Dennis Nowicki, chief of police, eagerly pointed out that some of the homicide detectives were Black (as if to suggest that such would automatically rule out racial bias). "That's ridiculous," he barked in a 1994 interview with media about the case. "Pardon me, but that [accusations of racism] offends me, it offends my officers, and it offends my community."[61]

However, neither most of the victims' families nor local Black community leaders were convinced that the police conducted a sufficient investigation into the murders. Even the appointment of a Black homicide detective, Gary McFadden, as the lead investigator only hours before a press conference in which police were confronted by frustrated community members and reporters was viewed suspiciously as the mostly white police department's attempt to mitigate accusations of racism. "The community hated me, and, in a way, I felt like a scapegoat," McFadden later said in an interview.[62] In the *20/20* episode, McFadden disclosed the anxiety police felt when they finally had to notify the public about Wallace's arrest. "How are we going to tell the public?" he recalled asking. "When we made that announcement, the city ate us alive! The media ate us alive." Undaunted by media and community criticism of the actions of homicide investigators, a stoic Larry Snider, deputy chief of the CMPD, stated, "Our investigators worked tremendously hard and did an excellent investigation of all these ten cases." Then, with apprehension, he lamented, "We're sorry that we did not get him to identify earlier. Had we done that maybe we could have saved the lives of some of these women."

Adding fuel to the fire that raged among the public toward the actions of police were comments made by local media as details of the investigation came to light. The managing editor of the city's only Black newspaper, the *Charlotte Post*, pointed out the investigators' failure to run a sufficient background check on Wallace after he was arrested several times while living in Charlotte for petty theft offenses. "They had him and they let him go," Herbert L. White said. "This, when they routinely run FBI checks on people for broken headlights."[63] It was not until Wallace was suspected in the last three homicides did police conduct a deep dive into his past and discover a possible link to another homicide in South Carolina. Reporter Cathy O'Hara acknowledged the media's failure to make connections in the murders while pointing out the CMPD's weak investigation. "For myself, as a reporter, I keep thinking, 'Why didn't we start putting two and two together?'" O'Hara mused to *20/20*. "Then you have the police who are trained to do these kinds of things. Why didn't *they* do it?" She later expressed sarcasm at police leadership's attempt to portray the investigation in a positive light. "I remember the police coming out and saying 'We have a serial killer. But you know what? Our officers did a great job!'"

Glenn Counts, another WSOC-TV news reporter in Charlotte, remarked that the Black community's anger at Charlotte police was attributed most to a belief that police were indifferent to the victims because of their race. "The community became outraged," he said. "There were some in the community who criticized the Charlotte police, saying that they didn't prioritize these murders because the victims were Black women." Dee Sumpter agreed. "There was not a level of caring," she said. "This is where the racial disparity comes in."

Jeri Young, a former reporter for the *Charlotte Post*, reported on Sumpter frequently, highlighting the grieving mother's focus on police dismissing the victims because they were working-class Black women. "We covered Dee," she said in her interview for "Lock the Door Behind You." "We covered her press conferences and one of the things she made everyone think about and talk about is 'if these had been white women who were dying in South Charlotte [a largely white area of the city], these killings would have been a huge story.'"

Yet, despite excoriation from the press and the public, police officials remained resolute in their denial that the race of the victims hindered their investigation efforts. "All of these cases were professionally and competently handled," said acting deputy chief Jack Boger. "Nothing was given a short shrift." But even Gary McFadden had to acknowledge the Black community's accusations of racial bias.

"Race is always a factor in criminal investigations," he explained in an interview. "Until America sees that it is not a factor or we have to mention it or do an interview, race is always going to be a factor."

When reporter Glenn Counts exclaimed to *20/20* reporters his disappointment with Charlotte police, "It was like you guys blew it! How could you miss this?" Gary McFadden offered an explanation. "It's not that we missed it, it's just that we were overwhelmed with the cases. We didn't have the technology. We didn't have the manpower, and we definitely didn't have the resources. All of those cases were on the desks of six homicide detectives in the nineties."

In 1993 the city of Charlotte experienced a noticeable increase in homicides. That year, 129 people were victims of violent death. Between the two years that Wallace sexually assaulted and murdered the ten victims, there were 300 homicides altogether. The majority of the killings took place in East Charlotte and were linked to the drug trade, according to McFadden.[64]

Also in 1993, Charlotte had a resident population of approximately 452,000 people. The city budget's allocation to policing was close to $57 million, and there were 930 full-time sworn officers in Charlotte. However, only 6 were assigned to the homicide unit to handle 129 murders, averaging 21 cases per officer.[65] An uptick in homicides would necessitate a more efficient use of police resources by increasing the number of homicide detectives, yet only a paltry number of investigators were handling an overwhelming number of cases, including the victims of Wallace. And, to complicate matters further, the responsibility for investigating the Wallace homicides were assigned to different officers throughout the homicide unit. One could question why there were fewer homicide detectives available since most of the murders were occurring in the largely Black areas of East Charlotte, as McFadden claimed. It wasn't until the murders of Betty Jean Baucom and Brandi Henderson that a task force (that included assistance from FBI's famed criminal profiler Robert Ressler) was formed to look at the cases collectively.

More than twenty-five years after Henry Wallace was arrested, convicted, and sentenced to death for the murders of nine of his ten victims—though he confessed to Sharon Nance's murder, he was not tried for her homicide—several questions remained, despite police emphatically attributing their poor investigation to a lack of manpower as opposed to racial bias.

- Is it possible that police didn't initially look closely at Wallace's background because police were indifferent to the murders of Black working-class young women?
- Did police indifference due to the victims' race play a role in investigators failing to obtain a list of acquaintances of the victims from family members, especially since there were signs that the victims knew the killer?
- Why didn't police attempt to locate stolen vehicles or other property stolen from victims by Wallace?
- As Dee Sumpter alleged, did police fail to secure crime scenes and launch a timely investigation into the murders?

As the proverbial adage goes, "Hindsight is 20/20," and Charlotte police assert that lessons were learned from the Henry Wallace serial homicide cases. "It made us better detectives, and it made the Charlotte police department a better homicide unit," Gary McFadden told *20/20* producers. One of the immediate remedies was to increase the number of homicide detectives in the unit and to "implement regular mandatory meetings to better identify related cases."[66] McFadden also advised that officers listen to the families of the victims who serve as the "voices" of their deceased loved ones. This was echoed in my interview with Dee Sumpter, who told me that she and Judy Williams, Shawna's godmother and the cofounder of MOMO, began helping to train homicide investigators on more empathetic ways to interact with the families of homicide victims, particularly in the cases of Black victims.

We went in and did an unpaid two-day seminar, intense eight hours in the police department downtown Charlotte, and literally walked them through Homicide 101, because I told them, "Give me the book that you get when you are training." I looked through it as I was talking, and I said, "So, in essence, what they are training you to do is to interview inanimate objects. You're not talking to human beings. But let me get real down and dirty with you. You're not talking to a Black woman or a man. You are mostly talking to Caucasians, right?[67]

Sumpter told me that the mostly white officers became "beet red" in the face and visibly uncomfortable at her question.[68]

Today, Henry Wallace remains in a North Carolina prison, where he awaits execution, although no official date has been set.[69] For the loved ones of Wallace's victims, the pain is still acute. Dee Sumpter struggles daily to simply get out of bed and face the day without her daughter, as echoed by family members featured in "Lock the Door Behind You." Linda Moore, the sister of Debra Slaughter, the last of Wallace's victims, told *20/20* reporters that what was important to her is that her sister and the other victims are not simply viewed as women murdered by a serial killer.

"I just want people to not forget, you know, what happened to these girls in Charlotte, North Carolina," she said. "I don't want people to go around and hear the name of Henry Wallace and not know who he is. Because he was a Black serial killer who killed a lot of Black women. I want the world to know what happened and that these girls' lives mattered."

Each of these young women were more than their short lives and brutal deaths. Therefore, it is imperative to remember:

- Sharon Nance, the shy young woman with a sweet smile . . .
- Caroline Love, the hardworking college student and fast-food worker with a younger sister who desperately awaited her return . . .
- Shawna Hawk, the best friend, soulmate, and dedicated daughter of her still grieving mother . . .
- Audrey Spain, the independent and "spirited" young woman from South Carolina who looked forward to her new life in the Queen City . . .

- Valencia Jumper, a senior at Johnson C. Smith University who majored in political science and worked two jobs to support herself and pay for her education . . .
- Michelle Stinson, a young mother who worked to support her two sons . . .
- Vanessa Little Mack, a young mother of two daughters who worked in health care . . .
- Brandi Henderson, the eighteen-year-old mother who called her infant son Tyreece "her masterpiece" . . .
- Betty Jean Baucom, a committed employee who had recently been promoted to assistant manager at the Bojangles restaurant and adopted a young daughter . . .
- And Debra Slaughter, a stunning beauty with a perfect smile, who left behind her young son, Eric.

The grievous apathy of the CMPD in the investigations of these young women's tragic murders underscores the lack of humanity that many police departments hold for Black homicide victims. This is a systemic issue, rooted in the devaluation of Black lives that has been pervasive in this country since slavery. While Charlotte police now acknowledge the shortcomings in their investigation of these young women's tragic deaths, time fails to erase the devastation of the victims' families, and their frustration with racially biased police indifference. And it is this indifference that leads to deadly consequences when predators, like Henry Wallace, target victims they believe police are more likely to ignore.

CHAPTER 4

"NO HUMANS INVOLVED"

Police Apathy and the Tale of the Grim Sleeper

A T FIRST GLANCE of Princess Berthomieux's school photo, one notices her large and expressive eyes, her head slightly tilted to the left, her sweet closed-mouth smile, reminiscent of Leonardo da Vinci's sixteenth-century painting *Mona Lisa*. She is wearing a lavender sweater, her hair in neat, curly, shoulder-length braids, as her eyes gaze upward, not at the photographer. The lack of a direct stare conveys the personality of a shy, perhaps awkward, preadolescent reluctant to pose for the obligatory school picture but who bravely musters a smile nonetheless. Given the name Princess at birth, a moniker that would suggest parents who regarded their daughter as precious, her life was anything but.

Abandoned by her birth mother as an infant in 1986, she was raised by a father whose abuse was so sadistic that, by the age of three, Princess was removed from his custody after being rushed to the hospital for cocaine poisoning. It was there that doctors discovered that the toddler had been both physically and sexually abused—allegedly by multiple men who were friends of her father—and bore rope burns from restraints on both her tiny wrists and ankles.[1] She was also malnourished, didn't smile, and could barely speak. Unlike many foster children, Princess was immediately placed in a home with a devoted and affectionate foster mother who would love the toddler like her own and immediately put Princess under the care of a therapist and enrolled her in private schools. Tragically, ten years later, her caregiver died of cancer, and her foster father became too ill to continue providing care to the girl, now in her early teens.

Samara Herard, the foster family's older daughter, tried taking guardianship over Princess to continue raising her, but Princess began acting out due to the grief and fear from losing the only mother she had ever known. Sadly, the young girl would again enter the foster care system, placed from one home to the next, until, disillusioned and wary of being further abused, she began running away. Once more, Princess became the victim of sexual trauma. She was sexually exploited and trafficked by an older man and raped by a thirty-year-old cab driver who was later arrested.[2]

Still, the worst was yet to come.

Death would claim her before she reached her sixteenth birthday. At age fifteen, Princess Berthomieux became the youngest victim of serial killer Lonnie David Franklin Jr.[3] On March 19, 2002, several months after she was reported missing by her last foster mother, Princess's nude body was found under a shrub in an alley in Inglewood, a neighborhood in South Central Los Angeles.[4] She had been raped, beaten, and strangled to death.

The man accused and convicted in Princess's murder, Franklin, was referred to as the "Grim Sleeper." Police initially speculated that Franklin, a married city sanitation worker and the father of one son, had been on a thirteen-year hiatus from a killing spree that began in 1985 in Los Angeles, but then later discovered that his rape-murders of Black women did not cease. LAPD investigators believed Princess Berthomieux to be Franklin's first victim after he emerged from a self-imposed "retirement" in 2002. By the time he was arrested in 2010 for the murders, Franklin had murdered at least ten victims, although it is believed he killed far more women than the ones for which he was convicted.[5] While police were aware that women were being killed in similar fashion, they failed to alert the victims' families and other members of the community that a killer was hunting women in their neighborhood. Not only were police accused of failing to conduct a sufficient investigation to apprehend Franklin, but it would also be revealed that police callously referred to the homicides as murders with "no humans involved."[6]

DEATH STALKS BLACK WOMEN IN SOUTH CENTRAL LOS ANGELES

The year 1985 ushered in several impactful, albeit chaotic, world events. A serial killer dubbed the "Unabomber" claimed his first victim; the US health-care system began screening blood donations to stop the spread of HIV/AIDS; Philadelphia police dropped a bomb on the West Philadelphia residential compound of a Black activist group called MOVE, killing six adults and five children; an earthquake hit Mexico City and killed at least nine thousand people; and Michael Jackson and a host of other celebrities gathered together and wrote the timeless anthem "We Are the World" to raise fifty million dollars to mitigate famine in Ethiopia.[7]

On an 81-degree day on August 10, 1985, the body of twenty-nine-year-old Debra Jackson, an African American mother of three children, was found in an alley in the mostly Black Vermont/Slauson neighborhood of Los Angeles. She was sexually assaulted and shot three times in the chest with a small caliber gun. Unfortunately, Debra's murder was barely covered by the press; it was one of many killings that year. The 1980s saw a rise in drug-related homicides resulting from a growing crack cocaine epidemic that devastated many communities that were both largely Black and urban. Police initially assessed that Debra was a prostitute whose murder was related to the deadly crack cocaine trade.[8] However, she was employed as a cocktail waitress at a local bar and was last seen alive leaving her friend's house to catch a bus home to her apartment.[9] According to her friends and family members, Debra was recovering from an addiction to crack cocaine. After she successfully completed a drug treatment program, she was on the verge of being reunited with her children, who had been removed from her custody by the state. Debra had also enrolled in a cosmetology program to become a licensed beautician, taking steps to create a future for herself and her children. When her body was found discarded by the killer in an alley, police classified her as a "Jane Doe" until she was identified by family members several months later.[10]

Exactly one year later, in August 1986—and less than two miles from the location where Debra Jackson was murdered—thirty-five-year-old Henrietta Wright was found shot to death in an alley in the

South Central LA neighborhood of Hyde Park. Her killer had attempted to hide her body under a discarded mattress. Similar to the murder of Debra Jackson, Henrietta was shot several times in the chest with a .25-caliber pistol. She was also gagged with a long-sleeved shirt that the killer stuffed down her throat.[11] Decades later, during the murder trial of Lonnie David Franklin Jr., Henrietta Wright's daughter, Rochelle Johnson, steeled herself to look at the crime scene photo of her mother's body that had been projected onto a screen in the courtroom. She identified Henrietta as "my beautiful mother."[12] The heartbroken daughter seemed determined to counter the narrative that each of Franklin's victims were "crack addicted prostitutes."[13]

Even though Debra Jackson and Henrietta Wright died under comparable circumstances, at the time police made no connection between the two homicides. Their deaths were simply viewed as more casualties of South Central LA's burgeoning drug trade. Additionally, Debra Jackson's and Henrietta Wright's homicides were overshadowed by a string of brutal slayings taking place in East Los Angeles, a more affluent and predominantly white area of the city. At least sixteen people were slain in their homes and another twenty-one injured or sexually assaulted by a shadowy serial killer dubbed the "Night Stalker" by the press. Each subsequent murder seemed to rivet the attention of not only the residents of California but also the entire nation, with nonstop coverage on the evening news. The victims were bludgeoned, stabbed, shot, and, in some cases, tortured by a man who would later be identified as twenty-five-year-old Richard Ramirez.

An unemployed drifter, Ramirez was apprehended on August 31, 1985, via a "citizen's arrest" by a group of residents, including the husband of a woman Ramirez attempted to assault on a residential street. The woman's screams alerted her husband and neighbors, who chased and beat Ramirez with a steel rod and held him until police arrived.[14] So terrified were the people of California of the serial murderer that the arrest of Ramirez even prompted a triumphant reaction from the city's mayor, Tom Bradley, who declared that his capture allowed the state to "breathe a sigh of relief tonight."[15] This myopic comment crystallized the fact that Ramirez's murders of mostly white victims seemed to resonate more viscerally with Californians, while the deaths of Black women did not. Bradley's statement also seemed to suggest that Ramirez's capture neutralized a threat of predatory violence that posed a danger to residents in general, as opposed to only people living in a specific neighborhood. Rarely do killings of Black people in urban environments have the same ubiquitous effect.[16] So, while the predominantly white population of Californians could now nestle safe and soundly in their beds at night, knowing that Ramirez was in police custody, there would be no such peace in the impoverished, violent landscape of South Central Los Angeles.

The murders of Black women continued.

That following year, three additional women would die violently in an eerily similar manner. On January 10, 1987, the body of twenty-three-year-old Barbara Ware was found under a pile of trash in an alley in the neighborhood of Central Alameda. She had been shot several times in the chest with a .25-caliber gun, a plastic bag pulled over her head and upper body.[17] A short time before midnight, 911 operators received a call from a witness who claimed to have seen Barbara's body being dumped by a man driving a blue-and-white van, even providing the license plate number of the vehicle. Despite this detailed information and police later tracking the location of the van to a church parking lot, no additional follow-up was conducted to find its owner, which media would later speculate could have provided the identity of Barbara's killer.[18] This seemingly intentional blunder would be one of many that outraged and frustrated the victims' families and other members of the community, who believed the police to be indifferent to the murders of Black women.

Three months later, on April 16, 1987, Bernita Sparks, age twenty-five, was shot to death, her nude body found dumped in a trash bin in an alley in the Gramercy Park area of South Central Los Angeles. On Halloween night, October 31, 1987, the nude body of twenty-six-year-old Mary Lowe was found less than a half-mile away in the same community of Gramercy Park. She, too, had been shot to death with a small caliber gun, and the killer attempted to cover her body with trash. Several months later and shortly before

January 1988 came to an end, twenty-two-year-old Lachrica Jefferson was found shot to death—approximately one mile from Mary Lowe's murder—and buried under a discarded mattress in an alley in the Westmont neighborhood. In a final act of humiliation, the killer wrote "AIDS" on a napkin and placed it over her face. Almost a year would pass before September 1988, when the killer struck again, murdering eighteen-year-old Alicia Alexander. The teen was shot, strangled, sexually assaulted, and found nude beneath a blue foam mattress in an alley in the Vermont Square neighborhood. Like most of Franklin's victims, Alicia Alexander had a history of sex work and using crack cocaine.

Detectives theorized that because many of the victims struggled with drug addiction, Franklin was able to entice them with crack cocaine. He'd lure the women into his vehicle, where he often took photos of them—in some cases after they were deceased—and would then sexually assault them before shooting or strangling them to death. Twenty-five years after he allegedly murdered Debra Jackson, the first of the Grim Sleeper homicides, police uncovered more than 180 photos of women and teenaged girls. Even as late as 2016, police were still asking the public for help in identifying the young women and teen girls in the photographs.[19]

As noted earlier, police initially surmised that Franklin ceased killing women in 1988 and then began again in 2002, with the rape and strangulation of Princess Berthomieux. Two more victims would be added to this grim tally. In 2003, Valerie McCorvey, thirty-five, was found strangled and sexually assaulted in an alley in the Westmont neighborhood. Several more years would pass before the body of twenty-five-year-old Janecia Peters was found dumped in the same alley where Franklin was later accused of discarding the body of Bernita Sparks twenty years before. Like the other victims, Janecia was sexually assaulted, then shot and strangled. But, unlike with previous murders, it would be the Janecia Peters homicide in January 2007 that finally prompted cold case detectives to reexamine evidence that linked the deaths to a single perpetrator.

Most residents of the South Central LA community did not agree with the LAPD's assertion that Lonnie Franklin took breaks in his killing spree; they were cognizant that murdered women were still found discarded in alleys throughout the neighborhood, even when police believed he had ceased killing women. Furthermore, there was suspicion that Franklin was not alone in his lethal predation. Margaret Prescod (whose tireless work to warn the community about a serial killer and pressuring the police to solve the crimes will be discussed later in this chapter) maintained that more than one killer was targeting Black women in the area. As it turned out, she was correct. It is estimated that more than one hundred Black women living in South Central Los Angeles were murdered between 1984 and 1993— an astounding number by any account, especially in one specific area of a city.[20] Prescod's organization, the Black Coalition Fighting Back Serial Murders, was formed in response to the overwhelming number of murders of Black women in the city and what was described as inaction on the part of police to stop them. Prescod also bristled at the media's portrayal of the killings as "prostitution murders," which not only discounted the value of the victims' lives but also anaesthetized public outrage to their deaths. Furthermore, not all of the women killed were sex workers, but many of them did engage in illicit sexual activity to procure crack cocaine, leaving them exposed to men who preyed on their addictions. By the time Franklin was arrested in 2010 for at least ten of these murders, three other men were convicted and sentenced to death for the rape-strangulations of multiple women—serial killings that overlapped and, frighteningly, showcased South Central Los Angeles as both a haven and a playground for men who sought to kill Black women.

One of three convicted serial killers, Chester Turner, thirty-six years old at the time of his arrest in 2002, sits on death row in San Quentin State Prison for the murders of ten women he was accused of killing over an eleven-year period in Los Angeles. At the time of his conviction, prosecutors described Turner as the city's "most prolific killer."[21] His victims were: Diane Johnson, twenty-one; Annette Ernest, twenty-six; Anita Fishman, thirty-one; Regina Washington, twenty-seven (who was almost seven months pregnant at the time of her death); Desarae Jones, twenty-nine; Andrea Tripplett, twenty-nine; Natalie Price, thirty-one; Mildred Beasley, forty-five; Paula Vance, thirty-eight (whose rape and strangulation was captured on a nearby trailer park's surveillance video); and Brenda Bries, thirty-seven. After DNA testing was conducted by the LAPD cold case unit on murder cases dating back to the 1960s,[22] Turner was linked to four more slayings of Black women: Elandra Bunn, thirty-three; Deborah Williams, twenty-eight; Mary Edwards, forty-two; and Cynthia Annette Johnson, thirty.[23] Unfortunately, David Allen Jones, a mentally disabled twenty-three-year-old man, was convicted of the four cold case murders Turner allegedly committed in 1995. The innocent man was exonerated and released in 2004 after serving nine years in prison.

At an imposing six foot two inches and 220 pounds, Michael Hughes, a former security guard with a criminal history that included assault and sexual offenses, was convicted in 1993 for the rape-murders of four Black women whom Culver City police chief Ted Cooke described to the press as "essentially prostitutes."[24] The victims, Teresa Ballard, twenty-six; Brenda Bradley, thirty-eight (the niece of former Los Angeles mayor Tom Bradley); Terri Myles, thirty-three; and Jamie Harrington, twenty-nine, were strangled and found nude or partially nude and dumped in alleys in both South Central Los Angeles and Culver City between September and November 1992. While incarcerated for those murders, police found evidence that linked Hughes to three additional rape-strangulation killings between 1986 and 1993 that included Yvonne Coleman, a fifteen-year-old high school student; Deborah Jackson, thirty-two; and Verna Williams, thirty-six. In June 2012, then-fifty-six-year-old Hughes was sentenced to death after being found guilty in the murders of the teen girl and two other women.[25]

The last of the three serial predators was Louis Crane, described in the press as a thirty-two-year-old illiterate construction worker. Crane was convicted and sentenced to death in 1989 for the rape-strangulations of three women in the same South Central LA neighborhoods where the victims of Lonnie Franklin and Michael Turner met their deaths. In my research there was no mention of the names of the women Crane was accused of killing, nor were there any personal details about their lives on any media news sites. Yet these articles readily used the dehumanizing label "prostitutes" when referring to the victims of these horrific killings. One news story suggested that police's refusal to publicly release the names of the victims or their cause of death was deliberately manipulative; police attempted to obfuscate any connection between victims or common characteristics in the homicides that would point to multiple serial predators operating in South Central Los Angeles at the same time.[26]

It is difficult to consider the onslaught of murdered Black women in one Los Angeles community without raising questions about the quality of investigative work by the LAPD. Why were police slow to classify the killings as serial murders? Is it possible that some lives could have been saved had police warned women in the community that serial killers were stalking them? Would there have been as many murders if police conducted a serious investigation into the homicides from the onset? Is it possible that police inaction emboldened these men to kill with impunity? And what role, if any, did the LAPD's strong-armed handling of rampant crack cocaine addiction in mostly Black and Brown communities play in their paltry response to these homicides?

Undoubtedly, the crack epidemic plaguing South Central Los Angeles at that time had a catalytic part in making most of the victims vulnerable to a serial killer. Autopsy toxicology reports revealed that all but one of the Grim Sleeper victims had cocaine in her system at the time of her death.[27] But this revelation should not be justification for treating these victims with contempt nor viewing their murders as simply an occupational hazard. Rather, it demands a consideration of the multifaceted tragedies that exposed these women to predatory violence: drug addiction, misogynoir, and the LAPD's callous disregard for Black women as human beings during America's so-called war on drugs.

BETWEEN THE DEVIL AND THE DEEP BLUE SEA: BLACK WOMEN AS COLLATERAL DAMAGE IN THE WAR ON DRUGS

On September 5, 1990, while sitting before a US judiciary committee on the first-year anniversary of President George H. W. Bush's war on drugs, LAPD police chief Daryl Gates made a statement that stunned not only members of the panel but also the nation at large. "Casual drug users should be taken out and shot!" he boldly exclaimed. Gates, referring to recreational users of marijuana, argued that they fueled the "enemy": street gangs and dealers of illicit substances. Later, when interviewed by the press following his Senate testimony, Gates doubled down on his caustic comments and unapologetically maintained his stance. "We're in a war," he blustered. "And even casual drug use is treason!"[28]

The president's drug policy involved a national strategy that focused on the implementation of four steps, the first (and most consequential) being an increase of funding and authority to law enforcement. "We need more jails, more prisons and courts, and more prosecutors," Bush stated emphatically.[29] The government earmarked $1.5 billion in federal spending for law enforcement; $50 million would be used to specifically target public housing projects, where Bush claimed the crack problem was most acute.

In major US cities, city officials put the Bush drug policy into practice, including one of the most controversial enactments of the law enforcement strategy orchestrated by Chief Gates. Gates's approach, which was called "Operation Hammer," utilized every militarized tool available to arm local police with tanks, battering rams, full body armor, and semiautomatic rifles, along with counterinsurgency war tactics to target individuals distributing and using crack cocaine in predominantly Black neighborhoods in Los Angeles. Gates also instructed his officers to patrol from their vehicles, eschewing any personal interaction with community members.[30]

Daryl Gates's comment about executing casual drug users was hypocritical, to say the least. His own son was struggling with drug dependency, yet the police chief attempted to make the distinction between his son's addiction to narcotics and what he saw as the hedonistic pursuit of recreational drugs.[31] Gates clearly did not understand (or, perhaps, didn't care) that crack cocaine is one of the most highly addictive illegal substances, and that very few users are "casual" in their consumption of it.[32] Unsurprisingly, the Bush administration's zero tolerance antidrug policies, Gates's unrelenting use of hypermilitarized police tactics to address both the sale and use of crack, and the ensuing gang violence resulted in devastating consequences for Black women in South Central LA neighborhoods. His openly hostile contempt for drug addicts (primarily those of color) translated into police actions that wreaked havoc on the Black women and their children who lived in low-income housing. Arrests and incarceration rates for Black women during this period skyrocketed, and doctors were more likely to notify police when blood tests of pregnant Black women during delivery revealed traces of cocaine in her system.[33] Even women who were not drug users endured the brunt of police brutality that culminated in the destruction of their homes, personal property, and even the loss of custody of their children.

One such raid occurred on the night of February 6, 1985, when Daryl Gates and LAPD officers used a fourteen-foot battering ram to plow through the wall of a home that was suspected of being a drug den (or "rock house," as it was often called) in the predominantly Black Pacoima neighborhood. Occupants inside the home included two mothers and their three children who were eating ice cream and watching television. With guns drawn and threats issued to shoot anyone who moved, police searched the residence and found only a small amount of marijuana. Twenty-four-year-old Linda Brown, who lived at the property with her husband and five-year-old son, was charged with child endangerment, and her young child was temporarily placed in protective custody. Her husband, twenty-five-year-old Antonio Johnson, was not at home at the time of the raid but was later arrested and charged with suspicion of selling cocaine.[34]

As it turned out, the home was not a drug house, and the community was outraged that the lives of innocent mothers and their children could have been lost due to faulty information. Police apparently assumed that steel bars on the windows and doors (which were installed by the landlord six months before Brown and her family moved in) served as evidence of a drug house as opposed to protection from neighborhood gang violence. Yet, despite virulent criticism by media and city officials about the raid, Gates remained unrepentant for the misconduct on the part of himself and LAPD officers. Not only did he accompany the police in the raid, but, when asked by reporters about the lack of drugs in their search of the home, Gates stated, "I suspect they sold out! That happens all the time."[35] No warrant was presented during the raid, and Gates suggested that the lack of physical harm to the women and children was "proof in the pudding" that care was taken to protect the minors.[36]

Such a problematic action on the part of Gates and the LAPD in the Pacoima raid was only one of several examples of police overreach that threatened Black mothers and their children. Three years later, in August 1988, police again used battering rams to completely obliterate two apartment buildings on Thirty-Ninth Street and Dalton Avenue in the southwest area of Los Angeles. The violent destruction of property was extensive. According to the *Los Angeles Times*, police "smashed furniture, punched holes in walls, destroyed family photos, ripped down cabinet doors, slashed sofas, shattered mirrors, hammered toilets to porcelain shards, doused clothing with bleach and emptied refrigerators."[37] In a move of stunning hubris, police even spray-painted their own graffiti of "LAPD Rules," and "Rollin' 30s Die" to intimidate neighborhood gangs.[38] Ten adults (mostly Black women) and twelve minor children were left homeless and required emergency housing through the American Red Cross. Undeterred and without apology, Gates justified the raid by arguing that surveillance of the properties revealed that drugs were sold in front of the building (as opposed to from inside the residences), but the raid netted no stash of drugs in any of the apartments. The city responded with a $4 million settlement for damages to the property and victims of the violent raid. Christopher Darden—the Black deputy district attorney who would later participate in the O. J. Simpson trial—charged three of the officers with misdemeanor vandalism, but each was acquitted by a jury in 1991.[39]

It is not without irony that the proliferation and sale of crack cocaine in South Central Los Angeles was documented in a number of sources as the result of collusion between the Reagan administration and the CIA to fund the sale of arms to Contra guerrilla fighters in Nicaragua.[40] This facilitated and escalated the trafficking of crack cocaine and the epidemic of addiction that ravaged Black communities not only in LA but in other urban areas throughout the United States. Interestingly, a decade later, in the 1990s, the Bush administration raged an all-out war on drugs under Chief Gates that led to the mass incarceration of Black men and women, and the development of a threatening and overly militarized brutal police force in inner-city neighborhoods across the country.[41]

For most Black and Brown people living in communities dubbed as "war zones" by an overzealous presidential administration and an authoritarian police chief, daily life was precarious and fraught with tension. Yet this anxiety was particularly heightened for women who were addicted to crack cocaine and participated in sex work to support their drug habits. Almost all of Lonnie Franklin Jr.'s victims were Black women who suffered from addictions to crack cocaine and practiced sex work to obtain the highly addictive substance. These women were not only discounted as victims by police, but they also were subjected to derision and predatory violence by both drug dealers and serial killers. Norm Stamper, a former police chief in the city of Seattle who began his career in 1966 as a "beat cop" in San Diego, California, revealed in his memoir, *Breaking Rank,* that he personally heard police officers dismiss the deaths of sex workers, particularly those who were Black, as "misdemeanor murders":

> I've heard some police officers refer to prostitute slayings (or the slayings of blacks) as "misdemeanor murders," employing an unofficial code for them: NHI, no humans involved. "Sex workers" as many in the trade prefer to be called, are vilified, stigmatized, and written off. They're immoral. They engage in sinful, illegal activity. . . . Dehumanizing or demonizing sex workers makes it easier to ignore them when they go missing or are found dead.[42]

Stamper goes on to question whether "these officers of the law would respond to the murders of forty teachers" in the same manner.[43] Rarely if ever viewed as damsels in distress, these Black women were between the devil and the deep blue sea, with little hope of protection or rescue.

In a 2014 study, Tanya Telfair LaBlanc and Barbara C. Wallace investigated the impact of crack cocaine addiction and sex work on poor Black women and their families. The researchers emphasized the diminishment of social status for women who often exchanged sex to support their drug habits and were stigmatized, dehumanized, and exposed to violence from both drug dealers, police, and the larger community. For many unemployed Black men in these neighborhoods who were also struggling with addiction and feelings of inadequacy, social power could be gained through forcing these women to participate in "degrading and dangerous" sex acts in exchange for crack.[44] If they were also mothers who lost custody of their children, this further reinforced community-wide disregard for them. Consequently, for victims of men like Lonnie Franklin Jr. or Chester Turner, the LAPD's anemic response to their murders reinforced the view that neither the lives nor the deaths of these women mattered. As was the case in the Roxbury murders of Black women living in Boston in the late 1970s, the police officers overtly exhibiting contempt for and brutally treating residents in communities of color would be the same police called on to protect the women of these neighborhoods from men who sought to kill them.

A FILM EXPOSES POLICE DEHUMANIZATION AND DEADLY MISOGYNOIR TOWARD THE GRIM SLEEPER VICTIMS

The ruthlessly hazardous environment of South Central LA was crystallized in Nick Broomfield's gritty 2014 award-winning documentary, *Tales of the Grim Sleeper*. Taking camera and courage (Broomfield was violently threatened on camera several times by men in the neighborhood while filming) into South Central Los Angeles, Broomfield interviewed the male friends of Lonnie Franklin Jr., Franklin's son Christopher, and women in the community (including those who barely escaped Franklin's murderous assaults) to examine how Franklin was able to kill repeatedly and avoid capture for more than twenty years. *Tales of the Grim Sleeper*, described as a "film about disposable human beings," takes the viewer deep into the underbelly of the neighborhoods that Franklin and others made their predatory playground.[45]

Activist Margaret Prescod is prominently featured in the film as the unrelenting crusader for justice for the murdered women.[46] Prescod became a virtual thorn in the side of police officials, including former mayor of Los Angeles, Antonio Villaraigosa. She and her organization, the Black Coalition Fighting Back Serial Murders, remained unwavering in their support for victims' families as well as their pressure campaign on the LAPD and LASD (Los Angeles Sheriff's Department) to sufficiently investigate the killings and warn women in the community about serial killers.

The murders of Lonnie Franklin's victims took place against the backdrop of Los Angeles's most deadly decade. From 1980 through 1990, the city's murder rate averaged more than five hundred homicides a year, with a significant number of them occurring in neighborhoods that made up South Central Los Angeles.[47] The disproportionately high Black unemployment rate coupled with gang violence and drug turf wars made murder an almost twice-daily occurrence. Initially, the deaths of many of these victims failed to raise the alarm for most of the community, and any suspicion that Franklin could be the man behind the killings was nonexistent.

Until it wasn't.

Franklin, unlike his neighbors, was gainfully employed as a city sanitation worker and operated as a fence for stolen automobile parts and appliances. As one of Franklin's neighbors commented in the film, "Lonnie could get you anything you needed!"[48] Men who described themselves as Franklin's neighbors and friends offered a full-throated defense of Lonnie. Many commented that the convicted killer was "a good guy," and that the street they lived on "is a close block," so they would know if a killer walked among them. Some even credited Lonnie Franklin as being so "anti-crack" that his animus fueled his ability to "shut down drug houses in the neighborhood."

From the beginning of Broomfield's conversations about Lonnie Franklin with his male neighbors and friends (the only women interviewed were victims of his violence), the men vehemently balked at accusations that Franklin was the person responsible for the murders. But as time went on, and they became comfortable speaking with the filmmaker, they began to doubt Franklin's innocence. It became clear that, since many of these men did odd jobs for Franklin and considered him the "richest man" in the neighborhood, Franklin used his position to buy their silence and complicity in his criminal exploits and violent treatment of women in the community. Several troubling scenes in the documentary make it clear that information they shared with Broomfield should have been reported to police and might have led to Franklin being arrested sooner.

For instance, one friend related that Lonnie Franklin showed him a .25-caliber automatic weapon and a pair of handcuffs—this after police began to publicly divulge details about the gun used in most of the killings after the death of Janecia Peters in 2007. The man said he was surprised that Franklin presented such damning evidence to him while hinting slyly that he was indeed the real killer, but the friend never went to police with this information. Another friend volunteered to Broomfield that he was routinely paid to destroy stolen cars after Franklin had stripped them of valuable parts to sell. On one occasion, the man noticed that a car Franklin asked him to burn had a bloody back seat with women's underwear on it. Despite his discomfort and suspicion that something was awry, the man did not question Franklin, but instead torched the vehicle. This, too, was never divulged to police.

Still another friend of Franklin's claimed he was riding in a car with him when Lonnie spotted a woman walking down the street and quickly pulled the car over to the curb. According to this witness, Franklin jumped out and began to physically beat the woman—an assault that was witnessed by police in the area. Officers quickly intervened and arrested Franklin and his friend. Within hours, both men were released from custody, and no charges were filed against either man in the case. The friend was shocked that police didn't even take mug shots or fingerprints as part of their arrests, and both men were freed without incident. Franklin also once worked as a mechanic on police vehicles, and this may have contributed to the LAPD's biased favor toward him.

Perhaps the most disturbing moment in the documentary was an interview the filmmaker conducted with a man referred to as "Tony." He described being an eyewitness to Franklin's sexual assault and torture of women that both men picked up for sex with the promise of crack and a few dollars. When Broomfield asked Tony if he believed Lonnie Franklin hated women, Tony's response included graphic details of Franklin's violent treatment of the sex workers he accosted. Tony described observing Lonnie Franklin sodomizing women with screwdrivers, with Franklin laughing while his victims cried out in pain. He also denied taking part in the sexual attacks and smoked crack while watching with indifference. The picking up of sex workers to rape and torture was treated as a "routine" recreational event initiated by Franklin, according to Tony.

> I would say, whoa, we would go out every week, everyday! On weekends would just be fun for us. Like I say, there's a lot of strawberries [street term for crack-addicted sex workers], lot of females out there on cocaine—crack—and they would do anything. I mean, we'd pick a female, we'd give two dollars to, both of us! We gave her two dollars! I can't sit there and make no stuff up because I was there. Actually . . . myself, I was there! And I know what we did![49]

Tony also insisted that he never saw Lonnie Franklin kill any of the women he raped. Several women confirmed Tony's accounts and described their own violent encounters with Lonnie Franklin, but said they were too distrustful of police to report them. One by one, they looked directly into the camera and described the horror of being forced to pose for pornographic pictures, wearing a dog collar around their necks, and being sodomized and beaten. Some believed they would be murdered by Franklin afterward.[50]

Nana Gyamfi, a community activist and member of the Black Coalition Fighting Back Serial Murders, explains why members of the community are reluctant to seek help from police, and why their actions are sensible. In the film, she said that it is not surprising that Black people living in South Central Los Angeles rarely contacted police with information, mainly because of their fear that police would not believe them, or that they themselves would end up brutalized or arrested. "You cannot just as a Black person walk into a LAPD station or a LASD office and just say 'I have something to report' and start describing something and think that you're going to be treated with dignity or treated with kindness," Gyamfi said. "Treated with concern and be able to leave feeling good, you know? Warm coddles of the heart that, yes! I've done something. It is a 99 percent chance that this is going to be an unpleasant situation for you."[51]

Broomfield's interviews with Tony and other male acquaintances of Lonnie Franklin elucidates a darkly toxic environment where these men mirrored the same lack of regard toward Franklin's victims held by police. In another telling interview between Broomfield and two more of Lonnie's acquaintances, the misogynistic disdain of these men toward Franklin's victims and women who abuse crack in general is fully displayed as they joke about the physical violence they saw Franklin perpetrate against drug-addicted sex workers. One of the men laughs when he describes what Franklin would do when he saw a female "crackhead" walking the street. "He would say [motioning with his finger], 'Come here'! And whoo!" The man cackled. He then imitated Franklin attacking the woman physically. When Broomfield asks the obvious question—that if Franklin hated "crackheads" so much, why would he offer them crack cocaine?—the men responded in unison, "To get them in the car!" Then, one sinisterly adds, "You get in his car?! [Shaking his head and giggling] You ain't comin' out of it!" He begins to laugh harder, barely able to speak. "You ain't comin' out lest you dead!" The scene ends with the men laughing at their joke that a woman getting into Franklin's vehicle is a dead one.

However, not everyone in the community was oblivious to women being murdered. One tireless advocate who championed the cause of protecting Black women and girls in South Central Los Angeles was Margaret Prescod and other members of the Black Coalition Fight Back Serial Murders. Prescod is an indomitable figure who is as supportive and compassionate with victims' families as she is unyielding, confrontational, and unintimidated with members of the LAPD and city officials. For her, what is most important above all else are the lives of Black women and girls. Broomfield interviewed both Margaret Prescod and Nana Gyamfi, as well as Laverne Peters, the mother of Janecia Peters, who was believed to be the last of the Grim Sleeper's homicide victims. Laverne Peters, a soft-spoken woman with mournful eyes, describes her daughter Janecia, an attractive young woman with smooth brown skin and perfectly straight white teeth, as her "baby girl and the love of my life." Sitting beside her at a picnic table in a nearby park, Prescod explained that when she expressed her concern about the safety of women in the community to the LASD, the chief of the department countered, "Why are you so concerned? He's only killing hookers!"[52] Stunned by the police official's comment, Margaret Prescod said she could hardly believe a police officer who has taken an oath to serve and protect the public would respond with such callous and cruel disregard for murdered Black women. And yet, publicly, the LAPD vehemently denied ever using the term "No Humans Involved" or the acronym "NHI" associated with the crimes.

As part of their effort to alert Black women and girls, Prescod and her organization distributed leaflets in 1985 to warn women in the community about the murders of Black women. "Very few people . . . women . . . knew there was a serial murderer in the neighborhood," she explained. She believed that, in 1985, a serial killer had been killing Black women in the community for at least three years and alleged that there were seventeen murders of women who had been raped and stabbed or strangled even before the first known victim of Lonnie Franklin, Debra Jackson, was killed. Her assertion that there were at least ninety murdered women for the decade of the 1980s was confirmed by police, but, according to Prescod, "only eighteen are on the books," suggesting that police either downplayed or minimized the actual number of killings to avoid criticism. She referred to the actions of police as "unconscionable" and added, "There are very few communities in LA outside of a Black community that this would have happened to." This was echoed by Gyamfi in her interview with Broomfield.

> You've allowed Black women to walk around here when someone is hunting them. Not knowing that they are being hunted. Imagine if they would have treated victim number three as if she were a student over at UCLA with blond hair and blue eyes. How many other people might still be living? But the lack of concern allowed for this hunting ground to just be free and open for this person. And for me that is the real, real, tragedy, you know . . . the real tragedy is just the lack of concern that allowed so many more people to be murdered.[53]

According to Thomas Hargrove of MAP, it is not uncommon for police to underreport the number of homicides committed in a particular city or state. A study conducted by his organization in May 2020 found that police failed to report close to three thousand homicides compared to the number of murders reported by medical examiners and coroner offices across the country.[54] Interestingly enough, California is one of the states that underreported homicides to the FBI's annual Uniform Crime Report (UCR) in 2018.[55] One of the reasons police choose to minimize or obscure the actual numbers of murders in a community is because unsolved homicides may be perceived by the public as evidence of poor policing. And the ramifications of underreporting homicides are significant. A decline in clearance rates of violent crime, particularly murder, is positively associated with a rise in homicide rates. This is especially true in cases of serial murder.

It is a vicious circle—police fail to solve murders and those who murder continue to kill. And the survivors of victims are left wondering if their loved one would still be alive if a killer was caught sooner. These include family members, like the mother of murder victim Barbara Ware, who faithfully took the bus from her job to the courtroom to watch Lonnie Franklin's murder trial. She wanted to make sure Franklin understood that her presence signified that Barbara was loved and cared for by her family, a family that was middle class, with a father who owned his own business. And . . .

> that Barbara had a daughter she loved
> that Barbara graduated from high school
> that Barbara was an avid roller skater
> that Barbara attended church on most Sundays

This, before she became addicted to crack cocaine and crossed paths with the man who raped and then shot her, leaving her dead in an alley with a trash bag covering her face.

Another stunning scene in the documentary occurred at the film's conclusion, when Broomfield focuses on the survivors of Franklin's sexual violence. One of these victims, Enietra Washington, was a woman whom police believed to be the only victim who lived to testify in court, about the night she escaped death at the hands of the Grim Sleeper. Enietra was shot in the chest and raped by Franklin after accepting a ride from him at a neighborhood convenience store to a friend's party. She described Franklin's easygoing manner and non-threatening demeanor, which convinced her it was safe to get into his car, but she said her feelings of safety quickly shifted after he turned the corner and proceeded to drive up an alley. She described Franklin almost immediately shooting her in the chest and her struggling against him as he began sexually assaulting her. She passed out during the rape.

After the assault, Franklin pushed Enietra Washington out of the car and sped away. She stumbled to a nearby home for help and was taken by ambulance to a hospital. Doctors removed a .25 caliber bullet from Enietra's chest; ballistics tests indicated that it was the same type used in eight of the previous killings. Broomfield points out that information about the ballistics evidence was not released to the public for another twenty years. In fact, there was no coverage of most of the murders in the Los Angeles Times or other newspapers, so many residents in South Central Los Angeles had no idea that one or more serial killers were stalking the community.[56]

When interviewed by police, Enietra Washington provided a description of the orange-colored Pinto that Franklin picked her up in (another witness described the same vehicle as the one she saw victim Mary Lowe get into), and a description used for a sketch of the assailant who raped and shot her. The sketch was never released by police to the public, and, despite her taking police to Franklin's home (he drove her past his house before turning into the alley), Washington was later dismissed as an "unreliable" witness; the police falsely assumed she was a sex worker. When criticized for their lackluster investigation into the killings, the police defended their decision not to release the sketch of the assailant, saying that eyewitness descriptions can be unreliable—a curious position for police to take, when sketches of suspects in violent crimes are frequently released to the public.

Yet, despite receiving eyewitness testimony from Enietra Washington, a victim of an attempted murder and rape, as well as additional confirmation from another witness about Franklin's distinct orange Pinto, police failed to locate the car, even though Franklin made no effort to hide or stop driving the vehicle. This detail was also confirmed in a *Los Angeles Times* article covering Franklin's trial in 2010.[57]

Once media became aware of the murders of Black women in the city, members of the press also criticized the lack of police investigation into Franklin's killing spree. Christine Pelisek, an investigative reporter for *L.A. Weekly*, wrote extensive articles about the murders even before the *Los Angeles Times* began covering the killings and police finally identified Lonnie Franklin as the man responsible. She, too, questioned whether police seriously wanted to apprehend the man who took the lives of at least nine women and a fifteen-year-old girl. To give the case notoriety and put pressure on police to solve the homicides, the *L.A. Weekly* provided the morbid moniker of "Grim Sleeper" to get the larger community's attention about the murders of women in South Central Los Angeles.[58]

Contrary to the LAPD's protestations that they conducted an effective investigation into the Grim Sleeper homicides, even forming a task force (albeit not until 2008), and denied ever using the acronym "NHI," their actions belie their words. Their failings are many, and an examination of their supposed investigatory work is both perplexing and frustrating. Christopher Franklin, Lonnie Franklin's son, revealed his shock at how some members of the sheriff's department wanted to shake his hand and were excited to meet the son of a man they admired for killing women they saw as less than human, or, as they put it, "cleaning up the streets."[59]

He said in Broomfield's documentary: "I've walked into sheriffs that were like glorified that they were able to talk to me. 'Oh, you're his son, dude?! That's fuckin' crazy!' and they are there all pumped up, and I'm just sitting there like, 'Just please put me in protective custody away from you and the other fools over there.'"

It was due to the DNA of Franklin's son that led to Franklin's arrest and conviction as the Grim Sleeper. While Christopher was being held in jail on a felony weapons charge, police collected a sample of his DNA and submitted it to the FBI's CODIS (Combined DNA Index System) database, which is protocol in solving cold cases. When a positive match was made between Franklin's son and DNA found on the victims and at crime scenes, police believed that it was more than likely familial and not an indication that Christopher was the actual killer but was a relative of the perpetrator. By this time, police considered Lonnie Franklin a person of interest in the cases but lacked irrefutable evidence. To obtain the father's DNA, a police officer posed undercover as a restaurant busboy and collected utensils and a half-eaten slice of pizza that Franklin enjoyed while attending a relative's birthday party.[60] Police were able to positively match Franklin to the Grim Sleeper murders once the DNA was tested.

Unfortunately for many of the victims' families and members of the Black Coalition Fighting Back Serial Murders, the actions of police in apprehending Lonnie Franklin were too little, too late. The egregious missteps and overt apathy displayed by the LAPD for more than twenty years has been blamed for the deaths of so many Black women and young girls who police not only failed to protect but also failed to see as worthy of such protection.

THE INVESTIGATION THAT WASN'T: EXAMINING THE ACTIONS OF THE LAPD IN THE GRIM SLEEPER HOMICIDES

In July 2020, I conducted an interview with Thomas Hargrove about his organization's ability to use a mathematical algorithm to detect serial homicide in a geographical location. During our conversation, Hargrove made a comment that I believed expressed one of the most flagrant missteps on the part of the LAPD in their response to a series of murders of Black women in the city. He said, "Americans have a right to know whether or not they are being murdered and whether or not they are safe, and whether or not those murders are being solved." This is the primary driving force behind the Murder Accountability Project's (MAP) mission to work with police to detect serial murder and inform the community being impacted.

But this is not what happened in South Central Los Angeles.

For more than twenty years, Lonnie Franklin terrorized a community of women with little attention from media and no credible investigation into his crimes from police. After all, as Margaret Prescod was told, "he's only killing hookers." How else can police explain their anemic reaction to characteristics of murders that would strongly suggest that the killings could be linked to a single offender? Not only did police refuse to consider that murders of Black women on the south side of Los Angeles were the work of a serial predator, but they also refused to alert the community that these killings were even taking place. It was the work of Margaret Prescod and other members of the Black Coalition Fighting Back Serial Murders that kept an ongoing tally of the sexual slayings of Black women and girls in their neighborhoods, assiduously reached out to media outlets for coverage of the killings, distributed flyers throughout the city (including the more affluent Beverly Hills neighborhood), and held community meetings to warn women that they were not safe.

Yet city officials were quick to credit police with exemplary work that led to the eventual capture of Lonnie Franklin for the homicides. In July 2010, mayor Anthony Villaraigosa, LAPD police chief Charlie Beck, and state attorney general Jerry Brown (who was elected governor of California that following year) held a press conference on the arrest of Lonnie Franklin Jr. as the Grim Sleeper. The mayor boastfully attributed the capture of Franklin to "more than two decades of dogged investigative work on behalf of exhausted detectives and twenty-five years of reviewing and reexamining evidence." News cameras captured the awkward moment when the conference was interrupted by Margaret Prescod, who boldly stepped to the podium, took the mic, and emphasized the role her organization played since 1985 in pressuring the LAPD and LASD to conduct a rigorous police investigation into the murders and warn women about serial killers stalking their community. She held up a file with documents she claimed supported her statements, but the footage of the incident was edited out of the media coverage shown to the public that evening; video evidence of the moment can only be found through a meticulous internet search.[61] The mayor and police chief were obviously embarrassed and flabbergasted by the audacity of Prescod's interruption, but neither of them could refute the obvious truth of her assertions. It could hardly be denied that what Mayor Villaraigosa described as twenty-five years of investigative work included questionable actions by police that would challenge whether investigative work occurred at all. Consider the following:

- Over a three-year period (1985–87), seven women were raped, shot to death with the same weapon, and dumped in alleys and trash bins throughout South Central Los Angeles, yet police failed to connect the cases.
- The same gun Franklin used in his attempted murder of Enietra Washington was later linked to seven other homicides, but this connection was not made until 2008, when the LAPD began to investigate the cold case murders in earnest.
- Enietra Washington described the vehicle Lonnie Franklin drove the day he attacked her as an orange Pinto, the same car a witness described in the Mary Lowe murder in 1987. Police claimed to have canvassed the neighborhood to find this car and were unsuccessful in their search, yet Franklin continued to drive the car every day, according to his neighbors. Police also failed to provide a description of the car to the media to generate tips.
- In 1987, 911 operators received a call from a man who claimed that he had just witnessed a body being dumped in an alley from the back of a van that he described in detail, even providing a license plate number. The victim was Barbara Ware, twenty-three, the third of Lonnie Franklin's known victims. Police traced the van to a church parking lot but did not pursue any further investigation into the matter. Moreover, the LAPD failed to notify the public through media or a press release about the vehicle or search for the witness who made the call.[62]
- The 911 call made by a man who claimed to witness a man dumping a woman's body in an alley was not released until 2008, again depriving the community of an opportunity to identify the voice on the call. Years later, police disclosed that they believed the caller to be Lonnie Franklin, based on voice analysis technology.
- It was not until the 2007 murder of Janecia Peters, believed to be Franklin's last victim, that cold case detectives began to

compare facets of previous unsolved murders and connect the
victims to a single offender. DNA found on Janecia matched
other victims, and ballistics analysis showed that the same
weapon was linked to the other homicides.
- Neither media nor the public were informed until 2008—
twenty-three years after the killing of Debra Jackson in 1985—
that the same gun was used in at least seven of the homicides.
- During the stint of multiple LAPD police chiefs over the years
(Daryl Gates, 1978–92; Willie Williams, 1992–97; Bernard
Parks, 1997–2002; and William Bratton, 2002–9), none held
a press conference about the killings, and, therefore, most of
the public was unaware that at least ten Black women may
have died violently at the hands of a single offender.
- According to L.A. Weekly reporter Christine Pelisek, when
she requested an interview with William Bratton about the
department's investigation into the killings, Bratton's press
aide responded that the chief was "too busy" and instead de-
ferred the matter to a lower-ranking police official.[63]
- However, Bratton summoned the press to discuss the LAPD's
apprehension of the "Silverware Bandit," a thief with a pen-
chant for stealing eating utensils and china place settings
from homes in more affluent communities in the city.[64] So insignificant were the deaths of Black women to Bratton that he
elevated the theft of silverware as a more urgent issue requiring the public's attention.
- The sole media outlet to notify the public about the murders
was the L.A. Weekly, a free alternative newspaper founded
in 1978 that typically covers the art scene and current events
throughout the city. Families of victims became aware of their
female relatives possibly being a victim of a serial killer from
this news source.[65]
- Some LA City Council members, including former police
chief Bernard Parks, expressed shock and anger about the
lack of notification by police about the homicides.[66] Parks
also claimed that even as someone who once headed the police department, he still found it difficult to get information

from police chief William Bratton about the investigation into the Grim Sleeper murders.

- Mayor Hahn and Chief Bratton were excoriated by media, city council members, and the larger Black community for not making the investigation into the murders a priority and devoting necessary resources not only to solve them but also to protect other potential victims.
- After the killer struck again in the years 2002 and 2003, investigative reporter Christine Pelisek noted in her article that one of the police captains demurred that a "taskforce wasn't even needed."[67]

The LAPD cold case unit, a division created by Bernard Parks during his tenure as chief in 2001, reexamined evidence that led to the arrest and conviction of Lonnie Franklin Jr. in 2010. Parks was the second of two Black LAPD police chiefs in the city's history until he was ousted from the position by mayor James Hahn and replaced with William Bratton in 2002. Once he became aware of the series of killings as a city council member, Parks was instrumental in procuring a $500,000 reward for the capture of the serial killer and placing billboards throughout the city to solicit tips or information leading to his arrest.[68] Even though Franklin was arrested in 2010, the case slowly made its way to trial six years later, much to the consternation and frustration of the victims' families. On June 6, 2016, Lonnie Franklin Jr. was found guilty of ten counts of first-degree murder and sentenced to death. He died on March 28, 2020, while awaiting execution on death row in San Quentin Prison.

CONCLUSION

In 2010, when police obtained a warrant to search Lonnie Frankin Jr.'s residence and property, they uncovered 180 Polaroid photos of Black women and teen girls. Some of the images were sexually graphic, some eerily appeared to depict women who were deceased, and almost all of victims of the Grim Sleeper killings were found among this macabre gallery. Even more unsettling were pictures police found of victims from unsolved murder cases whose deaths had not been linked to Franklin, but were killed and dumped in a similar manner to his other victims.[69] One of the pictures was that of surviving victim Enietra Washington, who seemed to be unconscious; blood could be seen on her exposed chest.[70]

To date, the total number of women who died at the hands of Lonnie Franklin Jr. and other serial killers operating from the 1980s through the early 2000s in South Central Los Angeles is unknown. However, what is clear is that the lack of an aggressive investigation by the LAPD and LASD into the murders of Black women for more than twenty-five years can be partly to blame for the demise of many of these victims. The LASD sheriff who allegedly made the comment to Margaret Prescod that her concern was misplaced since Franklin only targeted sex workers seemed to suggest that women who were *not* sex workers were safe. Not all of the one hundred victims murdered over a ten-year span were sex workers or used crack cocaine. Even if that were true, police still have a sworn duty to serve and protect members of the community—regardless of the victim's occupation or criminal involvement. When police discounted the humanity of these women, they emboldened the men who saw them as easy prey.

According to news sources, Franklin was arrested fifteen times over the course of forty years and was charged with a number of serious crimes that included receiving stolen property, car theft, assault, false imprisonment, and assault causing great bodily harm.[71] He rarely spent more than a few months in jail, and, after being sentenced to three years in prison in 2003 for the crime of receiving stolen property, he only served 270 days, and was released. Within months of his release, the body of thirty-five-year-old Valerie McCorvey was found in an alley, yet another casualty of the man the world would come to know as the Grim Sleeper.

For many of the disheartened relatives of the victims who were angry at the obvious apathy shown by police, the capture and conviction of Franklin did little to assuage their pain and anguish. For instance, Laverne Peters believed that her daughter's murder could have been prevented if police had notified the community about a predator stalking and killing young women. For Porter Alexander, a man whose nineteen-year-old daughter Alicia was raped and murdered by Franklin, even disposing of his daughter's possessions would take decades to do; her belongings remained in his home "because she's not gone from my heart," he explained to the court during Franklin's sentencing.[72] For Samara Herard, the foster sister of Franklin's youngest victim, Princess Berthomieux, the grief of not being able to protect the tragic teenager from the serial killer haunts her still. She recalled a final conversation with Princess after she had been placed with another foster family and the girl worried that her abusive biological father was trying to contact her. "We [Herard's family] sheltered her because we were determined to never let anyone else hurt her ever again," she testified to the jury. "The person I was trying to protect her from was the wrong person."[73]

Media coverage of the killings of Black women in Los Angeles noted numerous times that the significant majority of victims were engaged in sex work in exchange for crack cocaine, indirectly intimating that these women put themselves in harm's way. Is it reasonable, then, to expect that police would treat victims of this nature with the same regard as women considered "deserving victims" of violence?[74] An examination of other serial homicides involving victims who participated in sex work yields observable differences that demand an explanation.

Within the course of a year in 1988, eleven women, ten of them sex workers, were murdered in Rochester, New York. The women were raped, beaten, and strangled or suffocated, their bodies dumped in wooded areas and river gorges throughout Upstate New York. After the first few victims' bodies were discovered, police examined the evidence and determined that the murders appeared to be the work of a single offender, or, in common vernacular, a serial killer. Rochester homicide investigators convened a task force that included FBI agents, New York State police officers, and the Monroe County Sheriff's Department.[75] An extensive search involving both air and ground surveillance was implemented to apprehend the killer. Sex workers who were reported missing were immediately added to task force search parties in hopes of locating the women—dead or alive. Police warned women selling sex in Rochester's red-light district that a serial killer was targeting them. All were encouraged to contact Rochester police immediately if they had an encounter with anyone exhibiting violent or bizarre behavior that made them feel uncomfortable. Police patrols increased significantly, and, in less than two years, police arrested forty-four-year-old Arthur Shawcross, a paroled murderer and sex offender who was married and employed in low-wage factory work.[76] Shawcross was spotted near the area where the body of a missing sex worker was found by police search teams.

Overall, police response in the Shawcross murders was practically textbook and reminiscent of television detective shows, where police coordinate a team of exemplary investigators to find the assailant posthaste. The murders were determined early on to be the work of a serial killer. The task force did not take twenty-five years to find the man responsible for as many murders as Lonnie Franklin Jr. Sex workers were not only warned, but police also solicited their assistance in reporting any man that they felt warranted a closer look by investigators. Police provided information to the press, and nightly news programs broadcast details about the homicides to generate tips from the public. Searches were conducted to find sex workers reported missing by family members and friends, despite the fact that these women were known prostitutes. Indeed, ten of the eleven women killed were "just hookers," but they were also something else.

They were white women.

It is evident that when it comes to police conducting a thorough, immediate, and serious investigation into a series of violent murders, it is a matter of choice. Such was the case with Arthur Shawcross, Gary Ridgeway, Joel Rifkin, and other serial killers who targeted victims who were sex workers but were also primarily white. It is also clear that when the lives of victims' matter, regardless of vocation or background, their deaths matter also. The commendable actions of the Rochester Police Department in apprehending Arthur Shawcross extended beyond Shawcross's capture and conviction. Charles J. Siragusa, the prosecutor in the Shawcross trial, explained, "We have to be sensitive to the fact that unfortunately in any given year a number of prostitutes may be victims of homicide. This year we've seen an increase in the homicide rate."[77] Therefore, to protect women who engaged in sex work, police began a crackdown on prostitution in the city by arresting clients who purchased the sexual services of women. Siragusa also wanted to address the underlying issue that drove many of these women into sex work, drug addiction, and, in a coordinated effort with Rochester police, law enforcement set up a program to "steer female prostitutes into drug treatment instead of jail in an effort to reduce recidivism."[78]

These extraordinary efforts to shield vulnerable victims of serial homicide recognize their humanity and exemplify police's sworn oath to serve and protect. In short, police actions of this caliber see the lethal violence perpetrated against these women as murders *involving human beings*. Yet, for murdered Black women with or without a history of sexual solicitation, law enforcement has yet to collectively recognize *their humanity*.

The victims of Lonnie Franklin, Michael Hughes, Chester Turner, Louis Crane, and other faceless men who stalked, raped, terrorized, and then murdered them, can no longer speak for themselves. They cannot express that, despite their crack addictions and their desperate attempts to support a drug habit through the exchange of sexual acts, they were still human beings with families and children who loved them.

In the LAPD's apparent discounting of the lives of these women, their deaths were also treated with derision and disregard. Equally tragic were the men of their community, acquaintances of Lonnie Franklin Jr., who ignored or mocked their suffering, thus affirming the bitter pessimism of Malcolm X's view of unprotected Black women.

Broomfield's film concludes with several women who had violent sexual encounters with Lonnie Franklin speaking anonymously about their experiences. Perhaps the words spoken by a woman who barely escaped Lonnie Franklin's brutal sexual sadism speaks for the women who were not as fortunate:

You know I didn't mock his body. And then you want to kill me?! I didn't do that! I didn't try to rob you! I didn't set you up, I didn't do any of that! Yeah, OK, yeah, I was out there [selling sex]. But that doesn't mean I'm nothing. [*Crying*] It doesn't mean I'm nothing.

Like I'm a piece of trash. I was trapped! [*Having difficulty speaking through her tears*] I was trapped. It's not what I wanted! This is not the life I wanted.

She begins to weep, unable to continue speaking. And then the screen fades to black.

CHAPTER 5

CLEVELAND IS DANGEROUS FOR BLACK WOMEN

Serial Murders in a House of Horrors

A FTER BEING CHARTERED as a city in 1911, East Cleveland began as a suburb of great wealth and stately mansions. Oil baron John D. Rockefeller was just one of several über-wealthy residents with opulent homes in the small city; he owned a 248-acre estate, which served as his summer home, overlooking a lake on Euclid Avenue (also referred to as "Millionaire's Row"), where he hosted exclusive parties with some of the country's wealthiest people in attendance.[1] With a geography of a little over three square miles, East Cleveland can be described as a "city within a city" whose glory days have long passed. Today, it has more vacant homes than people, boasting a dwindling population of approximately fifteen thousand residents.[2]

By the 1950s, most of the wealthy families living in East Cleveland were replaced by upper-middle-class whites, who were soon joined by members of the working class, who purchased smaller, more affordable homes. In the next decade, of the mid-to-late 1960s, socially mobile Black families desired homeownership, and, due to education and better-paying jobs, they began to move into East Cleveland from greater Cleveland's east-side neighborhoods. Like most cities that were the destination of Black migrants fleeing racial terror and the suffocating grip of Jim Crow segregation, Cleveland, Ohio, was and remains a trenchantly segregated city. Most of the Black population reside in a handful of neighborhoods along the eastern corridor, in communities referred to as Collinwood, Maple Heights, Euclid, Mount Pleasant, and Buckeye-Woodhill, to name a few.[3]

Predictably, as Black families moved into East Cleveland, whites panicked and fled in record numbers. Blockbusting,[4] by greedy and disingenuous real estate agents, took advantage of white fear by encouraging homeowners to sell quickly and move to the suburban neighborhoods on the west side of the city and across the Cuyahoga River, which divides Cleveland into western and eastern regions.[5] In 2023, East Cleveland was 93 percent Black, with a poverty rate of 41.8 percent, almost four times the national average.[6] In contrast to East Cleveland and the east-side neighborhoods of Greater Cleveland, the west side of the city has a vastly different demographic, with neighborhoods (Kamm's and Old Brooklyn, among several others) comprised of at least 80 percent white residents.[7]

East Cleveland has its own municipal government and mayor, Brandon King, who was elected to office in 2016 and barely survived a recall vote in November 2022 after being accused of misappropriation of funds, using city contractors for personal use, and overseeing a police department with nine officers indicted for public corruption, civil rights violations, and abusive violence against Black city residents.[8]

Due to the dwindling number of homeowners and the loss of tax revenue from vacated businesses, city services are woefully inadequate. In 2016, East Cleveland's then-mayor, Gary Norton Jr., had to request an ambulance from neighboring Oakwood Village because the city's fire department had no emergency transportation.[9] Additionally, with fewer cars and traffic on the roads, the Ohio Department of Transportation (ODT) justified the removal of traffic lights on major roads in 2012, an action that, tragically, was blamed for the death of Terra Nolden, a thirty-seven-year-old Black mother of seven children who was struck by a vehicle while attempting to cross Euclid Avenue—a busy street where the traffic light was removed—after shopping at a Family Dollar store in January 2020.[10]

The ODT, at the request of Governor Mike DeWine, expedited the replacement of the traffic light at Euclid Avenue and other high-traffic areas throughout the city, but little else has been done to increase the reinvestment in East Cleveland that would spur economic revitalization.[11] East Cleveland, in short, has become an abandoned and neglected ghost of its former glory.

To complicate matters further and compound the stress of East Cleveland's residents already grappling with crushing poverty, an absence of quality food markets, and a high violent crime rate is the epidemic of police violence. Several high-profile fatal police shootings of Black residents put Cleveland, Ohio, on the map as a particularly treacherous landscape for civilian encounters with law enforcement. Between 2012 and 2014, there were three incidents of police violence that clearly illustrate the fraught relationship between East Cleveland police and the Black population it has sworn to protect and serve.

One of the incidents that gained national attention was the November 29, 2012, police shooting deaths of a Black couple, forty-three-year-old Timothy Russell, and his thirty-year-old girlfriend, Malissa Williams, after a high-speed chase on the suspicion of drug activity. Police claimed that they fired their weapons at the couple's vehicle after mistaking a backfiring engine for Russell and Williams shooting at the officers.[12] Despite being unarmed, the couple were each shot more than twenty times and were killed instantly.[13]

Two years later, on November 13, 2014, thirty-seven-year-old Tanisha Anderson would also die at the hands of East Cleveland police. After family members phoned 911 for assistance while Tanisha was having a mental health crisis (she was diagnosed with bipolar disorder in 2004), police arrived on the scene and events escalated quickly, according to Tanisha's family.[14] Her mother, Cassandra Johnson, claimed that police were openly hostile, and that their behavior further agitated Tanisha, who became more distrustful and began to resist police attempts to place her, handcuffed, in the back of the police car.[15] One of the officers, Detective Scott Aldridge, then grabbed Tanisha and slammed her to the ground, striking her head against the pavement, and placed his knee and body weight in the center of her back. (Significantly, Aldridge was one of the officers involved in the high-speed chase and shooting deaths of Malissa Williams and Timothy Russell.) Moments later, Tanisha stopped breathing. The coroner ruled her cause of death as a homicide from cardiopulmonary arrest, "in association with physical restraint in a prone position in association with ischemic heart disease and bipolar disorder with agitation."[16] Tanisha's body also bore multiple abrasions and contusions, as well as a fractured sternum.

There was also the humiliating spectacle of the young Black woman lying on concrete, handcuffed by police, with her nightgown hiked around her waist, exposing her partial nudity. She remained in this state for a full forty-five minutes before the ambulance arrived on the scene. In the interim, police did not provide resuscitation nor cover for Tanisha Anderson in the cold night air.[17]

Almost ten days after Tanisha's death, another police killing would completely eclipse the incident and shock the nation.[18] On November 24, 2014, twelve-year-old Tamir Rice was shot to death while playing in a park with a toy air gun by Cleveland police officer Timothy Loehmann. The officer claimed the child aimed a gun at him when Loehmann commanded him to drop the weapon. However, a video that captured the shooting showed the officer fire his revolver at Tamir Rice less than three seconds after arriving on the scene, seemingly discharging the weapon as he exited the police vehicle.[19]

A heartbreaking detail in Rice's death is that Tamir's fourteen-year-old sister, who was playing nearby, rushed to the scene, screaming at officers that her brother was just a child, but was thrown to the ground, handcuffed, and placed in the back of the police car only to watch her brother die while police failed to give aid.[20]

These incidents of police violence, among others, did little to cull the growing anger, fear, and resentment that Black people living in East Cleveland felt toward law enforcement. For Black residents of East Cleveland, as well as of the numerous Greater Cleveland east-side communities, brutal encounters with police are a frequent part of their reality, and oversight investigations into police conduct have yielded confirmation for their dread. In March 2023, the Cuyahoga County Prosecutor's Office, accompanied by the FBI's Cleveland Division, brought indictments against sixteen East Cleveland police officers on charges of public corruption and numerous civil rights violations that included kicking and beating unarmed and handcuffed residents. The charges stem from incidents that occurred over a four-year period, from June 2018 to July 2022.

According to local media coverage regarding the indictments, bodycam footage displayed officers engaged in acts of terrorism toward Black residents, [21] where cops were shown "stomping on the faces of handcuffed victims, brutally beating victims whose hands were up, and then bragging about it afterwards."[22] Several years prior to these indictments, the US Justice Department conducted a two-year investigation into civilian complaints against Cleveland police and found that officers routinely used their service weapons to "pistol-whip" residents during arrests and, on occasion, accidentally discharged them in the process.[23] As a result, Cleveland's police department entered into a consent decree with the Justice Department to cease using their guns as an impact weapon during arrests.

The troubled history between East Cleveland's Black residents and police force has been a source of deep distrust and friction, not atypical in many urban communities across the US. When people live in neighborhoods that are under siege from both violence at the hands of criminals in their community *and* law enforcement officers, this duality exacerbates the stranglehold of fear and hopelessness many people feel living under these conditions. And Black women, unlike their white counterparts, are not immune from violence at the hands of police.[24]

Since numerous police officers have perpetrated violence against the neighborhood's Black population, there is little confidence they will in turn conduct thorough investigations that ensure their safety and facilitate justice for those victimized by crime. While requesting assistance from law enforcement officers (*the same people who have committed violence against them*), Black residents in Cleveland have experienced police being indifferent and, at times, mocking in response. More pointedly, police brutality, in combination with their pernicious apathy, has cultivated a killing field in which Black women in East Cleveland are the prey, and where predators hunt without fear.

DANGEROUS CLEVELAND

East Ninety-Third Street is a major thoroughfare in the heart of East Cleveland. It is an avenue that is central to residents in their everyday traverse, and it stretches miles across the city. The more suburban sector touts the Cleveland Clinic, a renowned medical institution revered for its state-of-the-art health care for chronic diseases; the Cleveland Museum; and the eastern campus of the sprawling Cuyahoga Community College, Ohio's largest community college district. Yet, to many people living in East Cleveland, the East Ninety-Third corridor has a more sinister reputation: as a killing lane. The avenue is near the sites of numerous unsolved murders of Black women in the city and is haunted by the disappearance of countless other victims.

On a cold wintry morning in January 2017, fourteen-year-old Alianna DeFreeze left her home to catch two busses along East Ninety-Third Street to get to E. Prep and Village Prep Woodland Hills School, as she did each day. Her commute began before 6 a.m. and she often arrived to school by the time the morning bell rang. But, on January 23, 2017, the bubbly, petite teenager never made it to class; she was kidnapped shortly after exiting her first bus route on East Ninety-Third Street by Christopher Whitaker, a forty-five-year-old convicted sex offender. He accosted and then forced the young girl into an abandoned home on Fuller Street, steps from her East Ninety-Third bus stop. There, she was gruesomely tortured, raped, bludgeoned, and stabbed to death. Her body was found three days later, in a blood-splattered room on the vacant property.[25] I chose to spare the readers of this book the explicit and traumatic details of Alianna's homicide. Even as a researcher attempting to remain emotionally disconnected from my data, I found myself overcome with grief and horror while reading the autopsy report and court record of the case. In short, Alianna's death was a prolonged and excruciating one.

The teen's mother, Donnesha Cooper, reported her daughter missing after she failed to return home from school at 4 p.m., and police immediately commenced a search for her. Alianna had a developmental disability, making her particularly vulnerable, as someone who behaved younger than her actual age. Her parents blamed the school for failing to notify them that the 5'2", 115-pound ninth-grader never made it there—a very unusual occurrence, given that she kept near-perfect attendance.[26] They successfully sued the school and were awarded $1 million in a settlement. School administrators were found liable after they lied about sending a notification to Cooper and then claimed the system malfunctioned.[27] Ohio's then-governor, John Kasich, signed a bill into law named for Alianna DeFreeze that required that schools immediately notify parents of a child's absence.

Based on a review of Christopher Whitaker's lengthy violent criminal history, it is astounding that he was released from prison in the first place. In 2005, Whitaker was convicted of third-degree sexual battery and second-degree felonious assault of a woman whom he knew casually through a mutual acquaintance. After showing up at the victim's home under the pretense of needing to use the restroom, he emerged from her bathroom with a pair of scissors and began violently attacking her, choking her until she fell unconscious. She awoke a short time later, naked from the waist down, and was sexually assaulted and stabbed in the neck twice.[28] Despite committing an act of potentially lethal violence against his victim, Whitaker was sentenced to only four years in prison.

When Whitaker was sentenced to death for Alianna DeFreeze's murder in 2018, Cleveland police were certain Whitaker had killed before. During my interview with Thomas Hargrove, the founder of the Murder Accountability Project (MAP), he discussed Alianna's murder and the suspicion he and the Cleveland police had that Alianna was not Whitaker's only victim. "We kind of think, he, you know, there's just no way a forty-four-year-old man did that to Alianna DeFreeze and that was his first murder," he said. "That just did not happen."[29] Despite police believing Whitaker to be a serial offender, they have not been able to link him with any other unsolved murders in the city of Cleveland.

Hargrove also stressed that his algorithm, which pinpoints clusters of unsolved killings with similar victims in a similar location to indicate patterns of serial murder, zeroed in on East Ninety-Third Street as a prime location of danger for women in the community. These murders, he explained, also have "a very unnaturally low clearance rate," meaning that they go unsolved for long periods of time. Since 2004, there are at least sixty unsolved murders of mostly Black women in the city of Cleveland, and today they remain ice cold and unlikely to be solved.[30]

Between the years 2012 and 2017—the year of the DeFreeze homicide—the bodies of five other women were found in the same neighborhood bordering East Ninety-Third Street.[31] The first victim, thirty-seven-year-old Jameela Hasan, was found stabbed to death in her upstairs apartment on December 17, 2012, only a few blocks from the location of the DeFreeze murder five years later. Four months later, on March 24, 2013, the body of Jazmine Trotter, twenty, was found in an abandoned home on the 3900 block of East Ninety-Third Street; she had been beaten and strangled to death. Less than one week later, on March 28, police would discover the body of forty-five-year-old Christine Malone, the mother of eight children, strangled and dumped in a field near East Ninety-Third. Several months after the discovery of Malone's body, twenty-one-year-old Ashley Leszyeski was found dead after being stabbed multiple times in the head and neck and left in a vacant lot in the 3500 block of East Ninety-Third Street on May 28, 2013.

These four women were murdered within a span of five months.

One year later and two miles away from the abandoned home on Fuller Street where Alianna's body was discovered by police, Jessica Coleman, twenty-six, was shot to death and found near train tracks on East Eighty-Third Street and Rawlings Avenue.[32] Each of the victims except for Ashley Leszyeski were Black, and to date all five murders are still unsolved. In a March 2023 interview with Cleveland 19's local news, family members of the victims were upset that, ten years after these homicides, the killer or killers of their loved ones had yet to be found. Shana Johnson, the daughter of victim Christine Malone, expressed her frustration with both police and the community at large that the killings remain unsolved. "I think it's connected," she said. "It's not just a coincidence that all four of these women were killed on East 93rd Street and nobody's saying nothing. They were all loved." She criticized the police investigation as ineffective. "They [police] come with a scratch pad and pictures, and basically, it's like a kindergarten class. What do you have? There's no DNA?!"[33]

Shana Johnson's lack of confidence in police was not without merit, given the shocking debacle of police work in the murders of almost a dozen women in 2009 in a home near East Ninety-Third

Street. Eleven women would die violently at the hands of a serial killer, despite three survivors escaping the killer and reporting their assaults to police, and the persistent and noxious smell of death that overwhelmed a community.

THE IMPERIAL AVENUE HOUSE OF HORRORS

When I was a nineteen-year-old sophomore attending college at Wayne State University in Detroit, I used to catch the bus to school one block from my home on the city's northwest side. One day in late fall, as I neared the bus stop, I was suddenly overwhelmed by a sickly sweet and putrid odor unlike anything I had ever smelled before. The stench was coming from a building directly across the street from the bus stop on Grandriver Avenue. The structure was an abandoned storefront, where the upper level was rumored to be what was then referred to as an "after-hours joint"—an illegal speakeasy where drinking, drug use, and gambling took place. Present at the scene was a medical examiner's van and several Detroit police vehicles.

As I and another individual covered our noses and watched in horrified curiosity, police carried what appeared to be a corpse in a body bag on a stretcher out of the building and loaded it into the back of the coroner's van. Although the memory of that day dates back almost forty years, I would know that smell immediately if I ever encountered it again.

The stench of death is concomitantly indescribable and unforgettable.

So, when residents living on and near 12205 Imperial Avenue in East Cleveland were overcome with the odor of human decomposition, they began to complain in earnest to police and city officials that something was dangerously amiss. The first complaint about the rotten smell came from a neighbor who lived across the street from Anthony Sowell, the occupant of 12205 Imperial Avenue. The woman phoned her local councilman at the time, Zach Reed, and told him that the smell was so overpowering it seemed like that of a "dead body."[34] Councilman Reed dispatched health department inspectors to investigate the odor, and technicians flushed the drainage pipes and even replaced a sewer line, but the malodorous scent remained.[35] Some people in the neighborhood accused Ray's Sausage Shop, a meat-processing plant that sat next door to Sowell's home, of being the source of the rank scent of decay. Convinced, the shop's owner replaced the shop's drainage line and grease traps and had the gutters cleaned with bleach, yet the smell lingered and even amplified.[36] "People thought the stink was me," Ray Cash, the shop's owner, explained to reporters when the bodies were discovered.[37] Even the employees at the meat factory preferred the smell of rotting meat to the odor that lingered just outside the door of the plant, and they kept the windows shut even during summer.[38]

What the community did not know at the time was that the source of the smell emanated from something more nefarious and horrifying than frustrated residents could have even imagined. In a well-kept, two-story walk-up home surrounded by abandoned and crumbling edifices,[39] fifty-year-old Anthony Sowell, a quiet loner and convicted sex offender, lured, beat, raped, and murdered eleven women and buried them in his backyard, upstairs crawl space, basement, and other scarcely furnished rooms of his home.[40]

Sowell was released from prison in 2005 after serving a fifteen-year sentence for the 1989 choking, battery, and rape of a pregnant twenty-year-old woman in his apartment in a different Cleveland neighborhood. Despite being bound by the wrists and ankles, the woman was able to escape from a third-story window and summon help.[41] Anthony Sowell pled guilty to attempted rape and was sentenced to fifteen years in prison.

However, beginning in May 2007—two years after Sowell was released from prison—women who lived near his Imperial Avenue home began to disappear. In November 2009, police would discover the bodies of eleven women buried in his backyard and home. The women murdered by Sowell had long histories of crack cocaine addiction, arrests, and incarceration, and many were mothers who had lost custody of their children. They were vulnerable and unprotected, most of them estranged from family, who tried in vain to save them from their drug addictions and then, later, tried to find them when they disappeared. In 2011, two years after their bodies were discovered, reporters from the *Cleveland Plain Dealer* newspaper, Stan

Donaldson and Margaret Bernstein, dedicated a series of stories about each of the victims titled "The Women of Imperial Avenue." Many of the victims' loved ones complained about the disregard they felt from police and the way media underscored the victims' histories of drug addiction and criminal activity. Donaldson and Bernstein sought a way to humanize and pay tribute to each individual victim. Such poignant coverage is rare for women of color.[42] The details about the victims and their lives in this chapter were taken from their reports.

- Crystal Dozier, a thirty-eight-year-old mother of seven children, was reported missing by family members in May 2007. Although she lost custody of each of her children due to her crack addiction, when her eleven-year-old son passed away from complications from asthma, her drug use spiraled. For two and a half years, Crystal's family would not know that she was murdered by Anthony Sowell until her body was found among his other victims in 2009.[43]
- Tishana Culver, a thirty-three-year-old mother of four who lived only a few houses from Anthony Sowell, was last seen in June 2008. She was remembered by family and friends as a kind soul who would feed the homeless and was generous with whatever meager possessions she owned. Before her drug use worsened after the suicide of her boyfriend, she earned a cosmetology license and worked as a nursing assistant. She was arrested several times on drug charges and gave birth to her last child while incarcerated. Paternal relatives as well as her mother and sister took custody of her children. According to news reports, Tishana was not reported missing by family members, since she often disappeared for days or weeks at a time due to her addiction to crack cocaine.[44]
- LeShanda Long, twenty-five, disappeared in August 2008. She was a troubled mother of three children and the youngest of Sowell's victims. Raised by an aunt after being removed from the custody of her mother, who suffered from a drug addiction, LeShanda began to rebel at age fourteen and was placed several times in juvenile detention centers. By the time

she was seventeen, she had given birth to three children. Although she lost custody of her children to relatives due to her own crack cocaine addiction, she maintained a strong love for them and was arrested several times after attempting to run away with them after visits. Months before her disappearance, LeShanda spoke with the aunt who raised her and apologized for "not listening" to her advice. Her skull was recovered from a bucket in the basement of Sowell's home.[45]

- Tonia Carmichael, fifty-three, was reported missing in 2008. She was the mother of three daughters, a former student at Cuyahoga Community College, a licensed barber, and a medical secretary before she became addicted to crack cocaine. Buried in Sowell's backyard, Tonia would be the first of Sowell's victims to be identified by police.[46]
- Michelle Mason, forty-five, a mother of two sons, had been sober for several years after a prolonged addiction to crack cocaine and heroin. She credited a gunshot wound that cost her her left eye as the reason she turned her life around. After being diagnosed with HIV in the 1990s, she became a volunteer at Cleveland's AIDS Task Force. She was reported missing by worried relatives in October 2008. Like some of Sowell's other victims, she lived in the same neighborhood as her killer.[47]
- Kim Yvette Smith, forty-four, was the only one of Sowell's victims who had no children. Childless and with time on her hands, she generously became the caretaker of her disabled, wheelchair-bound father, who, according to news reports, was equally devoted to his daughter. Kim, like most of Sowell's victims, struggled with an addiction to crack cocaine and had a history of incarceration for petty drug offenses. Her father covered the expenses for her substance abuse treatment, desperate to free his daughter from the disease. She was last seen by her father in January 2009, three days before his birthday. He reported her missing after he had not heard from her for several days.[48]

- Nancy Cobbs, forty-four, a divorced mother of three children and grandmother of five, lived three blocks away from Sowell's home. Sowell befriended Nancy and would even drink beer with her occasionally on the porch of her mother's home. Family members said that they knew him by face, but not by name, and never suspected he was dangerous. When Nancy went missing in April 2009, family members and friends searched abandoned homes looking for her. She was found dead in November 2009 after police discovered the bodies of Sowell's victims in his home.[49]
- Amelda Hunter, forty-seven, an avid reader of classic fiction, was the mother of four children and affectionately known by family and friends as "Amy." Impregnated at fourteen with her first child by a teacher, the child was born deaf and had cerebral palsy. She later gave birth to three more children with a longtime boyfriend. Her last-born daughter passed away from a birth defect, and, according to family, the death of the child and the disability of another exacerbated her drug use. Despite a history of drug addiction, Amelda had a work history as a hair stylist and a home health aide. She was the only one of Sowell's victims that did not live in the same neighborhood as her killer but visited him often and viewed him as a friend, according to relatives. She was last seen in April 2009 and found among other victims in November of that year.[50]
- Janice Webb, forty-eight, was divorced and the mother of one child, a son, and the grandmother of three. She was remembered by her close-knit family as a prankster who loved to sing. She became addicted to crack cocaine after being introduced to the drug by her husband's relatives when visiting them in California. The couple's drug use eventually led to their divorce. Her husband became sober while Janice tried and failed several times at sobriety. She went missing in June 2009, and her body was found among Sowell's victims five months later, in November.[51]

- Telacia Fortson, thirty-one, lost custody of her three children due to her addiction. Placed in foster care at age six and adopted at age nine, Telacia was separated from her birth sister and never overcame the trauma and feelings of abandonment. As a teen, she rebelled and frequently ran away from home and used drugs. According to a family friend, she seemed to be on an endless quest to find love. Although she was last seen in June 2009, she was not reported missing by family until August. Loved ones tragically learned of her fate when her body was found in Sowell's home in November 2009.[52]

- Diane Turner, thirty-eight, was the last of Sowell's victims. The mother of six children had a difficult childhood filled with abuse, neglect, and abandonment. Diane also suffered with seizures from epilepsy that she attributed to being hit on the head as a child with a hammer. Troubled, she began experimenting with drugs at a young age and then, later in life, became addicted to crack cocaine. She was arrested on drug and prostitution charges numerous times as she ebbed between addiction and failed attempts at sobriety. Each of her first five children were removed from her care and placed in the foster care system, but when she became pregnant with her sixth and final child, a daughter, Diane stopped using crack, maintained her sobriety throughout the pregnancy, and enrolled in an in-house parenting program. However, officials stepped in and removed her daughter from her care, claiming that she was neglecting the baby due to Diane's frequent seizures. Her child's father obtained partial custody of the baby, whose godmother became the custodial parent. According to media reports, Diane's crack use increased, and she was arrested several more times on drug and prostitution charges. She had been missing since September 2009, and when her remains were found in a third-floor bedroom of Sowell's home, it would take more than thirty days to confirm her identity. Since she had no contact with biological family, her youngest daughter's father took the seven-year-old to the coroner's office to test the child's DNA. The results confirmed that the last body found was that of Diane Turner.[53]

A KILLER GOES UNCHECKED

The violent and sexually predatory behavior of Anthony Sowell began when he was barely an adolescent.

According to his niece, Leona Davis, from age ten she was brutally raped on a daily basis by Sowell, who was eleven years old at the time.[54] Orphaned at age eight after her mother died, Leona and her five siblings were cared for by Sowell's mother and grandmother, who, she testified at Sowell's murder trial, beat her and her siblings with extension cords while they were naked. After she turned ten, Sowell began to take her to the third floor of his grandmother's home in East Cleveland and rape her under the threat of violence.

In 1989, Sowell was accused of raping and attempting to choke to death a pregnant twenty-year-old woman whom he had lured to his apartment. Fortunately, she was able to escape and report the assault to police. He was convicted in 1990 of attempted rape in a plea bargain that resulted in a prison sentence of fifteen years. Eerily similar to his later crimes, three women were found murdered in Sowell's neighborhood between 1988 and 1989, but the police never investigated him as a potential suspect. The victims—Rosalind Garner, thirty-six; Camilla Karen Prater, thirty; and pregnant thirty-year-old Mary Thomas—were each beaten and strangled with cords (many of Sowell's Imperial Avenue victims were also strangled with cords). Camilla Karen Prater, who lived on the same street as Sowell, and Mary Thomas were found in abandoned buildings near Sowell's home at the time Rosalind Garner was killed in her home.[55]

The eleven victims who died in Sowell's Imperial Avenue home did not live to identify and report him to police, but several women managed to escape from Sowell's murderous grip. At least two of these survivors told the media that they reported the attacks to police and were ignored.

In 2016, documentary filmmakers Laura Paglin and Nels Bangerter interviewed survivors of Anthony Sowell for the film *Unseen* to highlight the invisibility of Sowell's victims and the frustration of the victims' family members with the police investigation. To provide a fuller examination of the scope of violence Anthony Sowell committed against his victims, I delved into a number of resources ranging from interviews from the film, media coverage of his trial, and public court records.[56]

In September 2008, Anthony Sowell approached then-thirty-four-year-old Vanessa Gay and told her that it was his birthday, but he had no one to celebrate it with. Gay agreed to follow Sowell to his home after they spoke for a short time, with the promise of him providing her with alcohol and crack cocaine. Gay said she felt comfortable with Sowell, who also told her he was once in the military and was a good cook.[57] After entering Sowell's home, Vanessa's nightmare began. She first noticed a horrid scent (not yet knowing the source was decomposing bodies) before being taken upstairs to his bedroom. Despite the squalid conditions of Sowell's home, she did not immediately leave because she hadn't been sleeping in the best conditions. At the time, she was sheltering in "bandos" (a term for abandoned homes) after being estranged from her family, due to her addiction.[58] Vanessa testified in court that when they entered Sowell's bedroom, he lit a crack cocaine pipe, took a "hit," quickly turned toward her, and punched her in the face. Throughout the night and into early morning, Vanessa said she was repeatedly raped and beaten.

Despite her terror, she never tried to escape or injure Sowell, even as he periodically fell asleep. In the morning, bruised and bloody, Vanessa asked permission from Sowell to use his bathroom. She said she was surprised that he agreed to her request, and he left the room for a short period of time and came back to escort her. Vanessa testified she immediately noticed that a plastic sheet that had been draped across the doorway of a room across the hall from where Sowell raped her had been removed, and, to her horror, she looked in the doorway and saw a headless torso of a body lying in the center of the room.

Vanessa told the court she believed the killer deliberately removed the plastic sheet that covered the door so she could see the grotesque sight to instill even more fear into her.[59] After using the restroom, she composed herself and did her best not to show her terror. After assuring Sowell that she would not tell police about the assault, he escorted her downstairs and out of the home, setting her free. Vanessa stated that she phoned police to report Sowell's attack along with his address but was "rudely" told that she needed to come to the station to file a report. She said that she was badly injured and did not have a way to get to a police station, so she did not report the assaults at that time. Then, in 2009, a few months before human remains were found in Sowell's home, Vanessa changed her mind and went directly to police and told them about Sowell repeatedly raping and beating her, but was "laughed at" by police, who did not take her allegations seriously.[60] Prosecutors became aware of her rape and beating by Sowell during a probation hearing in 2010, when she explained to a judge that the violence she suffered attributed to her probation violation.[61] She was then asked by prosecutors to testify at the killer's trial, since she was the only witness who could link the bodies directly to Anthony Sowell; the other survivors had not seen any of Sowell's deceased victims while in the residence.

In 2021, while being interviewed by reporters about surviving the trauma of escaping Anthony Sowell, Vanessa Gay's psychological distress was still noticeable. She was disappointed that the prosecutors did not charge Sowell for her rape and beating and only used her as a witness, thereby ignoring her as one of Sowell's victims.[62] She was also excluded from an undisclosed settlement the city of Cleveland made to two other victims who survived Sowell's attacks.[63] "Police took me on a tour of the house on Imperial," she said. "I'm the only woman who had to go back in there and no one wanted to fight for me."[64]

In December 2008, two months after Vanessa Gay's attack, forty-two-year-old Gladys Wade would battle Anthony Sowell for her life, shortly before Christmas Day. Gladys described walking past Sowell as he stood in front of his home. He greeted her with a friendly "Merry Christmas." At Sowell's murder trial, she recounted that immediately after speaking to her, he grabbed her and dragged her into the residence.[65] She stated that she fought hard for her life, struggling against him as he pulled her up the stairs to the third floor. Gladys was choked and beaten in the face repeatedly, but she continued to fight back, clawing at his face and neck. Once they reached the top of the staircase, Gladys claimed that she grabbed him around the waist and threw herself and Sowell down the steps. At the bottom of the stairs, near the front door, the struggle continued until she grabbed him by the groin as hard as she could, causing him to release her. Then she was able to make her escape out of the house.

Gladys Wade ran to a nearby business, Bess Chicken and Pizza, where she begged the employees to call the police. She said she was laughed at and told to leave the store because she was bleeding from her injuries. She then flagged down a police car, and officers took her to the precinct and photographed her wounds. In the *Unseen* documentary, viewers are shown police photos of deep, bloody marks and bruises around Gladys' neck and back. Police arrested and interviewed Sowell, who claimed that she had entered his home willingly and then attempted to rob and attack him. After hearing his version of events, officers released Sowell. Prosecutors concluded that there was "insufficient evidence" to support Gladys Wade's claim of assault. Traumatized and disheartened eight years after the attack, she told producers of the film, "They [police] don't listen to women on drugs. They don't listen. They're [victims] nothing." Gladys Wade was one of two victims who received compensation from the city of Cleveland for police failing to adequately investigate the complaint she filed against Anthony Sowell.[66]

Tragically, six more women were murdered by Anthony Sowell after his attack on Gladys Wade.

In October 2009, Shawn Morris was captured on video from the nearby Bess Pizza and Chicken restaurant falling out of a second-floor window of Sowell's home. She was nude and bleeding from her injuries. The video also showed a naked Sowell run out of a side door of the home and attempt to pull Shawn from the ground toward the house. Employees of Bess Pizza immediately called the police, and two men came to render aid. Shawn also appeared in the *Unseen* documentary. In her interview, she described going to Sowell's home after he promised to supply her with crack cocaine. As soon as they entered the second-floor bedroom, Sowell began choking her from behind and ordered her to undress. She complied and was sexually assaulted by Sowell.

When the rape ended, Shawn Morris said she noticed one of the bedroom windows, ran to it, and tried to climb out of it, praying that

God would not let her die. At Sowell's trial, she testified that Sowell attempted to pull her back in, but became frustrated and pushed her out of the window.[67] She lost consciousness after she fell to the ground. According to witnesses who saw her fall from the window, Sowell told them that Shawn was his wife and tried to pick her up and bring her back into the home. He was stopped by two men at the scene who covered her with a T-shirt until the ambulance arrived.[68] After waking up at the hospital, she asked for a phone to call her husband. She was then told by a nurse that "your husband rode with you in the ambulance." Shawn replied that that man was *not* her husband, but she did not disclose that it was Anthony Sowell and that he had raped her. Out of shame, she lied to hospital staff and told them she was injured in a car accident and did not report the assault to the police. She came forward to testify at Sowell's trial when the victims' bodies were discovered in the Imperial Avenue house. When cross-examined by Sowell's defense attorneys about why she initially failed to identify Sowell as her attacker, Shawn Morris was resolute in her response. "I'm telling the truth now," she said. "I'm the voice for them [the women Sowell murdered]!"[69]

A week after Sowell attacked Morris in October 2009, Latundra Billips, thirty-six, was approached by Anthony Sowell who invited her to his home to smoke crack and drink beer. According to Billips, Sowell was not a stranger to her; she had been to his home before to get high. They went to the second floor and entered a room that she described as almost empty, but she noticed a piece of extension cord on the floor in the middle of the room. She said that Sowell left the room briefly and entered again, carrying a chair. After putting down the chair and asking her if she had a stem (a glass tube used to smoke crack cocaine), Latundra reached into her pocket and handed him one. She said that Sowell then turned his back to her as if to light the stem and then suddenly turned toward her and forcefully punched her in the face.[70] He then began to choke her, forcing her to the floor and onto her stomach, at which point he wrapped the extension-cord ligature around her neck and tightened it.

Latundra said she lost consciousness and after some time, woke up to find Sowell naked and sitting in the chair watching her. Sowell had undressed and raped her after she passed out. She said he seemed "shocked" that she was still alive. Curiously, he began to apologize to her, told her that he had "been going through a lot of things lately," and allowed her to dress. Then he walked her down the stairs and out of the home. Latundra said that she maintained her composure, casually walked down the driveway and past several houses, and then broke into a run, fleeing to the emergency room of a nearby hospital, where she was treated for her injuries and a sexual assault evidence kit was collected. Police were notified by medical personnel, and officers came to the hospital to interview her.

Police would not contact Sowell for another three weeks to follow up on the rape allegation. When they arrived at his home, he was not on the premises. Yet the horrific smell coming from the house prompted them to enter and discover two decomposing bodies on the floor of one of the rooms.

Latundra Billips sued the city of Cleveland and was awarded a $240,000 settlement on the basis that police's failure to charge Anthony Sowell in the attempted rape and physical assault of Gladys Wade led to Latundra Billips's brutal sexual assault. Detective Georgia Hussein was accused of "shoddy police work" in the investigation into the attack on Gladys Wade. Detective Hussein did not review evidence and photographs collected by police officers when she took the case to prosecutors, nor did she inform the district attorney's office of Sowell's previous rape conviction.[71] Likewise, the families of the six victims murdered by Anthony Sowell after Gladys Wade's assault successfully sued the city of Cleveland for Detective Hussein's mishandling of Sowell's case and were awarded $1 million, to be divided among them.[72]

Not only would the court excoriate Cleveland police for their failure to stop a killer who preyed upon women in the Mount Pleasant community of East Cleveland, but family members and friends of the victims also would level criticism at the police. Loved ones of the missing and murdered women, in addition to the proprietors of neighboring businesses, expressed frustration that police did not seem to care when women were reported missing nor when survivors of Sowell's violence notified police. Barbara Carmichael, the mother of Tonia Carmichael, told reporters that her attempts to report her daughter's disappearance to police were met with laughter and derision. "They belittled it and made jokes," she said. "They told me to wait a while because she would return once all the drugs were gone."[73]

Sandy Drain, the aunt of Gloria Walker, a woman who disappeared two years before Sowell's victims were found, echoed a similar complaint about police. She told reporters that she organized her own search parties to scour abandoned homes for her niece, even soliciting the help of neighborhood children to put up flyers around the community after police refused to look for Gloria. "It was pretty obvious the police weren't going to help us," she said. "If you're from this neighborhood, you come to expect that."[74] Gloria Walker was not found among the victims in the Imperial Avenue home, and she remains missing at the time of this writing—a disturbing reality for many families living in East Cleveland.[75]

Fawcett Bess, the owner of Bess Chicken and Pizza, expressed concern about police inaction regarding the violence they witnessed from Anthony Sowell toward women in the community. Bess said he personally called police when Sowell pushed Shawn Morris out of his bedroom window. Yet when police showed up at the residence two hours after the incident to interview Sowell, Bess claimed that the police never spoke directly to him. "Nobody did anything because she was a girl walking the streets," Bess told reporters.[76] One month after Morris's sexual assault, the restaurant owner said he witnessed another woman run into his establishment, bruised and bloody, with visible neck injuries, asking for help notifying police. Bess also confirmed that the victim in that attack, Gladys Wade, was not believed by police when she identified Anthony Sowell as the person responsible.

In their own defense, the police acknowledged to *New York Times* reporters that they were aware of accusations of sexual violence by Anthony Sowell by women in the Mount Pleasant neighborhood but claimed they did all they could to adequately investigate the allegations. "There were several incidents at the house that we were aware of, and we investigated everything we heard about," said Lieutenant

Thomas Staccho of the Cleveland Police Department while the search of Sowell's home was underway in 2009. "We are doing everything we can."[77]

Despite comments from law enforcement officers that they expended all efforts to investigate the murders of Black women in East Cleveland, as well as their continued declarations that they took missing person reports seriously, the community remained unconvinced. One pressing fact that contradicts police statements is that an overwhelming and putrid odor of decay blanketed Imperial Avenue and several surrounding blocks, and yet the police never investigated it. It is very likely that cadaver dogs would have immediately seized upon the source of the odor, yet dogs were not brought to the scene until police found the decomposed bodies of two of Sowell's victims on the floor of his home.

Still, the stench did not alarm police when they came to the Imperial Avenue address to follow up on a victim's complaint, nor when parole agents verified Sowell's residence as that of a registered sex offender. In fact, media reports indicate Sowell had regular contact with law enforcement authorities and followed all reporting requirements after he was released from prison in 2005.[78] It is very likely he did so to obscure his murderous predation of Black women in the Mount Pleasant neighborhood.

It seems incredulous that police and members of the sheriff's office visited Sowell's Imperial Avenue home to confirm that he lived at the address, even entering the home to personally interview him, but were oblivious to the smell emanating from the residence. According to Kristen Anderson, the director of the sex offender tracking team in Cleveland in 2009, the extent to which police can track a registered sex offender boils down to a question of "offender rights and privacy versus public safety."[79] Anderson acknowledged, however, that methods used to locate and track sex offenders are insufficient.

Given Anthony Sowell's violent rapes, strangulations, and murders of more than a dozen women, despite adhering to sex offender reporting requirements, Anderson's use of the term "insufficient" is a blaring understatement.

A resident contacted East Cleveland city councilman Zack Reed to complain about the stench. He tried to address the issue through the Department of Health and expressed disbelief that law enforcement failed to sufficiently investigate the smell. "What happened from there, we don't know," he told reporters. "It was no secret that there was a foul odor. We don't want to point fingers, but clearly something could have been done differently."[80] However, other residents of Cleveland were more direct in blaming apathy on the part of police as the reason why Black female victims of predators like Anthony Sowell were targeted. "We have a lot of women of color who disappeared, and police just never bothered to look for," explained Judy Martin, the director of Survivors/Victims of Tragedy, a community activist group in Cleveland.[81] This sentiment was echoed by Mary Mason, the sister of Michelle Mason, one of Sowell's victims. She scoffed at the notion that police did everything in their power to search for the victims after they were reported missing, as well as follow up on complaints from women who had been assaulted or attacked by Sowell. "The police are still in the mindset that some people don't matter," Mason said. She believed that police were not only indifferent to the smell of decomposition blanketing the neighborhood, but they also dismissed missing person reports filed by victims' family members. "Shouldn't the police have noticed that we had so many Black women missing before this?" she asked.[82]

Mary Mason's question is a fair one. At least eleven women were reported missing by family members from the same neighborhood, yet police did not appear to actively investigate their disappearances. And, even more egregiously, Anthony Sowell seemed confident that police indifference toward his victims would allow him to escape detection. Sinisterly, he told several of the women who lived through his rapes and physical assaults, "Scream, bitch! No one will hear you. You could just be another dead crackhead, and no one gives a fuck about what happened to you."[83]

As in many impoverished communities grappling with the proliferation of the illicit drug trade, Black women struggling with drug addiction are particularly vulnerable to killers like Anthony Sowell.

Men preying on these women use crack cocaine and alcohol to lure victims into their homes or cars, abandoned structures or alleyways. And when police are slow to investigate missing person reports or follow up on complaints of sexual assault and violence by women fortunate enough to escape death, Sowell and others are more emboldened to kill.

Not surprisingly, Anthony Sowell's murderous disregard for Black women in his community inspired another case of serial murder in the same East Cleveland neighborhood four years later. However, this time police seemed to learn from their mistakes and reacted quicker to a resident's complaint about a bad odor.

In July 2013, Shauen Childs called police to report a bad smell emanating from the garage of the apartment building where he worked.[84] Police officers brought cadaver dogs to the scene and shortly afterward arrested thirty-five-year-old Michael Madison, a registered sex offender, for the kidnapping-slayings of three women: Angela Deskins, thirty-eight; Shetisha Sheeley, twenty-eight; and Shirellda Helen Terry, eighteen. The women's bodies, wrapped in plastic bags, were found in the dilapidated garage of the apartment where Madison lived on Shaw Avenue in East Cleveland. Madison provided his mother's address as his residence when he registered as a sex offender, yet he lived at a different address than the one on record—a violation that should have been investigated by police.[85]

The victims were in a state of advanced decomposition, to the point where they were not easily identified, nor the cause of death readily determined. An autopsy would later reveal that at least two of the victims were strangled, and that Shirellda Terry was sexually mutilated "with a sword."[86] Police believed that Madison, a local marijuana dealer who lured women with his never-ending supply of the drug, admired Anthony Sowell and sought to copy his lethal predation of women in the community.[87] Madison's youngest victim, Shirellda Terry, was described by her family as a "good girl" who attended church, loved hugs, and disappeared after leaving her summer job at an elementary school.[88] Overcome with grief and rage at the teen's killer, Van Terry, the girl's father, would lunge at Madison in court when the killer smirked at him during his victim's impact statement.[89] Shortly before she was murdered, Shetisha Shee-ley, described in the press as "troubled" with little family support, was recently released from jail on a weapons charge that was later dismissed.[90] Angela Deskins worked in customer service, once attended Cleveland's Cuyahoga Community College, and came from a middle-class family. Deskins's father owned a demolition company that contracted with the city to tear down abandoned buildings to prevent crime; ironically, his daughter's body was found in one.[91]

The murders committed by Anthony Sowell in 2009 and Michael Madison in 2013 would send the city of East Cleveland reeling and the nation questioning why Cleveland appears to be so dangerous for Black women, especially those who are Black and poor. Furthermore, only two months before Madison's victims were found, three young women, Michelle Knight, Georgina DeJesus, and Amanda Berry, would be rescued by neighbors from a home in Tremont, a village near downtown Cleveland, after being kidnapped as teens by Ariel Castro, a school bus driver, who repeatedly beat and sexually assaulted them for more than a decade. Although Tremont is a largely white, working-class community, and Knight and Berry are white, while DeJesus is Latina, police again were criticized for failing to follow up on neighbors' complaints of screams, loud noises, and even one neighbor's claim to have witnessed one of the victims crawling around naked in the backyard of Castro's home.[92]

For years now, the city of Cleveland, Ohio, has been besmirched with the reputation of not just being one of the most dangerous cities in the nation but the most unsafe city in the state of Ohio.[93] And, with two cases of serial homicide committed within four years of each other, Cleveland found itself in the center of news coverage that blamed the rate of violent crime on a crumbling infrastructure of a city left behind. "This is what happens when you have poverty," former Republican governor of Ohio John R. Kasich explained during a press conference after Michael Madison was arrested for the murders of three women. "It's what happens when you have individuals who are very dangerous inside the community and somehow lose track of them."[94] East Cleveland more specifically has been plagued by a municipal budget steeped in debt, a plethora of poorly performing schools (many are permanently closed), 2,600 abandoned homes littering blocks with a paucity of occupied ones, and a relentless plague of crack cocaine addiction.

Combine these factors with a police department wracked with accusations of brutality so shocking that sixteen officers were fired for pistol whipping and sadistically beating handcuffed citizens, what is left is a perfect storm for predators like Sowell, Madison, and possibly several others responsible for the unsolved murders of at least sixty-one Black women in Cleveland at the time of this writing. Majority-Black areas of the city have for many decades been neglected by an indifferent state government that facilitates corporate investment and gentrification in areas west of the mostly Black east-side neighborhoods, including East Cleveland, leaving these communities behind. In this vacuum of poverty and high unemployment, the sale of street drugs proliferates. Moreover, women living in those areas have been subjected to violence at the hands of individuals who take advantage of high-risk lifestyles that are an offshoot of their crack cocaine addiction and sex work necessary to supply their insatiable compulsion for the drug.

This point was crystallized by a 2013 *New York Times* article that described East Cleveland as one filled with "semi-abandoned neighborhoods where social bonds have weakened, and women seemed especially targeted as victims."[95] Likewise, Ronnie A. Dunn, associate professor of urban studies at Cleveland State University and a member of the NAACP's criminal justice task force, connected the murders of Sowell's victims with the state government's neglect of East Cleveland. Dunn dubbed Anthony Sowell's murders of Black women as Cleveland's "Hurricane Katrina" for its exposure of the social and physical decay of a city where its residents felt ignored and its women at the mercy of violent predators. "Unfortunately, a lot of these crime victims, they tend to be African American women or minority women," he explained.[96] Jeffrey Johnson, a then-councilman for Cleveland's east-side Ward 8, referred to the fear that paralyzed members of the community and deterred some from reporting potentially dangerous individuals to law enforcement. "Most people living in inner cities are great people, but they are afraid," he said. "They won't talk about the crazy guy down the street who talks aggressively to women."[97] Yet the responsibility of keeping track of "crazy guys down the street" or dangerous criminals has been largely that of police, and, as was evident in the cases of Anthony Sowell, Michael Madison, and Ariel Castor, police failed miserably in that mission.

From the start, Black communities throughout the city of Cleveland have taken exception to police's initial handling of missing person reports of Black women. According to data collected by Ohio's Law Enforcement Automated Data System in 2021, roughly 70 percent of women reported missing in Cleveland have been Black, while they only make up 30 percent of the population in Cuyahoga County—a rate more than twice their proportion of the population.[98] And, in what has been a pattern for many Black families with missing loved ones, the onus of finding their missing has fallen to family members. Some of the relatives of Sowell's victims told reporters that police rebuffed their efforts to report the women missing, even at times laughing at them when they attempted to do so. Judy Martin, head of Survivors/ Victims of Tragedy, distilled the lack of action by police in missing person cases with Black female victims into one laconic sentence: "If you're white, you're looked for."[99] Martin's assertion is the personification of "missing white woman syndrome," a term in the modern lexicon to explain why white female crime victims garner significantly more attention than Black women who go missing or are murdered.[100]

Furthermore, Thomas Hargrove emphasized in his research that one motivation for serial predators is the high rate of unsolved homicides. This, in turn, leaves some groups more exposed to danger than others. Anthony Sowell's menacing reminder to the women he attacked that they were insignificant reveals a disturbing reality that predators like him know all too well: not all lives matter, and those who don't are easy prey. As Hargrove explained during our interview in July 2020, high rates of unsolved crimes, especially of those who are poor and Black and Brown, embolden killers to target certain kinds of victims. He was direct in his assertion that when a serial killer is confident police are less likely to investigate homicides of victims for which they lack regard, a killer becomes "a walking, talking, breathing testament that there are no sanctions to homicide."[101]

Hargrove and his team of researchers at the Murder Accountability Project (MAP) published a special report in February 2019 that analyzed unsolved killings with Black victims nationwide and found a troubling trend compared to victims of other racial categories.[102]

As can be observed from figure 5.1, from 1976 to 1979, the clearance rate for homicides with Black victims was almost 78 percent, on par with other racial groups. However, that rate dropped by almost twenty percentage points three decades later, by 2017. For all other victims (Asian, American Indian/Indigenous, and white), each group saw an increase in the number of homicides solved by police. Black victims were the only group to see a substantial decrease.

With respect to Cleveland specifically, Hargrove stated that the rate at which police solved murders "plummeted" from more than 75 percent to 45 percent from 2012 to 2017.[103] He attributed this drop to a limited number of homicide detectives (only thirteen in 2017) investigating over one hundred homicides a year and the rapidity in which caseloads grow, given the high rate of violence. However, there is also another disquieting pattern of police behavior that reinforces the city's image of apathetic policing: the deliberate underreporting of homicides to the FBI's Uniform Crime Reporting System (UCR).

Each year, approximately 18,000 police agencies (including city, state, college and university, county, tribal, and federal) voluntarily report to the FBI Bureau of Statistics crime in the communities for which they are responsible. According to Hargrove, the number of homicides reported by law enforcement agencies in Cleveland varied considerably from what local records revealed. For example, in 2014, there were 102 homicides recorded by police in the city, but only 63 were reported to the FBI.[104]

FIGURE 5.1: *Solved Homicides (Offender Identified) by Race/Decade*

	ASIAN	BLACK	AMERICAN INDIAN	WHITE
1976–1979	67%	78%	78%	74%
2010–2017	77%	60%	84%	79%

Additionally, since the year 2003, Cleveland police had not reported even one death by strangulation, even though records maintained by police indicate that there have been thirty such homicides.[105] This is significant, since unsolved slayings of women by strangulation provide a strong indication that a serial killer is at play.[106] Thomas Hargrove described the underreporting (and, in some cases, nonreporting of homicides) by police agencies in Cleveland's Cuyahoga County as being "among the worst," and his algorithm detected unsolved murders that were "flashing 'red alert' for serial killers."[107] To make this stunning assessment, Hargrove collaborated with reporters from Cleveland's *Plain Dealer* newspaper as well as the medical examiner's office to get a more accurate count of unsolved murders (particularly strangulation deaths) in the city that were indicative of serial homicides. His research led to two areas that suggested that victims in those communities—the East Ninety-Third corridor and Euclid Avenue—were killed by serial predators.[108]

In my interview with the self-described "homicide archivist," Hargrove specified these same areas as being veritable "playgrounds" for serial killers, especially when the clearance rate drops lower than 50 percent. His concern was that a high rate of unsolved homicides "inspires" others (such as Michael Madison by Anthony Sowell) and provokes vigilante justice by families of victims frustrated by police inaction. "In Chicago," he explained, "a very significant number of murders are committed because of revenge. Murder and unsolved murder, especially."[109]

It is important to note that Hargrove pointed to the small number of homicide investigators assigned to an overwhelming number of cases as one of the reasons why so many homicides go unsolved, especially in East Cleveland and in the predominantly Black neighborhoods on the east side of Cleveland proper. Due to this lack of manpower and investigative resources, homicides that are not solved in a matter of days, expeditiously become "cold cases," making them even more difficult to resolve.

While I agreed with Hargrove's explanation, I found myself questioning why there is such a small number of investigators given how much revenue is provided for public safety in Cleveland's municipal budget.

According to data provided by Policy Matters Ohio, a nonprofit research institute, for the year 2021, $371.5 million or 56 percent of Cleveland's General Revenue Fund (GRF) of $665 million was spent on public safety (which encompasses police, fire, emergency services, and animal control). And, of the allotted public safety funding, police received the largest share—a whopping $281.2 million.[110] Even in the impoverished city of East Cleveland, more than half of their piteous budget is spent on public safety. In a meeting with city residents who complained about the lack of streetlights and increasing violence in their neighborhoods, mayor Brandon King explained, "I go to these groups, and I say, 'Look! Here's our annual budget. Out of the $10 million, $6 million automatically goes to police and fire.' Out of what we have left, I'll spread this around so that everyone gets something."[111]

Aware that more money is needed to curb violent crime in East Cleveland, the mayor and city council proposed a merger with the larger city of Cleveland in 2016, but this proposal was rejected by Cleveland's city council president Kevin Kelley. Kelley balked at demands of members of East Cleveland's city council to maintain their salaries as a newly formed "advisory council," as well as their request that the city maintain control over East Cleveland parks with Cleveland's Metro Park System footing the costs for maintenance.[112] Left without additional revenue for public safety in East Cleveland, the city has had to rely on the cumbersome process of appealing to the federal government for grants. Thus, financial resources needed to increase the number of homicide detectives remains lacking. But shouldn't a collective concern for residents in the state of Ohio, particularly Black women living in increasingly dangerous neighborhoods in East Cleveland, override the siloed provision of resources needed to protect them? It seems reasonable that money used to increase public safety would be spent where it is needed most—in high-crime areas where police are overwhelmed by higher rates of homicide. Why are there not more officers trained and promoted to work as homicide investigators? For what services specifically are public safety funds being used?

Perhaps the answer to these questions lies in the value (or lack thereof) placed upon the lives of Black women in Cleveland, Ohio.

Just as Los Angeles police officers referred to Lonnie Franklin's victims with the acronym "NHI" (no humans involved), this attitude has been demonstrated repeatedly in the murders of Black women examined in this book. It is evident that the value police place on crime victims matters most when it comes to investigating violent crimes, even more so than funding earmarked for public safety in municipal budgets. After all, if there is a scarcity of resources in a city's policing budget, some cases will have more priority than others.

Jennifer K. Wesely and Susan Dewey's 2022 study concluded that homicide detectives' attitudes about and perceptions of homicide victims even determines whether victim compensation funding is used to help the families and survivors.[113] Detectives interviewed by Wesely and Dewey further confirmed that there is a dichotomy in which police place victims in categories of "good/true" versus "bad/guilty," and, as such, some police believe that some victims "were responsible for their fate."[114] One sergeant explained, "In the mindset of a law enforcement officer, everybody's guilty. There's going to be some true victims and stuff, but when you're sitting down, you have your personal beliefs, I mean you know, when you start talking about— you're checking their backgrounds, you know who they are, you've seen them thousands of times selling drugs . . . and they end up dead or they end up as a victim of crime."[115]

The women murdered by Anthony Sowell had histories of crack cocaine addiction, sex work to support their drug habits, loss of custody of their children to foster care; some had extensive arrest records and were at times incarcerated. Perhaps for this myriad of reasons, when they were reported missing by their families, police were slow to respond or even investigate their disappearances. Some of Sowell's survivors chose not to report their sexual assaults to police for fear of being disbelieved or mocked, especially if they had entered his home willingly and engaged in illicit drug use with their attacker.

Nevertheless, these women are *real* homicide victims and, despite their circumstances, are deserving of serious attention by law enforcement and protection from the men who preyed upon them under the presumption that no one, especially police, would care. What is more, with sixty-one murders of Black women in Cleveland still unsolved since 2004 and heartbroken families reeling from frustration and grief, the demand for effective and committed police investigations into their deaths will not abate any time soon.

The apparent lack of action on the part of law enforcement and alleged callous treatment of the murdered women's loved ones reinforces an attitude that was apathetically summed up by a local business owner in the *Unseen* documentary. Assad Tayeh, the owner of Imperial Beverage, located only a few houses away from Anthony Sowell's address, expresses a shockingly dehumanizing view of the murdered women. In heavily accented English, he says to the interviewer, "I know you tried to interview about Anthony Sowell, you know, but I hate to say that. I want to say that. You know, I'm not ashamed of it. I wish we have about a million of Anthony Sowell. I'm speaking the truth over here. OK?" The store owner looks directly at the camera. "He cleaned up the garbage. He clean up those garbage." The interviewer asks, "Who's the garbage?" Tayeh responds with a dismissive shoulder shrug. "The ones he killed. Those garbage!"

Not human beings. Not mothers, sisters, lovers, friends, daughters, or grandmothers. Garbage.

CHAPTER 6

"SAY THEIR NAMES—ALL FIFTY-ONE OF THEM"

Unsolved Murders in Chicago

S EVERAL YEARS AGO, while delving into cases of the serial murders of Black women and girls as a possible topic for this book, I discovered that a Roosevelt University professor and *Chicago-Sun Times* journalist, John Fountain, had assigned my first book, *You're Dead, So What? Media, Police, and the Invisibility of Black Women as Victims of Homicide*, to his journalism students. Fountain used data and quotes from my book for his *Sun-Times* article about fifty-one unsolved strangulations of mostly Black women on the city's South and West Side neighborhoods since the late 1990s. He and several of his students embarked upon an ambitious project, "Unforgotten 51: The Untold Story of Murdered Chicago Women." Their goal was to name each of the fifty-one victims and provide a brief biography of their lives along with a photograph to humanize them for the larger society who all too often ignored or dismissed murdered Black women, especially when compared to white female victims.

Intrigued by his mission, I reached out to Professor Fountain by email and immediately received a reply that encapsulated the importance of dismantling the invisibility of murdered Black women and girls. "When I decided what topic we were going to focus on this semester, I went searching for related texts," he wrote. "And there was your book, shining like a light in darkness. From beginning to end, it is clear that it was a labor of love. You cared. And that compassion moved you to use your gifts and talents to seek to empower and change, to help even the least of these."

Sadly, I must admit that, prior to speaking with Fountain, I was unaware of the shocking number of unsolved homicides of mostly Black women in Chicago. Our conversation piqued my interest, and I began to research the cases. It was during this exploration that I first stumbled upon algorithmic data found on the Murder Accountability Project (MAP) website, which identified a cluster of fifty-one unsolved murders in Chicago. Additionally, Thomas Hargrove published a series of articles trumpeting that a serial killer (or several) seemed to be targeting women on the city's South and West Side areas. As I noted in the last chapter, Hargrove made the same assessment of cases in the city of Cleveland as well.

Surprised that more than fifty Black women and girls had been murdered in Chicago, primarily on the segregated South and West Sides of the city, and that the cases remained unsolved, I began to probe media sources and MAP's research, as well as Fountain's capstone project with his students, to learn more.

One case in particular, the murder of twenty-one-year-old Diamond Turner in 2017, crystallized the virulent criticism that the Chicago Police Department (CPD) has received from not only victims' families and the Black communities in Chicago but also from media. The *Sun-Times* described police actions in bringing Turner's killer to justice as "languishing" above all else.[1] The man accused, fifty-two-year-old Arthur Hilliard, was considered the "prime suspect" in Turner's murder, yet he remained free for three years before an arrest was made. Police officials blamed the delay in Hilliard's arrest on slow DNA testing.[2] However, in the time that police awaited confirmation that blood found at the suspect's home matched that of the victim, Diamond Turner, police suspected that Hilliard murdered two additional victims.

It began on a cold March night in 2017 on Chicago's South Side, when the body of the attractive young woman was found in a trash bin behind the apartment of Arthur Hilliard, a man Diamond Turner had been dating. She was found partially nude and had been asphyxiated and bludgeoned to death. Diamond's family reported her missing after failing to hear from her the morning after a night out at a neighborhood bar. What her loved ones did not know at the time was that she left the bar with Hilliard, who was more than twice her age and the father of six adult children.[3] Hilliard lived in and managed an apartment building across the street from Diamond's residence. He had several roommates, who later shared information with police that identified Hilliard as a primary suspect in Diamond's homicide. One of Hilliard's roommates, Michael Parks, provided several disturbing details to police:

- Diamond was a frequent visitor to their apartment and was seen in Hilliard's bed the night of her disappearance, telling Parks that she was "annoyed" with Hilliard.
- Parks awoke to Hilliard mopping a trail of blood on the floor of his bedroom to the kitchen's back door, claiming to have injured his leg—an injury none of the witnesses observed on Hilliard's body.
- When Parks and the two other roommates asked Diamond's whereabouts, Hilliard told them that someone picked her up in a white vehicle in the middle of the night. However, her jacket and shoes were still on the floor in his bedroom.
- Parks alleged that, early the next morning, he saw Hilliard cleaning a hammer while sitting on his bed.
- Parks claimed that Hilliard asked him to retrieve a large trash bin and bring it into the kitchen. Shortly after, Hilliard snapped at one roommate "not to touch it." The roommate claimed to have seen the sleeve of Diamond's jacket sticking out of the top of the bin.
- Hilliard dragged his "soaking wet mattress" out of the apartment and discarded it in an alley across the street from his apartment building.[4]

On November 3, 2017, during an ABC-7 Investigative Team (I-Team) special news report on Diamond's murder, the family told reporters that Hilliard repeatedly called Diamond's mother, asking if she had returned home. Suspicious, the family insisted to police that

Hilliard knew more about Diamond's disappearance and murder than he claimed. Diamond's aunt Latonya Turner explained that the family became frustrated with the lack of police action to question Hilliard and decided to play detective instead. Diamond's mother, aunt, and cousins met with Hilliard in a neighborhood park and secretly tape-recorded their conversation with him as he told them that he had information about Diamond's death.

For twelve minutes, in a voice on the edge of frenzy, Hilliard described Diamond's murder in minute detail, claiming that his roommate, Michael Parks, killed her, and that Hilliard was an eyewitness to her death. "I'll tell you the whole story!" he exclaimed. "I've never seen nothing like this in my fucking life except on TV!" He went on, "He took a big ass hammer and hit her. He hit her again—bam! He hit her again and her head went that way (imitating how Diamond's head reacted to the blow). She died at 5:50 a.m. that Tuesday night or Wednesday morning. I remember it vividly!"[5] Hilliard even told the family where they could find the murder weapon, which he claimed was a sledgehammer. "Just open that basement door. You gon' go to that corner. Right behind that is the murder weapon, a big ass sledgehammer!" Parks denied any involvement in Diamond's murder and told her family, police, and reporters that the killer was Hilliard, who acted alone in beating Diamond Turner to death with a hammer.[6]

Confident that they had what seemed to be a confession on tape, Diamond's family took the recording directly to police and relayed to them that Arthur Hilliard was the last person seen with Diamond, and that Hilliard had described Diamond's murder in exact detail on the recording, including "her last words."[7] To their dismay, the police refused to accept their tape-recorded evidence. But after Parks reported to police the details of Hilliard's odd behavior, police obtained a search warrant for the apartment. There, investigators collected what appeared to be blood found in the floorboards of Hilliard's bedroom and sent the evidence swab to the state crime lab to verify whether the blood belonged to Diamond Turner. The Turner family would wait another three years on those DNA results and for police to finally arrest Hilliard for the murder of Diamond.

CPD police chief Charlie Beck blamed the Illinois State Lab for the delay. "He [Hilliard] was the prime suspect," Beck explained in a news conference. "You know we don't have the full ability, as with some other police departments, to analyze our own DNA. So, we have to rely on the state. And as soon as the DNA came back, the warrant was served."[8] Chief Beck's explanation provided little comfort to the family of fifty-two-year-old Andre Williams, a wheelchair-bound man police now believe Hilliard stabbed to death one year after Diamond's homicide. Williams sustained eight stab wounds to his head, neck, and abdomen before Hilliard dumped his body in an alley. This time, a security camera captured footage of Hilliard pushing Williams's body in a shopping cart into the alley where his body was discovered. Incredibly, Hilliard was not charged with *killing* Williams, but only with *concealing* a dead body. He served one year in jail before being released on probation.[9]

Why police and prosecutors did not charge Arthur Hilliard—a man with a long criminal history already suspected in the brutal bludgeoning of Diamond Turner—with Williams's murder is confounding. Outraged, Andre Williams's family blamed the CPD's delay in arresting Hilliard for killing Diamond Turner as a contributing factor in the death of Andre. "If they would have locked him up when Diamond got killed," Shawndra Williams, Andre Williams's sister, told the press, "He wouldn't have had a chance to hurt my brother or no one else. My brother is not the only one he hurt. He's been doing some stuff."[10]

The "stuff" Shawndra Williams alluded to was a third homicide that police suspected Hilliard committed: the stabbing death of another man who argued with Hilliard at an apartment complex. Police refused to disclose details to the press about the victim's name and cause of death, citing an ongoing investigation.[11]

Interestingly, for three years prior to Hilliard's arrest, ABC News I-Team reporters conducted their own investigation into Turner's beating death, taking action that Diamond's family accused the CPD of failing to do. Reporters confronted Hilliard on camera about Michael Parks's accusations as well as Diamond's family's taped recording of Hilliard's description of the manner in which the young woman was killed. Hilliard denied involvement in the homicide and once more pointed the finger at his roommate, boasting to reporters that he provided enough information for Diamond's family to get "street justice" against Parks for beating Diamond to death.[12]

As of 2023, Arthur Hilliard still awaits trial for the murder of Diamond Turner, while also being investigated by police for the homicides of Andre Williams and the other unnamed victim. In September 2018, a judge denied his bond request, referring to him as a "real and present danger."[13] The painfully slow resolution of the Turner homicide, as well as the subsequent murders of Andre Williams and the other unnamed victim, frustrated the victims' families and community activists. Andrew Holmes, a resident of Chicago's Englewood neighborhood and the president of Operation Restoring Innocence, expressed dissatisfaction with the CPD's investigations into the deaths of Diamond Turner and others, suspecting that Hilliard may be responsible for some of the unsolved fifty-one strangulation homicides. "The family (of Diamond Turner) is asking, I am asking," he said, "that the detectives look into all of those unsolved cases with females just in case there is some probable cause or evidence that these are linked."[14]

For close to two decades, CPD homicide investigators had been reluctant to connect any of the killings of fifty-one Black women in Chicago to a single perpetrator. However, recently under public pressure, police agreed to look at evidence that may confirm (as Thomas Hargrove and others suspected) that a serial killer is responsible for some of the murders. In 2019, detectives started testing backlogged DNA evidence to examine possible connections between murders that date back to 2001.[15]

But several troubling questions remain unanswered.

Why did Chicago police not only fail to monitor a clearly dangerous man like Arthur Hilliard? Why delay a thorough investigation of more than fifty unsolved homicides of mostly Black women? These questions are at the crux of the frustration and demoralization felt by Black South Side and West Side residents. To the people living in these communities, this is not a recent or isolated incident, but rather part of a historical trajectory that dates back to the Great Migration when Black people fled the South and white grievance-fueled terrorism in search of a promised land in the Windy City. Since that time, police have acted not as an institution that seeks to "serve and protect" Black lives, but rather to constrain and act as an occupying force to keep Black bodies within the margins of ghettoized borders.

And the past must be examined to provide context for the present.

THE TROUBLING HISTORY OF CHICAGO POLICE AND BLACK RESIDENTS OF THE CITY

A black-and-white photo of a family arriving in Chicago, Illinois, on August 30, 1920, has become a symbolic placard when searching for images of a period in US history known as the Great Migration. From 1910 to 1970, approximately six million Black people living in the South headed to Northern cities in search of freedom from overt Jim Crow oppression.[16] Posing in the photo is Scott Arthur; his wife, Violet; his four daughters; a son-in-law; and their school-aged grandson at the Chicago Polk Street Depot train station. The family had just arrived in Chicago from Paris, Texas, dressed in what appears to be their "Sunday best" and clutching battered suitcases full of everything of value they owned—which wasn't much. What is not evident from the photograph is the horrifying reason for the family's move from Texas. Given the shocking details of the catalytic event that sparked their journey, one must wonder how and why their faces appear so composed, with at least two members of the family attempting to smile for the camera.

Only two months before their arrival, Scott and Violet's two sons, Herman, twenty-eight, a World War I veteran who recently returned home from the front, and Irving, nineteen, were tortured and burned to death by a white mob of three thousand people after the eldest brother Herman shot and killed a white landowner named John H. Hodges, sixty-one, and his thirty-four-year-old son William.[17] The murders happened when the Arthurs—who worked for the Hodgeses as sharecroppers—attempted to leave Hodge's farm after John

Hodges refused to pay them fair wages, cheated them out of their share of the crop, and at gunpoint forbade the Arthur family from leaving the property. After John Hodges jumped on the family's truck and began throwing their furniture to the ground while his son held a gun on the family, Herman ran into the Arthurs' residence, retrieved a shotgun, and shot and killed both John and William Hodges. Herman and Irving Arthur fled the scene of the murders but were caught in Oklahoma and returned to Paris, Texas, where a large mob had gathered and lynched both brothers. Adding to the family's terror, the Arthurs' three eldest daughters were arrested and placed in the city jail for "protective custody," only to be beaten and raped by at least twenty white male assailants.[18] Several days after the young women were released, they united with their family and lived in the woods for weeks before Black Masons were able to raise enough money to ferret the family to Chicago for safety.[19]

The Arthurs were only one of millions of Black families and individuals who fled the South, propelled by white supremacy, racial violence, crushing poverty, and unrelenting dehumanization. Once they arrived in Northern cities, their dream of "yearning to breathe free" was met with disappointment and violence—once again—emanating from hostile white people and police, who heavily patrolled, harassed, and abused Black people living in de jure designated ghettos.[20]

The Arthur family, among countless other Black families, would soon learn that the city of Chicago was one of the worst destinations for those desperate for respite.

As Black people moved from the South to Chicago, white people reacted in what has become the customary fashion of panic: the implementation of policies to restrict the movement of Black bodies. Redlining, restrictive covenants, denial of home and business loans, and police and white mob violence were utilized to keep Black families and individuals cordoned in slum neighborhoods on Chicago's South and West Sides, which were referred to as "Black Belt," communities dispersed along Twelfth to Seventy-Ninth Avenue.[21] Homes in these neighborhoods were dilapidated and virtually uninhabitable, yet were leased to Black families for rents higher than those paid by white families. White people soon abandoned their properties when

Black migrants began to arrive in the city in large numbers.[22] The famed Black writer Richard Wright described the exploitative process by which Chicago property owners provided housing for the new Black migrants to the city:

> The Bosses of the Buildings [owners] take these old houses and convert them into "kitchenettes," and then rent them to us at rates so high that they make fabulous fortunes before the houses are too old for habitation. What they do is this: they take a seven-room apartment, which rents for $50 a month to whites, and cut it up into seven small apartments, of one room each; they install one small gas stove and one small sink in each room. The Bosses of the Buildings rent these kitchenettes to us at the same rate of, say, $6 a week. Hence, the same apartment for which white people—who can get jobs anywhere and who receive higher wages than we— pay $50 a month is rented to us at $42 a week![23]

So dangerous and crowded were these treacherous and densely populated neighborhoods on the South Side of Chicago, many homes were overrun with rodent infestation, and deadly fires were frequent. It was estimated that there were ninety thousand Black residents living in a square mile compared to only twenty thousand whites for the same perimeter.[24] Former first lady Michelle Obama grew up on the South Side of Chicago and described fire as "a fact of life, a random but persistent snatcher of homes and hearts."[25] In her memoir, she lamented the death of a fifth-grade classmate who burned to death along with two of his siblings in a townhouse only a block from Michelle's family's apartment.[26] In fact, a fear of dying in a house fire so consumed Michelle's older brother, Craig, that he routinely engaged in fire drills with his parents and sister, even practicing dragging their father, who became increasingly disabled by multiple sclerosis, down the narrow stairwell of their building.[27]

It is believed that the number of Black people who left the South during the Great Migration is an underestimation, since some avoided census takers, for fear of being returned by authorities for outstanding debts as sharecroppers or violent disputes with white people.[28]

Yet, according to available census data, the Black population in Chicago increased exponentially between 1910 and 1920 from 44,000 to 110,000 during what was referred to as the "first wave" of the Great Migration.[29] The arrival of Black migrants from the South stoked racial tension and fierce competition with white ethnic immigrants from southern and eastern Europe for jobs in factories. Over the course of two years, from 1917 to 1919, at least twenty-four homes of Black residents in Chicago were firebombed, even killing a six-year-old girl, and none of the crimes were solved by police.[30]

In particular, the year 1919 brought the end of World War I and the return of Black soldiers to segregated neighborhoods and murderous white hostility, culminating in a number of deadly riots across the country in what was referred to as the "Red Summer of 1919." In the city of Chicago alone, a six-day violent clash between white and Black residents resulted in the deaths of thirty-eight people (mostly Black), with five hundred others injured, and thousands were left without homes. What sparked the conflict was an attack on a seventeen-year-old Black teenager, Eugene Williams, who "accidentally" drifted across an invisible line that separated the white part of the beach from that reserved for "coloreds only." He was pelted with rocks by an angry white man named George Stauber until he drowned in the lake.[31] Enraged by Williams's murder and a white police officer's refusal to arrest his killer, Black residents began to fight with a crowd of white people on the beach, and the violence spilled over into the Black neighborhoods on the city's South and West Sides. Historians recorded Chicago's 1919 race riot as "some of the worst violence" that took place during that deadly summer.[32] The lethal incident shattered Chicago's supposed reputation as a "safe haven" or promised land for Black people seeking to escape the oppressive violence of the Jim Crow South. Furthermore, Simon Balto, a University of Iowa African American studies professor, pinpointed the 1919 riot in Chicago as the inception of biased and "repressive" policing by law enforcement against Black residents living in impoverished neighborhoods. Mob violence by white people in Chicago toward Black inhabitants was aided by police as a means to protect neighborhood boundaries to keep the two groups separate and, most importantly, to keep Black people in their place.[33]

Three years later, in 1922, the city of Chicago commissioned a panel of six white men and six Black men to investigate the causes of the riot. They concluded that the root of the conflict stemmed from the discrimination and segregation of Black people in the city and the "persecution by local police and the criminal justice system."[34] Although they created a list of reforms to be implemented as a result of their analysis, the recommendations were never put in place. Instead, segregation and biased treatment of Black residents was reified to a greater degree. This included an expansion of police harassment designed to restrict the movement of Black residents from migrating beyond the neighborhoods on the West and South Sides.[35]

As has been the pattern of post–Great Migration police violence, hostile relationships between law enforcement and Black residents living in low-income neighborhoods continues into the present day. Thus, Chicago, too, has been the site of shocking incidents of deadly interactions between Black citizens and police. The shooting death of seventeen-year-old Laquan McDonald in October 2014 and the subsequent attempt by police to shield the public from the bodycam footage of the killing sparked angry protests around the country.

Laquan McDonald's life began as tragically as it ended. He was born to a crack-addicted fifteen-year-old mother (herself a ward of the state) and was shuffled from one foster home to another until his great-grandmother assumed custody of him as a toddler. Laquan acted out as a teenager and had been arrested twenty-six times by his thirteenth birthday. It was at this time that he was diagnosed with "learning disabilities and complex mental health diagnoses," which included multiple psychiatric hospital admissions.[36] Sadly, his great-grandmother died in 2013, the year before Laquan was shot and killed by police, and he was then placed in the care of an uncle, as his mother attended substance abuse treatment and parenting classes to regain custody of her son. Grieving the death of his great-grandmother, he was arrested several more times for drug possession and tested positive for marijuana, cocaine, and heroin, violating his probation for a previous juvenile criminal offense.[37] On the fateful night of October 20, 2014, Laquan was shot sixteen times by Chicago police officer Jason Van Dyke, who claimed to have acted in self-defense after Laquan slit the tire of a police vehicle and then lunged at police with a knife. Laquan was suspected of breaking into trucks in a South Side neighborhood trucking yard.[38] A dashcam video released a year after the killing (after a request from journalist Brandon Smith and an order from a judge) contradicted Van Dyke's account and showed Laquan walking "briskly" away from police when he was gunned down by the officer, who emptied his service weapon into the teen's body.[39]

A spokesperson from the CPD police union used dehumanizing language to describe the teenager, saying that Laquan had a "100-yard stare" and stared "blankly" at officers, who alleged that they demanded repeatedly that Laquan McDonald drop the knife he was holding.[40] It should be noted that similar language was used in the killing of Michael Brown by officer Darren Wilson in Ferguson, Missouri, who described the eighteen-year-old Brown as having superhuman strength that made him feel like "a five-year-old struggling against Hulk Hogan." Wilson also testified at trial that Brown wore an angry facial expression that looked "like a demon."[41] There is a long history of police using subhuman language to describe Black people during confrontational interactions in the United States, including using the acronym "NHI" to describe them as victims of violence.

The controversial police killing of the troubled mentally ill teen Laquan McDonald and alleged cover-up resulted in a 2015 investigation by the US Justice Department into the behavior, community interaction, and practices of the CPD, particularly in Black and Latino communities. Investigators discovered that police lied about the encounter, and that both police officials and Chicago mayor Rahm Emanuel attempted to shield the video from the public. From their inquiry, the Justice Department released what was described as a "scathing" 164-page report that revealed "a lack of accountability for officers, a pervasive code of silence and disproportionate use of force against the city's Black and Latino residents" as well as police tendency to use "10 times" the use of force against Black people compared to white people.[42] Further, there was a woeful lack of investigations into citizen complaints of police brutality.

Despite Mayor Emanuel's creation of the Police Accountability Task Force and support of consent decrees negotiated by the CPD and the Justice Department to address problematic police practices and implicit bias, there appeared to be little progress made to improve relations between the Black community and police in Chicago.[43] In fact, there was another disturbing encounter in February 2019 between CPD officers and an older Black woman, and, again, a body-cam video captured the discomfiting incident.

Anjanette Young, fifty, a Black social worker, arrived home from work and was getting ready for bed when police burst into her apartment, claiming that they were looking for a man with a gun.[44] A terrified and humiliated Young, who lived alone, stood naked in her living room, demanded to see a search warrant, and then pleaded with officers that they had the wrong address. Ignoring her protestations, police pushed Young to the floor and handcuffed her as she continued to sob and insist at least forty times that officers had made a terrible mistake and had the wrong address.[45] For ten minutes, police ignored her, callously refusing to let her cover herself as she lay on the floor of her home. One officer covered her with a blanket, but Young was still forced to lie on the floor with no clothes on beneath it. Eventually, a female officer arrived and allowed Young to put on clothing.

A subsequent lawsuit brought by Young revealed that police realized early on that they had the wrong address, yet continued to raid her apartment for almost an hour.[46] She received a $2.9 million settlement, which included reforms that police execution of a warrant involve a written plan, and that officers use the least intrusive methods possible in their delivery. This reformed procedure, referred to as the "Anjanette Young Ordinance," failed to pass a vote by the city council in the fall of 2022. The only officer that suffered any consequences resulting from the botched raid was Sergeant Alex Wolinski. He was fired by the Chicago Police Board for failing to adequately provide oversight and monitoring of officers at the scene, allowing "disrespect to and maltreatment of any person" while conducting police business.[47]

The long history of abusive actions from police in the South and West Side communities of Chicago toward its Black residents significantly erodes their trust in believing that this very institution will launch serious and effective investigations into violent crimes committed against the people who reside there.

SAYING THEIR NAMES . . . FIFTY-ONE MURDERED WOMEN IN CHICAGO AND COUNTING

On June 14, 1999, thirty-two-year-old Angela Marianna Ford, a mother of two, left her West Side residence to pick up her children's report cards from school but never returned. She was found in an abandoned building after being missing for several days; she had been raped, severely beaten, strangled, and left to die. Ford remained in a coma for two years before finally succumbing to her injuries and dying on January 4, 2001.[48] She would be among the first of more than fifty women to die in a similar fashion in Chicago—mostly Black women whose bodies were discarded like refuse in alleys and abandoned buildings.

In their Unforgotten 51 capstone project, John W. Fountain and his journalism students at Roosevelt University attempted to provide a biography of each victim by meeting with family members and friends of the murdered women but found this to be an almost impossible task. For many of the families, talking about the homicides of their mothers, sisters, daughters, and friends further opened unhealed wounds, invoking frustration with what little media attention their deaths received. Instead, news stories focused more on victims' troubled pasts with addiction and sex work. Reporters who constantly positioned the women as "prostitutes" or drug addicts often undercut the public's willingness to feel compassion or sympathy for them as homicide victims.[49] Many of the Black women murdered in Chicago were, in fact, involved in sex work and the use of illicit drugs. The selling of their bodies was primarily a way to earn money to support their drug habits, making them more vulnerable to the men who preyed on them with the intent to do them harm. For many loved ones of the murdered women, the grief is twofold: it encompasses both the devastation of the violent death, and the sting of police indifference to it. Despite this, several families eventually agreed to interviews and told stories about the women's lives that had rarely been written about in mainstream media.

Samantha Latson, a former student in Fountain's journalism course at Roosevelt University who worked on the Unforgotten 51 project, explained why it is important to recognize the humanity of each of the women, regardless of their backgrounds. Her sensitive and empathetic approach is why she is successful when interviewing victims' loved ones and asking them to speak openly about their grief and experiences with homicide detectives. "When this [victims' personal stories] goes unnoticed and people aren't talking about it, you're basically saying that they didn't matter," Latson said. "That their lives weren't important. But it's important that we humanize these women and tell these stories because they were loved."[50]

This particular heartfelt acknowledgment did not alleviate all resistance to (or, in some cases, hostility toward) the media from victims' families, who already felt revictimized by those police and journalists who centered their stories on salacious backgrounds of many of the murdered women. Unfortunately, some victims were referred to as "prostitutes" by reporters, even when the victim had no history of sex work. Latson noted that this was the case for one of the victims featured in the Unforgotten 51 project. "Gwendolyn Williams had been labeled a prostitute, but her family said it wasn't true," Latson explained. "That's how they stigmatize these women, by blaming them for their own demise." She added, "Even if she was, so what? She was still a human being."[51]

I concur with Samantha's sentiment: that, despite their troubled pasts, these victims are still human beings. Therefore, in each of the earlier chapters, I included as many personal details about them as I could find in the press. When I was fortunate enough to locate and interview a victim's loved one, I included the information they shared with me. But, like Fountain and his journalism students, I found this to be a difficult and daunting undertaking. As much as possible, I have attempted to do the same for the murdered women in Chicago. The following table lists each of the victims, the dates that they were found dead, and their cause of death. I also highlight patterns that are evident in the homicides that would suggest, as in Thomas Hargrove's Murder Accountability Project, that a serial killer may be responsible for some of the killings (more on this later in the chapter).

TABLE 6.1: *Cold Case Chicago Victims, 2001–2018*

DATE	NAME	MANNER OF DEATH
January 4, 2001	Angela Marieanna Ford, 32	Strangulation
March 28, 2001	Charlotte W. Day, 42	Strangulation
August 2, 2001	Winifred Shines, 33	Strangulation
August 22, 2001	Brenda Cowart, 33	Strangulation
November 5, 2001	Elaine Boneta, 41	Strangulation
December 28, 2001	Saudia Banks, 39	Strangulation
February 16, 2002	Bessie Scott, 43	Strangulation
June 12, 2002	Gwendolyn Williams, 44	Strangulation
August 14, 2002	Jody Grissom, 20	Strangulation
August 25, 2002	Loraine Harris, 36	Strangulation
September 7, 2002	Dellie Jones, 33	Strangulation
December 20, 2002	Celeste Jackson, 37	Strangulation
March 19, 2003	Nancy Walker, 55	Strangulation
May 20, 2003	Tarika Jones, 30	Strangulation
May 20, 2003	Linda Green, 42	Strangulation
August 14, 2003	Rosenda Barocio, 20	Strangulation
August 16, 2003	LaTonya Keeler, 29	Strangulation
October 15, 2003	Latricia Hall, 21	Strangulation
October 15, 2003	Lucyset (Mary) Thomas, 38	Strangulation
December 26, 2003	Ethel Anderson, 36	Strangulation
July 15, 2004	Michelle Davenport, 40	Strangulation
October 16, 2004	Tamala Edwards, 37	Strangulation
November 5, 2004	Makalavah Williams, 18	Strangulation

DATE	NAME	MANNER OF DEATH
November 13, 2005	Precious Smith, 23	Strangulation
February 1, 2005	Denise V. Torres, 35	Strangulation
August 30, 2005	Wanda Hall, 33	Strangulation
December 25, 2005	Yvette Mason, 35	Strangulation
December 30, 2005	Shaniqua Williams, 40	Strangulation
January 12, 2006	Margaret E. Gomez, 22	Strangulation
July 14, 2006	Antoinette P. Simmons, 21	Strangulation
September 24, 2006	Kelly Sarff, 34	Strangulation
March 25, 2007	Veronica Frazier, 46	Strangulation
May 2, 2007	Mary Ann Szatkowski, 56	Strangulation
November 13, 2007	Theresa Bunn, 21	Strangulation
November 14, 2007	Hazel Marion Lewis, 52	Strangulation
October 9, 2008	Genevieve Mellas, 32	Strangulation
June 13, 2009	Charlene Miller, 54	Strangulation
July 5, 2009	LaToya Banks, 29	Strangulation
August 6, 2009	Shannon Williams, 36	Strangulation
December 9, 2009	Vanessa Rajokovich, 32	Strangulation
June 25, 2010	Laronda Sue Wilson, 43	Strangulation
July 16, 2010	Quanda L. Crider, 37	Strangulation
August 28, 2011	Angela Profit, 37	Strangulation
August 9, 2012	Pamela Wilson, 46	Strangulation
February 21, 2014	Velma Howard, 50	Strangulation
March 3, 2007	Diamond Turner, 21	Asphyxiation
June 22, 2017	Catherine Saterfield-Buchanan, 58	Strangulation
March 17, 2018	Valerie Marie Jackson, 49	Strangulation
March 25, 2018	Lora Dawn Harbin, 44	Strangulation
June 12, 2018	Nicole Lynell Ridge, 47	Strangulation
September 10, 2018	Reo Rene Holyfield, 34	Strangulation

A common pretext of the Chicago Police Department is that there is little evidence to support the presence of a serial killer in the fifty-one yet unsolved murders. Yet a cursory review of the table above would indicate that most of the killings fit a pattern:

- cause of death was asphyxiation or strangulation
- the majority of the victims had a history of both sex work and drug addiction
- their bodies were found partially nude
- the women were dumped in trash cans and/or alleys throughout the neighborhoods[52]

There were two exceptions to the pattern in which the bodies were disposed: Charlene Miller, fifty-four, and Mary Ann Szatkowski, fifty-six, were found dead in their homes. Two victims, Theresa Bunn, twenty-one (who was pregnant at the time of her murder), and Hazel Marion Lewis, fifty-two, were not only strangled but the killer also placed their bodies in trash cans and set them on fire. Both women were killed one day apart from the other. On the exact same date, two victims were found strangled and, again, left in alleys: Tarika Jones, thirty, and Linda Green, forty-two, were found murdered on May 20, 2003, while Latricia Hall, twenty-one, and Lucyset Thomas, thirty-eight, were found dead on October 15. These are patterns that can be observed from not only the table I provided but also from Thomas Hargrove's algorithm that identified clusters in the murders that Hargrove concludes "screams serial killer."[53]

The probability that each victim was killed in each case by a single offender is very unlikely. To assume that is to believe that fifty-one separate men were killing women throughout the city with the same modus operandi and disposing of the victims in a similar fashion.

That would be an extraordinary coincidence.

And if, indeed, there are fifty-one killers responsible for the deaths of these women, this would affirm a climate of impunity in which men can wantonly murder Black women on the South and West Sides of Chicago without fear of apprehension. And, for the residents of Chicago, that is still an urgent crisis in need of judicial resolution.

HEARTBREAK AND HOPELESSNESS:
VICTIMS' FAMILIES DEMAND JUSTICE

Riccardo Holyfield remembers his cousin Reo's smile, her tendency to break out in song, her love for peanut butter and jelly sandwiches, and the fact that she made "the best spaghetti."[54] Although they were actually first cousins, to him, Reo Rene Holyfield was his sister, and the two cousins had a special bond for most of their lives, especially since they were the first girl and boy grandchildren born in their family.[55] He considered her to be his protector, even though she was petite in size and only several years older. After thirty-four-year-old Reo's battered and strangled body was found September 10, 2018, in a trash can in an alley of a South Side neighborhood, Riccardo channeled his grief into community activism. In the memory of his beloved cousin, he started an organization called God's Gorillas to protect Black women in his community.[56] By 2019, the number of murder victims had increased from fifty-one to fifty-five, and Riccardo began to do what police failed to do: warn women that they were in danger of a serial killer and distribute flyers throughout the community that included pictures of some of the victims. In looking closely at the facts of the killings, Riccardo noticed that many of the victims had been killed in very close proximity to each other—another indication, according to Hargrove's algorithm, that the murders were committed by serial perpetrators. Riccardo was angry that police were not looking at the homicides as serial killings. "I don't know what information you're [police] looking at," he said. "Don't dismiss this. Don't keep trying to go about proving that there's not a serial killer."[57]

Riccardo's admonishments to police mirror the feelings of other victims' family members who feel dismissed and ignored when they seek answers from Chicago police about their efforts to find the killers. Latonya Moore, whose twenty-five-year-old daughter Shantieya Smith was brutally strangled and found dead in an abandoned garage in June 2018, grew so despondent when police refused to answer her questions or even return her calls that she took Shantieya's eight-year-old daughter and moved 145 miles away in hopes that her grief could somehow be abated. The devastation followed her to Kewanee, Illinois. "I call the detectives, but they never call back," she told reporters. "It'll be a year in June."[58] She expected an update on DNA tests or any evidence that may have been found at the crime scene, yet she has heard nothing from detectives in the case. I recall Jodie Kenney, the cousin of my friend Michelle Jackson, sharing emails with me that she sent to the Detroit homicide detectives, attempting to get information on the murder investigation, especially after Eddie Joe Lloyd was released from prison when his conviction was overturned. Like Moore, Jodie felt ignored.

Worse still, according to Latonya Moore, Chicago police superintendent Eddie Johnson met with her shortly after her daughter's murder and insinuated that Shantieya's involvement in sex work contributed to her death—a comment that further devastated the inconsolable mother. Despite his "soon after" apology, Moore made it clear that her daughter's humanity should be the only thing that mattered in finding her killer. "Whatever they was [sic], whatever they did," she told Superintendent Johnson, "they're still human beings."[59]

The issue of police failing to keep families updated about investigations into the murders and not returning their phone calls emerged as a consistent complaint with many of the murdered women's loved ones. When fifty-eight-year-old Catherine Saterfield-Buchanan was strangled to death in June 2017, her family recalled the last conversation they shared with her, only hours before her body was found. She told them, "I love you. Tell the kids I love them."[60] To the family's mortification, they were never interviewed by police to get information that would lead to an arrest in Catherine's murder. Police, however, disputed the family's report and countered that a relative was questioned by police, but family members say the person was a cousin who barely had a relationship with Catherine Saterfield-Buchanan.[61] The police also did not contact Breakthrough, the homeless shelter that Catherine was known to frequent when she was unhoused and tried to escape sex work and addiction. Moreover, not speaking with other sex workers who knew some of the victims is a missed opportunity, according to Cheron Massonburg, the director of Breakthrough, especially if officers are serious about solving the murders of these victims. Massonburg believes that women in her program possess information that could help find the individual(s) responsible for the killings, but they do not trust the officers. "People know what's happening on the street," she explained to reporters. "But they don't talk because they don't feel protected."[62]

Equally striking, some families were unaware their murdered loved ones were among the fifty-one unsolved cold cases of women who died under similar circumstances. After forty-two-year-old Linda Green was found nude and strangled to death in an alley on May 20, 2003, her sister Amanda Dudley sat horrified while watching a 2021 documentary series called *The Hunt for the Chicago Strangler* on the Discovery+ channel and saw her sister's name and death date appear among the fifty other victims. It was the first time she was made aware that Linda may have been the victim of a serial killer.[63] And still, twenty years after their sister's death, the family is angry that police have divulged little if any information about the investigation into Linda's murder. While their requests for updates on the search for Linda's killer received initial obligatory polite responses like "We'll call you if we know anything," as time passed, detectives stopped answering the phone altogether. "The phone would just ring," Hattie Green, an elder sister of Linda, explained. "I haven't heard anything since."[64]

Charles Green, another of Linda's eleven siblings, and her younger brother, strongly believes the reason police dismissed the family's inquiries and acted disinterested in finding Linda's killer is because, as a Black woman, her life simply has no value. "Do you think if these were 51 white women this would've happened?" he asked. "This would've been all on CNN and everywhere."[65] It was Charles who single-handedly conducted a search for Linda after the large, close-knit family did not hear from her for two weeks, especially on Linda's birthday, June 2. He also endured the grief and trauma of identifying her body at the county morgue. "I didn't want to believe it was my sister 'til I saw her," he said.[66] After viewing her battered body, Charles felt the need to protect his sisters from the brutality of Linda's homicide and did not share with them the condition of her body. Linda, whom he remembered as his protector, the provider of stylish clothes he wore in high school, the "cool sister every sibling longed to have," was forever lost.[67] Even after two decades, her remaining siblings are as heartbroken over her death as they were when police found her remains discarded by her killer in an alley.

Eventually, families and friends of victims grew increasingly frustrated and distrustful of police and reached out to community activists, who galvanized South and West Side residents to raise the alarm and demand justice for the victims and their families. An advocacy group, Stop Taking Our Girls Campaign, continues to apply steady pressure on the CPD to foment aggressive investigations into the unsolved murders and send a clear message to predatory offenders— that Black women and girls must be protected.[68] Part of the group's mission is to raise awareness of the constant threat of lethal violence targeting Black women and girls as well as provide self-defense classes and community outreach to improve neighborhood safety. The activists' amplified efforts to bring attention to the victims has caught the attention of media. A number of documentaries, podcasts, and investigative news reports have emerged to challenge Chicago police to find the person(s) responsible for so many deaths. They also openly question if the race of the victims plays a role in what seems to be an apathetic response by investigators.

Other community organizers and activist voices have called out the invisibility of Black women and the CPD's pallid response to their murders. Rosie Dawson, a vocal member of the Stop Taking Our Girls Campaign, sees the destruction of Black women having historical tentacles that reach back to enslavement in the US. "As far back as slavery, Black women have never got the proper respect or due when it comes to what people care about," she opined. "Black women are always being marginalized in every form. We just feel like some of the elected officials and the police are not putting as much effort into stopping this."[69] James Coleman, the community wellness director for the Westside Health Authority, a nonprofit organization that has provided a myriad of supportive services and resources to residents living on the West Side of Chicago, echoed the same sentiment. Taking aim at police officials' explanation that they are unable to solve cases in a timely fashion because the department lacks a city-owned crime lab, causing delays in DNA testing (as in Diamond Turner's murder investigation), Coleman stated plainly, "They prioritize their resources. So, they haven't prioritized the funding to do DNA testing, not just for missing girls but with everything else."[70]

Reverend Robin Hood (a name befitting his commitment to protect victims of violence) and his wife, Louvenia, are community activists and the founders of Mothers Opposed to Violence Everywhere (MOVE). The couple has forcefully spoken out against what they believe to be anemic and ineffective investigative work by the CPD. In an April 2019 interview on WBEZ-NPR, Reverend Hood shared his conviction that a serial killer was at work in Chicago, especially in 2007, the year he claims police stumbled upon the dead bodies of women in an illegal dump as part of a federal government effort to expose corruption among city officials and construction companies in a sting known as Operation Silver Shovel.[71] "There was a landfill where they dumped stuff, and when they [the city] had to clean it up, there were bodies found. And it was unbelievable because some of the bodies were still intact."[72]

Reverend Hood alleged that police never followed up with investigations into the dead women found in the landfill whose murders occurred simultaneously with other strangulation homicides throughout the South and West Sides.[73] I searched for independent sources to verify that police discovered bodies in the illegal landfill in 2007 during the city's cleanup of the debris, but I was unable to find confirmation of Reverend Hood's claim. However, if there was no police investigation nor media reporting the discovery of dead bodies, it is unlikely that the public would have access to this information. Robin and Louvenia Hood also blame media for the lack of police effort in solving the crimes early on, since news agencies were initially slow to report on the strangulation murders. "If this was happening in any other place, on the North Side, or in one of these suburbs, and it was people of another color," Robin Hood said, "there would be dragnets, we would have 24-hour round the clock media on it, because it's unacceptable."[74] The Hoods' criticism is not without merit. As I noted in my previous book, media and police have a symbiotic relationship: pressure from media embarrasses law enforcement into launching investigations into crimes that would otherwise be ignored.[75]

Shannon Bennett, another community activist and the lead organizer of Kenwood Oakland Community Organization, took exception
with the overall insensitive treatment police showed toward victims'
families, revictimizing them and compounding their grief. She stated:
"Those family members have gone through two traumas: one, the
loss, then two, the extra trauma of disrespect and just flat-out racism that the Chicago PD and other departments have really given to
these victims."[76] To demonstrate the cruelty of police to victims' loved
ones, Bennett referenced the heartbreaking case of the murder of an
elderly Black woman, sixty-six-year-old Daisy Hayes.

Months after Hayes disappeared in May 2018, police obtained
security footage from her apartment building that revealed her boyfriend, James Jackson, entering Daisy's building with an empty suitcase and shortly afterward dragging the bulging suitcase to a dumpster
behind the building.[77] Police and prosecutors believe that the body
of Daisy Hayes was in that suitcase and now resides in a landfill in
Indiana, where trash collected from the neighborhood was sent.[78]
Even without Daisy's remains, police arrested and charged Jackson
in her homicide. However, in April 2022, he was acquitted by a Cook
County judge who argued that the video alone was not enough evidence for a murder conviction.[79] For Theresa Smith, the daughter
of Daisy Hayes, her anger at Jackson's acquittal and grief over her
mother's death is deepened by an even greater tragedy. Police have
refused to assist her in retrieving Daisy's body from the landfill, leaving her daughter devastated and in disbelief. Theresa Smith said that
she "begged authorities" to recover her mother's remains, but she was
rebuffed and instead told that such an endeavor would cost "millions
and millions of dollars."[80] "I guess she's trash," Smith lamented. "I
don't understand why there has to be a dollar amount on someone's
life." The trauma of losing her mother, trying to solve the case on her
own, and not being able to bury Daisy's remains was made worse by
the insulting way she was questioned by police. According to Smith,
the investigator's line of questioning made her feel like a suspect in
her own mother's death. "It was terrible," she said.[81]

Frustrated that police refused to assist her in recovering Daisy's
body, as a last ditch effort, Theresa reached out to the Cook County

State Attorney's Office for assistance but was told the responsibility to locate her mother's body was that of the CPD, who released a public statement (in reaction to press coverage) explaining that finding Daisy Hayes's body in a landfill would be "an impossible task."[82] Police claimed in their statement that they consulted with experts, including the FBI, and "ultimately determined that the successful recovery of Daisy Hayes from a landfill would have been impossible, as no general landfill search has ever resulted in the recovery of a body."

This is not entirely true.

In September 2019, police in Missouri recovered the remains of Megan Schulz, a white woman who had been missing for thirteen years, in a city landfill. Police searched for her body for more than a decade after Schulz's husband confessed to her murder and to dumping Megan's body in a trash bin near their home.[83] Additionally, I looked for other instances where murder victims were recovered from landfills during a police search and came across the recent case of forty-year-old Rene Benedetti, who in 2023 was allegedly choked to death by her boyfriend and found in an Ohio landfill by police. Officers received a tip from a caller that Rene's body "might" be found in the Rumpke Recycling Landfill near Cincinnati, Ohio—ironically, a state that borders Indiana, where the landfill possibly containing Daisy Hayes's body is located. Rene Benedetti had been missing for more than a month before police commenced a search and found her remains.[84] The difference is not just a matter of location, but also of race: both Megan Schulz and Rene Benedetti were white women. Missouri and Ohio police officers felt that both women mattered to their loved ones, whom they chose to provide peace of mind, whereas the CPD did not hold the same regard for Daisy and her family. Theresa Smith also believed that her mother's race factored prominently in the CPD's reluctance to find her mother's body. "If she was a white girl or white woman," she said, "they would have done everything in their power to go get her remains."[85]

The callous indifference shown to Daisy Hayes' family concretizes the major thrust of this book: that the lack of concern, urgency, respect, and protection of Black women and girls by law enforcement is also obvious to the men who murder them.

SOUNDING THE ALARM: FIFTY-ONE STRANGULATION
MURDERS OF BLACK WOMEN GO UNSOLVED

When *Chicago Tribune* reporters Anne Sweeney and Ariana Figueroa knocked on the door of a home on the city's South Side to ask residents to comment on the murder of fifty-one-year-old Velma Howard, a woman whose frozen body was found in East Garfield Park in February 2014, they were met with a hostile reception.[86] An elderly man who answered the door was neither pleased to see them nor willing to answer their questions. However, he had several questions of his own, and he asked them, barely hiding his contempt. "Why are you here?" he angrily insisted. "Three years later? After all this time? Where were you?"[87] Shaking his head in disgust, he slammed the door in their faces. Almost immediately afterward, the man's adult son, who lived in the apartment beneath him, opened his door and spoke with the journalists. He explained why his father was upset: both he and his father witnessed the discovery of Howard's body, wrapped in a blanket, tied with rope, and buried in a snowbank, yet police did not ask them for statements. They were not interviewed that day, nor any of the days and the eventual years that followed. "They just picked up the body and left. We were looked over," he said.[88]

The elderly man's fury mirrored the growing anger Black residents in Chicago felt toward law enforcement and local media. According to the *Chicago Tribune*, since 2001 seventy-five mostly Black women were found murdered throughout the segregated South and West Side.[89] When dozens of women were found strangled and dumped in alleys from the late 1990s into the twenty-first century, police initially formed a task force of ten detectives in 2001 and solved at least forty of the murders.[90] At the time that the task force was created, detectives expressed commitment to finding justice for the victims, regardless of many of them having backgrounds in sex work. "Years ago, nobody cared about these girls," Sergeant Tony Kuta, a member of the task force, explained. "Well, they're homicide victims. They're people, citizens of Chicago and they deserve the same investigation, the same integrity of investigation as anyone else."[91] Despite this poignant commitment to attaining justice for the victims, the task force was mysteriously disbanded after a few years, and the murders "continued at a steady pace."[92] Thomas Hargrove argues that solving cases is vital to decreasing the homicide rate, as evidenced by the short-lived success of the CPD initial homicide task force. In an interview with journalist Ben Kuebrich, Hargrove stated bluntly, "Every day in America people die who did not need to die. Because every solved murder reduces the occurrence of murder."[93] In short, when murders go unsolved, it creates a toxic killing field in which violent offenders feel emboldened to kill with impunity.

The Chicago police have consistently denied the possibility of a serial killer in the still unsolved strangulation deaths, despite the history of serial predators striking on the streets of the South and West Side. In May 2010, a twenty-four-year-old man named Michael Johnson was arrested and charged in the rape-strangulation murders of four South Side women: Lutelda Michelle Hudson, twenty-nine; Siobhan Hampton, thirty; Eureka Jackson, thirty-eight; and Leslie Brown, thirty.[94] Again, all of the victims were found dead in abandoned buildings or storefronts. A fifth victim was sexually assaulted, beaten, and choked into unconsciousness, but survived the attack and later identified Johnson to police. Her identification and the DNA evidence taken from the victims' bodies led to the arrest of Michael Johnson, who in September 2015 was convicted of the murders and sentenced to one hundred years in prison.[95]

Still, police were slow to respond to MAP's algorithm, which identified a cluster of strangulations as possible serial killings. Chief of Chicago detectives Brandon Deenihan cynically scoffed at Hargrove's data when he initially viewed the analysis. "We don't work that way with . . . like dots on the map, and this says x, y, z, so it must be this," the chief explained. "We can only work with what we know and what we can prove."[96] Yet, with thirteen thousand DNA samples from murders throughout Illinois untested until 2019,[97] and five thousand active homicide investigations stifled by a backlog of DNA testing in state laboratories, how could police be so vociferous in their denial that the killings were the work of serial killers for close to twenty years?[98] How could they be certain without tests that would confirm (or disprove) linkages in the murders? After all, wouldn't DNA be the place to start to determine if there was a connection among the homicides?

I am not the only one asking these questions. Illinois state senator Patricia Van Pelt also expressed disbelief that police dismissed the possibility of a serial killer without incontrovertible evidence to confirm their position. "What I don't like is that, in the same story [Superintendent Eddie Johnson] is saying they've found no connection," she said. "You haven't even done the research yet, so how would you find it without doing the research?"[99] Van Pelt was additionally troubled by the lack of information about the killings police provided to the residents. "We had women missing on the west side, and there was very little information put out in the community except for what we had put out there to raise awareness," she explained. "We said then we believed it was a serial killer. We were told [by police] that it wasn't." She credited MAP for raising the alarm. "But when we had the Murder Accountability Project come in for the hearing I had, they laid it all out and clearly it's not 51 different murderers."[100]

Award-winning Chicago journalist and writer Ben Austen took aim at homicide detectives in his expansive article "Have You Seen These 51 Women?" and summed up the issue succinctly: "The list included 51 unsolved homicides. Fifty-one women murdered in Chicago, zero arrests. No public emergency alarms had sounded. The body count multiplied, and few seemed to care. The crimes were perhaps the work of a serial killer."[101]

The public was not warned by police, despite the mounting body count and similarities among the killings. The lack of urgency by police to notify women living in these neighborhoods put the women at risk of victimization. While many of the murdered women had what police repeatedly referred to as "high-risk lifestyles," this should not have precluded police from alerting the public—much in the same way Rochester police warned sex workers when Arthur Shawcross murdered eleven women in Rochester, New York, in 1989.[102]

The difference, however, was that Shawcross's victims were all white women.

CHICAGO POLICE BLAME LACK OF FORENSIC
LAB FOR LOW SOLVENCY RATE

When police were criticized for failing to arrest Arthur Hilliard sooner in the beating death of Diamond Turner, CPD superintendent Charlie Beck blamed the three-year delay in obtaining matches of a blood sample taken from Hilliard's home to Turner's body, and again, during that lapse, two more people were allegedly murdered by Hilliard. CPD spokesman Anthony Guglielmi argued that the city doesn't have the funding to build their own crime lab and test DNA in a timelier fashion. "If we had the resources to develop a lab for Chicago," he said, "we would. That's hundreds of millions of dollars."[103]

As James Coleman surmised, solving violent crime, especially in cities like Chicago with astronomical rates of violence, is in fact a matter of primacy. Moreover, for the city of Chicago, what takes precedence in determining whether the CPD can improve their clearance rate of cold cases is how funding is allocated in the municipal budget. Given the notoriety of Chicago's homicide rate, it is reasonable that residents often question how much money is spent on policing.[104]

In 2023, former Chicago mayor Lori Lightfoot asked for and was approved for an increase in public safety spending of $1.94 billion in a total budget of $16.4 billion—up more than $4 billion from the previous year's budget of $12.1 billion.[105] Could a reallocation of this funding be used to solve the city's DNA testing conundrum? First, one would need an exact accounting of how public safety funding is spent, and, according to Jonathan Silverstein, a former analyst in the City Council's Office of Financial Analysis, the numbers don't quite add up.

Silverstein conducted an independent review of police spending and concluded that the "true cost" of policing far exceeds Mayor Lightfoot's ask of $1.94 billion for the CPD, putting the actual amount over $3 billion.[106] Silverstein argues that there is a lack of transparency in how funds for policing are spent, and he highlights the city's ability to obviate a clear picture of where funding is expended by maintaining a budget category of "finance general," where costs are "dumped" without a specific breakdown of the amount of money disbursed on specific line items.

Laurence Msall, the former director of the Civic Federation, an organization that tracks police spending, explained that the use of a finance general category is problematic because the combining of costs in a catchall account complicates taxpayers' and "policymakers'" ability to see changes over time, while providing "enormous discretion" to the mayor's budget team "without real cost measurements."[107] Whether there is enough funding for the CPD to have its own crime lab is called into question when there is neither transparency nor accuracy in the amount of money spent on policing.

At present, DNA is tested through the Division of Forensic Services for the State of Illinois, with six operational laboratories throughout the state, one of those being in the city of Chicago. Yet the lab is under the jurisdiction of the state, and not the city itself. When the overburdened state lab is the only recourse for the CPD to analyze evidence for homicide investigations, this explains why the lab is handling such a backlog of cases. Further, this accumulation compromises the CPD's ability to efficiently solve homicides. How many other cities in the State of Illinois have a rate of violent crime comparable to Chicago's that would contribute to a delay in DNA testing? Could the bottleneck in evidence analysis be remedied with additional manpower, such as extra technicians?

To get an idea of the volume of DNA testing of crime evidence that Illinois forensic labs process, I compiled Illinois state homicide rates by city (see table 2) for the year 2019.[108] One can observe that for the top five cities with the highest rates of murder and sexual assault (violent crimes where DNA analysis has greater utility) in the entire state, Chicago far outpaced all other cities. Chicago had 492 murders and 1,761 reported sexual assaults, followed by East St. Louis, with only 36 homicides, and Rockford, with 125 reported rapes. Since Chicago leads the state in the two most violent crimes that depend on DNA evidence to solve, why doesn't the city have its own crime lab, or at least the ability to make their request for results

TABLE 6.2: *Violent Crime (Homicide/Sexual Assault) in Illinois*

CITY	MURDER/ NON-NEGLIGENT HOMICIDE	CITY	RAPE/SEXUAL ASSAULT
Chicago	492	Chicago	1,761
East St. Louis	36	Rockford	125
Peoria	25	Springfield	108
Joliet	18	Peoria	65
Rockford	14	Aurora	59

a priority? It is likely that Chicago accounts for the backlog of testing; therefore, the state should allocate more funding for additional technicians, especially when the CPD has a solvency rate that is so low that it was highlighted in the Justice Department's highly critical consent decree executive summary.

In October 2023, Black women made up 37 of Chicago's 297 homicide victims, compared to 8 white women victims and 8 Latina victims in the same year.[109] Disproportionately, Black women and girls are dying at almost five times the rate of both their white and Latina counterparts in the city. If Black women and girls matter as homicide victims in Chicago, it should be incumbent upon both city and state government to provide the funding necessary to find their killers and deter further slayings.

POLICE DENY SERIAL KILLER BASED ON DNA RESULTS

After almost two decades and unrelenting pressure from victims' families, community activists, and local politicians, as well as data provided by MAP's algorithm, in late March 2019, the CPD finally decided to investigate the more than fifty unsolved homicides as possible serial killings. Six detectives who were also FBI agents were assigned to reopen the cases and probe evidence collected from the crime scene and victims. Surprisingly, after the backlog of DNA tests were completed, police asserted that the twenty-one DNA profiles returned from the lab indicated twenty-one dissimilar male profiles—a finding that would otherwise challenge the community as well as MAP's belief that a serial killer was responsible for some of the murders.[110] However, police only collected DNA evidence from less than half of the fifty-one victims, but continued to deny any linkages between the murders.[111] Activist Shannon Bennett expressed his skepticism that the police would seriously investigate the murders as serial killings, since they seemed dead set against the possibility from the start. "The police department has been dragged to the party by our work and by the media," Bennett told a WBEZ-NPR journalist. "I mean, CPD has in one voice said, 'OK, we're gonna start this task force, but we don't believe there's a pattern [to these murders].' I feel you've already shown where you're gonna go with this. We're a little worried, because then they'll move on to the next thing."[112]

In his response to the variance in DNA results, Chief Deenihan expressed serious doubt that a predator would "skip the white prostitutes to kill Black ones, that doesn't make sense."[113] There are a number of assumptions in the chief's statement that can be disputed. It seems that Deenihan is suggesting that, if a serial killer was responsible, the killer is motivated solely by the vulnerability of his target, and that race is inconsequential to the hunt. Secondly, he infers that Black men don't fit the profile of serial killers, and that, therefore, each Black victim would have been killed by a separate perpetrator. Research, however, would undermine both assumptions. In previous chapters of this book, I have detailed cases where Black men were responsible for the serial murders of Black women, and these are only a few of many instances. In each of the cases I've examined, police initially denied that a serial killer was responsible for the deaths of Black women and girls until an arrest was made that proved otherwise. Third, it behooves a serial predator to choose Black women as their victims since it has been empirically shown that Black women receive less media attention and police response when they are victims of homicide, especially if they are involved in sex work.[114] In short, offenders know which victims are easy prey.

For example, when eighty-year-old Samuel Little, referred to by the FBI as plausibly "America's most prolific serial killer," was convicted on September 25, 2014, for the rape-strangulation murders of three women in Los Angeles during the 1980s—Linda Alford, Audrey Nelson, and Guadalupe Apodaca—he confessed to the murders of ninety-three women over three decades.[115] Police have confirmed that at least fifty women were killed by Samuel Little. Little told police that he stayed undetected for so long because he carefully selected victims that would "not be missed"—primarily Black women who suffered from drug addictions or were involved in sex work.[116] When interviewed in prison by New York magazine journalist Jillian Lauren, Little boasted: "I never killed no senators or governors or fancy New York journalists—nothing like that. [If] I killed you, it'd be all over the news the next day. I stayed in the ghettos."[117] It is important to note that Lauren is white. Despite the fact that Little was arrested almost one hundred times in his lifetime in different states across the country for violent crimes including rape, sodomy, kidnapping, and attempted murder, he served less than ten years in prison, and, again, the vast majority of the victims in these offenses were Black women.[118] Thus, Deenihan's assertion that a serial killer would not target one victim and skip another based on racial demographics is not evidentially supported.

Fourth, and finally, most murders are intra-racial: people tend to kill members of their own race.[119] For example, in 2019, the FBI Uniform Crime Report data indicated that 78 percent (3,299) white victims of homicide were killed by white offenders (2,594), while 88 percent (2,906) of Black victims were killed by Black offenders (2,574). This proportional data has remained consistent over time. And if there are, in fact, twenty-one different men who have killed twenty-one separate victims, is this not a virtual killing field that rises to an even greater level of urgency? Does this not reflect a lack of fear among violent criminals that they will be arrested by police for their crimes?

Undaunted by the DNA results, Thomas Hargrove questioned how investigators could remain resolute that no connections in the homicides existed without DNA evidence from *all* victims. In our interview, Hargrove stood by his assertion that there were multiple serial killers involved in the fifty-one unsolved strangulations. "First of all, we have no doubt that there are serial killers, more than one involved in this cluster, none whatsoever," he assured me. "It is not an uncommon thing for a serial killer to not have sex with his victim [thus there would be no semen evidence] and strangulation murders are a 'hands on' murder."[120]

Hargrove also asked Chicago's chief of detectives Brendan Deenihan why so little DNA evidence—from less than half of the victims—was collected, and, per Hargrove, Deenihan said he couldn't explain it. Hargrove was also frustrated with the CPD and Illinois crime lab shifting blame to one another for the yearslong backlog of untested DNA. "I don't know, and I don't care," Hargrove declared. "Just take it to the bank that we got multiple . . . at least three serial killers involved."[121]

Nevertheless, CPD spokesman Anthony Guglielmi continued to emphasize that initial DNA tests yielded little evidence of a serial killer behind the murders. "There is, just to be clear, there is no evidence that we can point to that there is an orchestrated movement to kidnap women in Chicago," he said. "We just don't have the evidence to prove that." He pointed to the sex work background of most of the victims as a primary factor in their victimization, yet strongly denied that this factor played a role in determining the level of police commitment to the investigation. He was adamant that solving these cases with a renewed task force was a "top priority" for the department.[122]

Yet the US Justice Department seems unconvinced of the CPD's determination to not only solve these homicides, but murders in general in the city of Chicago. In their 2017 consent decree with the CPD, the US Justice Department pointed out its piteously low murder clearance rate, which is 29 percent—less than half of the national average.[123] Moreover, US Justice Department investigators stressed the urgent need for Chicago police to increase trust among impoverished Black residents in the city who lack confidence that police "care about them and has not abandoned them, regardless of where they live or the color of their skin."[124]

A POSSIBLE SUSPECT IN THE KILLINGS EMERGES

There may be a break in solving some of the fifty-one cold cases, based on a 2014 confession from a man convicted in the murders of seven women in Gary, Indiana, a city almost thirty-one miles from Chicago, Illinois.

In 2018, Darren Vann, a forty-seven-year-old drifter, was convicted for the murders of seven women in the city of Gary: Afrikka Hardy, nineteen, originally from Chicago; Anith Jones, thirty-five; Teaira Batey, twenty-eight; Tracy Martin, forty-one; Kristine Williams, thirty-six; Sonya Billingsley, fifty-two; and Tanya Gatlin, twenty-seven.[125] Vann raped and strangled each of his victims, dumping most of their bodies in vacant houses throughout the city. He was arrested in October 2014 for the murder of nineteen-year-old Afrikka Hardy, whom he met through an online escort service before arranging an encounter at a Motel 6 in Hammond, Indiana (eleven miles outside of Gary). During what Vann described as "rough sex," he confessed to strangling Afrikka to death and leaving her body in the motel bathtub.[126] In his interrogation by Gary detectives, he disclosed that he had murdered six other victims in the city in addition to Afrikka Hardy, leading police to the bodies of his victims, who had been reported missing by family members.[127] And, in a surprising turn of events, Vann bragged that he killed "way more victims" in the city of Chicago, riding the north-south train line into the city on a hunt for victims that, he confessed, "relieved the pressure he felt when he wanted to kill women."[128]

After reviewing the list of victims in Chicago who were strangled and left specifically in abandoned houses, I counted eight women. Vann confessed that he began his murder spree in the late 1990s and continued to kill until he was arrested in 2014. Of the women who were killed on the South and West Sides of Chicago, at least four of the women were strangled between 2004 and 2010, and these cases remain unsolved. Hargrove's algorithm pinpointed that several of the fifty-one victims' bodies were found in alleys or abandoned buildings along the route of Chicago's Green Line elevated trains—the same route Vann took by train to the city.[129]

Hargrove's difficulty in convincing the Chicago homicide investigators that there is a serial killer in Chicago is reminiscent of the same resistance he encountered from investigators in Gary, Indiana, in the Darren Vann murder cases. He was particularly frustrated with Gary police when, in 2010, his algorithm identified a cluster of unsolved strangulation killings of Black women in the city that would later be linked to Darren Vann, but authorities ignored his warnings.[130] "I continued to suggest, 'have you really looked at these cases?," he explained to Ben Kuebrich on a podcast in June 2021.[131] After police stopped returning his calls, Hargrove became concerned, as he was about to release a story about the killings to the media, specifically reporting that the data pointed to a serial killer stalking victims in the city.

But, as it turned out, police were not investigating the killings as serial murders, nor had they seriously considered his data. "We needn't have worried . . . that was our fear," Hargrove said. "I even sent registered letters to the chief of police and to the mayor saying what we were about to do and if there's any issue they have or any conversation they want to have, for heaven's sake, call me."[132]

Despite his imploration, his calls were not returned. "We had total radio silence from those people," Hargrove scoffed. In a surprising turn of events, the Lake County Coroner's Office was pleased to receive Hargrove's data and immediately assigned the list of victim cases for further investigation. "They agreed with us that there were too many unsolved murders," Hargrove said. "She [the deputy assistant coroner] added three more cases that she thought belonged on that pile. We had identified fifteen, she added three, making eighteen that she thought were connected." Hargrove said that the coroner also attempted to have a conversation about the growing number of strangulation murders with the Gary Police Department, but to no avail. Moreover, Hargrove suggested that Vann was not the only killer who targeted women in Gary, Indiana, and that he was convinced that Vann was responsible for some of the Chicago killings—this despite a lack of DNA connecting some of the murders to a single offender.[133]

Although Darren Vann's interrogation by detectives in Hammond, Indiana, occurred in 2014, it wasn't until *Algorithm* podcast host Ben Kuebrich got access to the tapes through a Freedom of Information (FOI) request that the press became aware of Vann's revelations. When members of media confronted the CPD about Darren Vann confessing to some of the cold case murders in Chicago, police released a statement doubling down on their position that "there is no evidence linking the cases to each other or to suggest there is a serial killer."[134]

Police departments' resistance to declaring a series of unsolved homicides to be serial killings is par for the course, according to Brent Turvey, a renowned criminologist, professor at the Forensic Criminology Institute in Sitka, Alaska, and a cold case investigator. Turvey, who has more than twenty-five years of experience, is also part of an international team of investigators working on femicide cases in Latin America.[135] In a March 2020 podcast with John Fountain and Samantha Latson to discuss the prospect of a serial killer in Chicago and the CPD investigation into the fifty-one unsolved homicides, Turvey also explained why, in his experience, police have been reluctant to confirm that a serial predator is targeting a community.[136]

> If they have to admit there's a serial killer operating in an area, it means that one, they have not created a safe environment for a certain population, so that's a political problem, rife with all kinds of civil rights issues. Number two, it now puts them on the hook to be responsible for actually investigating a real "whodunit" type of crime, and that's not something they are capable of doing. . . . There is also a financial problem, and which is now you have to sit down, assign people to this task force, and that's a political nightmare. That's been my experience anyway. I've worked on probably five different serial murder task forces over the last 26 years.

Turvey provided a blunt and scathing critique of the Chicago Police Department. He painted a picture of law enforcement in general as disjointed agencies in competition with each other who fail to cooperate and are reluctant to share information that is critical to solving murder cases. When asked if he believed that some of the murders were linked, Turvey answered affirmatively that some of the cases were connected. "Some of them will be," he answered. "So, I would agree that there's probably a serial murderer in there, and more than one. I would say between three and five." The criminologist also confirmed that a lackluster police response to marginalized victims, specifically "prostitutes and drug addicts of a minority community," emboldens predators, who capitalize on their vulnerability, ultimately "banking on us [society at large] not caring and they're banking on law enforcement understanding that we don't care, and knowing that they [police] are not going to be held accountable."[137]

Unfortunately, Turvey expressed racially biased tropes about impoverished Black communities lacking solidarity, activism, and political engagement, factors that he believes hinder police and elected officials solving crimes in their communities. This is an assumption that shifts blame to the victims of violence instead of the people who are tasked with protecting them. The persistent activism of Reverend and Louvenia Hood's MOVE, Shannon Bennett's Kenwood Oakland Community Organization, and Rosie Dawson of Stop Taking Our Girls Campaign would refute Turvey's contention. It was the relentless and consistent pressure these groups put on media, police, and city and state officials that triggered a renewed investigation into murders that went unsolved for more than two decades. What has also emerged from these grassroots-level efforts and that of determined victims' families are a plethora of podcasts, documentaries, and investigative news reports that now have people around the country questioning whether racial bias is behind the CPD's inability (or unwillingness) to find the killers. Furthermore, it should be stated again that the background of the victims should be irrelevant when it comes to the administration of justice. Police should not solve cases based on how they feel about victims. They are sworn to protect and serve all citizens, not just the ones they deem worthy.

When police fail to that end, communities of color are forced to rise to the occasion, yet Turvey and others assume that residents are indifferent to the violence that plagues them. I am reminded of a conversation I had with a student a few years ago in one of my sociology courses. The student asked plaintively, "If Black lives matter, why don't they matter to Black people? Why are they not doing something about violence in their own communities?" For the record, this was a Black student living in the city of Detroit. I brought to her attention the work of Detroit's 300, a community activist group made up of Black men who routinely patrol Detroit neighborhoods, gas stations, and grocery store parking lots, especially in the evening, to protect

Black women from violence. In fact, the group was credited for working together with police to apprehend a number of violent sexual offenders, particularly one dubbed the "Bus Stop Rapist" in Detroit in 2011.[138] More recently, in 2019, the group canvassed communities on Detroit's East Side to garner information and tips that led to the arrest and 2022 conviction of Deangelo Kenneth Martin, thirty-eight, a serial killer and rapist in the murders of four women: Nancy Harrison, fifty-two; Travestine Ellis, fifty-three; Annetta Nelson, fifty-seven; and Tamara Jones, fifty-five. All of the victims, with the exception of Nancy Harrison, were older Black women, and all had been raped, beaten, and strangled to death.[139] Without national media attention on the efforts of activists in urban communities, many are unaware that, despite feeling under siege from poverty, high crime rates, and fraught relationships with police, Black and Brown people are fighting every day to make their neighborhoods safer. Thus, the assumption of inertia is a common one.

Turvey also cautioned that, in many cases, when police claim to have opened investigations into homicides, it is little more than a political smoke screen: no investigative work is actually being done. The declaration of a new probe by police is a disingenuous way to quell public unrest. "We have to remember that law enforcement is linked to politicians," he explained. "They only respond to negative press . . . things that relate to image."[140]

As I have reiterated throughout this chapter and others, victims' families are desperately trying to get answers, demanding dissemination of information to keep women in the community safe, calling for accountability from the police department for lethargic and ineffective investigations—often to no gain. Phone calls are unreturned, questions are left unanswered, and contact with victims' loved ones is avoided by homicide investigators. This despite these families paying the taxes that provide the salaries and funding for public safety for their communities. Contrary to Brent Turvey's assumption that victims' families are not demanding more from police, they are not idly standing by.

On the other hand, I agreed with one observation Turvey made about law enforcement and public pressure to solve cases, particularly in the Diamond Turner homicide investigation. He stated that police would name a "person of interest" without actually making an arrest to distract the public from the case not actively being solved: "Either you got somebody who is responsible for the crime, and you can make your arrest, or you don't. And you shouldn't be throwing names out there to the media in the hopes that everybody is sure to go for the 'shiny object.' . . . What they're trying to do is distract the public from the fact that they are not doing anything, and they've got no results."

The CPD used the arrest of Arthur Hilliard as proof that they were making progress in solving the fifty-one murders, but, by their own admission, they had suspected Hilliard as the killer of Diamond Turner from the beginning of their investigation, despite taking three years to arrest him.[141] Turner was not murdered by a stranger or a perpetrator unknown to law enforcement; therefore, her death did not fit the victim profiles of the other Chicago victims. Yet police hailing the arrest of Hilliard as "the first in the 51 strangulation murders" has been used to reassure the public that police are working hard to close the cases.[142] As Brent Turvey suggested, this kind of pronouncement reassures the public, causing people to move on, and any follow-up questions about progress from victims' families and community activists ceases.

As of the fall of 2023, no other cases of the fifty-one unsolved Chicago strangulations have resulted in an arrest of a suspect. The murders remain unsolved, but, as John Fountain poignantly urged, the victims remain . . . unforgotten.

CONCLUSION

N OCTOBER 2022, while in the throes of writing this book, a news story broke that sent shock waves across the country. A twenty-two-year-old Black woman from Kansas City, Missouri, escaped from the basement of a home in Excelsior Springs, Missouri, a predominantly white town approximately twenty-nine miles from Kansas City. There she had been held in captivity by thirty-nine-year-old Timothy Haslett Jr., a white man who allegedly raped and tortured her for almost a month. The victim (referred to as "T.J." to protect her identity) had been kidnapped from Prospect Avenue, in an area rife with poverty, violent crime, addiction, and illicit sexual activity. One day, when her kidnapper left the home to take his seven-year-old son to school, T.J. was able to make her escape and ran to nearby houses, frantically knocking on doors until an elderly woman pulled her into the safety of her home.

The terrified, trembling young Black woman, who was dressed in a trash bag fashioned into a latex dress with duct tape and a padlocked collar around her neck, repeatedly stated that Haslett was going to kill her. T.J. also told the woman that two of her friends "never made it out alive"—alleging that Haslett had murdered two other women (whom she knew personally) prior to him kidnapping her.[1] Police quickly arrested Haslett, who was indicted in February 2023 on one count of first-degree rape, four counts of first-degree sodomy, one count of first-degree kidnapping, two counts of second-degree assault, and one count of endangering a child. In December 2023, he was being held on a $3 million bond.[2]

What emerged from T.J.'s fortuitous escape from Haslett's basement dungeon was more than a story of a woman being kidnapped
and sexually assaulted. One month before, Bishop Dr. Tony Caldwell,
the founder of the Justice and Dignity Center, a community organization in Kansas City focused on activism and violence prevention
in the city's Black community, posted a video on his Facebook page
sounding the alarm about the possibility of a serial killer targeting
women in the area of Prospect Avenue.[3] The video was also reposted
on Twitter and TikTok and viewed more than one hundred thousand
times. Sitting in his car along Prospect Avenue, he broadcasted his
concerns to the public:

> I am a little upset right now. The reason I'm upset is because we
> got four young ladies that have been murdered within the last week
> here off of 85th and Prospect. We got a serial killer again, and ain't
> nobody saying nothing! The media's not covering it. We got three
> young ladies that are missing! Ain't nobody saying a word! What
> is the problem? Why can't we get some cooperation? Where's our
> community leaders? Where's our activists? Where's our public offi-
> cials? Where's our police department? Where's those folks at? Come
> on now! We need to start knocking on doors! We need to make sure
> this is brought to the light! We cannot continue to let this happen.[4]

Bishop Caldwell's comment "We got a serial killer again" is a reference to the 2004 murders of six women by Terry Blair, who was
convicted in March 2008 and sentenced to life imprisonment.[5] During
the time that Blair was committing these murders, police initially denied that a serial killer was responsible.

However, prior to T.J. escaping and telling police that Haslett murdered two other women, the Kansas City Police Department (KCPD)
again wholly dismissed Caldwell's concerns that a serial killer was
preying on women in the community as "completely unfounded."[6]
They used mainstream media outlets such as the *Kansas City Star*,
Newsweek, Fox 4 News, and KMBC to release the following statement to the public:

We are aware of the social media post circulating regarding the murder of 4 women in Kansas City, Missouri in the past week at the hands of a "serial killer" and the report of 3 additional women missing. We want to make the public aware this claim is completely unfounded. There is no basis to support this rumor. Furthermore, we notify the media any time we respond to a homicide. There is a daily homicide analysis which is also posted on our website. There has been 1 female homicide victim in the last six weeks which occurred in the 3600 block of Cypress Ave.[7]

There are several ways to counter KCPD's public announcement of no credible evidence to support the community's concerns about a serial killer. First, police are not obligated to report all violent crimes to the public. The Uniform Crime Report (UCR) statistics collected by the US Justice Department and the FBI gather crime statistics from police agencies who voluntarily report to the public database. Therefore, not all precincts cooperate or are transparent.[8] Public safety departments on college campuses are particularly wary of reporting data that might negatively impact student enrollment.[9] The numbers are not completely accurate.

Second, it is possible that some murders will not be known to the public. Homicides occur more frequently in impoverished, high-crime areas than in suburban, middle-class, and largely white communities. Many of these homicides are not covered by media nor broadcasted by police.[10] Growing up in inner-city Detroit, I remember knowing about murders that occurred in my neighborhood, but no newspaper or evening news programs covered the stories—the information was passed along by word of mouth.

Third, to get accurate numbers on strangulation murders of Black women in Gary, Indiana, Thomas Hargrove of MAP had to work with the county medical examiner, since police refused to provide this information to his organization. MAP staff utilizes coroner reports and other methods to track homicide numbers throughout the country. Because of this, the organization has more accurate and factual data in measuring violent crime in the US—more so than even the UCR.[11]

Finally, families were met with resistance by police officers when attempting to file missing person reports on victims, particularly if they had histories of drug addiction and engaged in sex acts in exchange for drugs. For the KCPD to suggest there are no missing women in these communities is disingenuous to say the least, especially when officers rebuffed efforts to report the person's disappearance in the first place.

The Kansas City Defender, a Black online news organization, was the only news outlet that took Bishop Caldwell's warnings seriously and reposted his social media video about a serial killer targeting Black women in the city, called for police to launch a serious investigation into reported disappearances and homicides of Black women in the Prospect Avenue neighborhood.[12]

Since his arrest in October 2022, police now suspect that Timothy Haslett Jr. was involved in the murder of another Black woman—thirty-six-year-old Jaynie Crosdale—whose remains were found in a blue barrel washed up along the Hills Island chute of the Missouri River in Saline County, Missouri. Jaynie, described by her family as "charismatic" and "full of energy and life," was classified by Kansas City police as a witness in T.J.'s rape and kidnapping.[13] However, Jaynie's family denies the police's implication that she was a witness to T.J.'s victimization by Haslett, since it suggests that she was somehow involved in the violence. Rather, Jaynie Crosdale's family asserts that Jaynie was in fact a *victim* of Haslett's violent sexual predation, since police publicly released her name as a "witness" one day before she went missing in January 2023, putting her life in danger.[14] Since Haslett was being held in jail on a $3 million bond since October 2022 for charges in T.J.'s case, police are now investigating whether Haslett had an accomplice in the murder of Jaynie Crosdale—especially after details emerged that police found blue barrels similar to the one containing her body in a search of Haslett's home.[15]

At the time of this writing, police have refused to release any information about Jaynie Crosdale's cause of death or to explain why they classified her as a witness in T.J.'s assault. Such vague details and lack of forthright transparency has outraged Jaynie Crosdale's family, who expressed that police have placed Jaynie "in a bad light" and created a "negative narrative" that intimates that she was an accomplice of Haslett's. "It's a slap in our face, as our family knows the kind of person Jaynie was," Nikiyah Crosdale, Jaynie's cousin, told the press. "She'd never jeopardize anyone else. The language could have been different."[16]

After the arrest of Timothy Haslett for his attack on T.J., police suspecting he played a role in the murder of Jaynie Crosdale, and T.J.'s account that Haslett killed two of her friends, police now confirm they are "actively investigating the possibility of two more victims" by Haslett.[17] Yet Kansas City police still refuse to use the term "serial killer" in reference to their investigation.

And thus, Bishop Caldwell joins the ranks of the Combahee River Collective in 1970s Boston; Dee Sumpter of Mothers of Murdered Offspring (MOMO) in Charlotte, North Carolina; Margaret Prescod in South Central Los Angeles; Reverend and Louvenia Hood, Rosie Dawson, and Shannon Bennett in Chicago; as well as Thomas Hargrove of MAP in reference to Cleveland, Ohio, and Gary, Indiana, who acted as modern-day Cassandras to sound the alarm that a serial killer was stalking women in the community, only to be ignored and/or dismissed by police.[18] And such indifference has cost Black women their lives.

Yet, as the old adage goes, the hits just keep coming. In December 2023, an Associated Press article was published excoriating Detroit police for failing to follow up on leads over a fifteen-year period that would have resulted in the arrest of thirty-eight-year-old Deangelo Martin for the murders of four women in the city—a case I referenced in chapter 6.[19] It was revealed that Detroit police had DNA evidence from a rape kit that dated back to 2004 from a sexual assault of a forty-one-year-old Black woman, Sylvia Sampson, by Martin, but this evidence languished on the shelf in an abandoned crime lab along with eleven thousand other untested rape kits. Martin's DNA was collected by police after a 2009 charge of receiving stolen property and entered into the FBI's CODIS database, and in 2012 the state crime lab (who by this time had begun testing the eleven thousand rape kits) informed police that Martin's DNA matched the semen evidence collected from Sylvia Sampson in 2004. It would take Detroit police another four years to investigate the sexual assault and reach out to Sampson, who by this time had died. Police then closed her case.

That same year, 2012, Detroit police were contacted a second time by the state crime lab regarding another sexual assault linked to DNA from Deangelo Martin, and, yet again, police did not issue a warrant for Martin's arrest. Then, in 2016, police were informed a third time by crime lab technicians that there was a DNA match linking Martin to the rape of a fifty-year-old woman who also had been physically assaulted by him and sustained injuries that "worried prosecutors" that the brutality of his sexual assaults of women had been escalating.[20] Still, police failed to issue an arrest warrant for the serial predator.

One year later, in 2017, a woman went to the emergency room at a Detroit hospital and reported to medical personnel that she had been raped. Semen evidence was collected and turned over to police. After a DNA hit linked Deangelo Martin to the sexual assault, police failed to follow up with the victim, since she did not file a police report about the attack, even though she sought treatment at a hospital and reported the rape to medical staff. Keep in mind that, by this time, Deangelo Martin had been linked to four rapes through DNA evidence.

By February 2018, police surmised that Deangelo Martin murdered his first victim, fifty-seven-year-old Annetta Nelson, who was strangled and beaten to death in an abandoned house. Incredibly, despite semen evidence collected from the victim's body that matched Martin, police again failed to apprehend him. Detroit police commander Michael McGinnis made a troubling statement to the press when asked to explain the delay in arresting Martin: "For all we knew, he might have been a consensual sexual partner, and the other male DNA could have been the murderer's." Here, McGinnis is not only alluding to the victim having multiple sex partners through sexual solicitation but also seems to be questioning if she was a victim of rape at all. This, despite Deangelo Martin's semen being linked to at least four violent sexual attacks.

Astonishingly, Martin continued to have run-ins with police and was arrested repeatedly for petty offenses, even spending at least two weeks in an Oakland County jail (a suburban county outside of Detroit) for domestic battery of a girlfriend. But he was never remanded to Detroit police custody for questioning in the rape-murder of Annetta Nelson, since police never issued a statewide all-points bulletin (APB) to locate him. Consequently, Martin would kill three more times, and, in each homicide, DNA evidence would be collected from the victims and matched to Martin as the perpetrator. Finally, in 2019, he was arrested after he raped a woman in his grandmother's basement. Later that same evening, Martin was apprehended "without incident" by police at a bus stop in Detroit. He pled guilty to four counts of murder and two counts of rape and was sentenced to forty-five to seventy-five years in prison on October 6, 2022.

For over a fifteen-year period, Deangelo Martin engaged in a campaign of murderous predation against Black women, didn't even bother to hide his crimes, and escaped detection by police. Despite numerous opportunities to stop him and protect potential victims, police failed to do so, leaving victims' families in a rage and reeling with disbelief that police could act with such a degree of apathy.[21] Thus, Deangelo Martin personifies the major tenet of this book: that a serial killer who boldly snuffs out the lives of Black women without fear of apprehension is capitalizing on the egregious indifference and lack of regard of police for Black women, whom they do not view as human beings worthy of protection.

The families of murdered Black women are well aware that seeking justice comes with a high cost to their emotional well-being. Despite their frustration and disillusionment with police and ineffective investigations that deny the possibility of a serial killer, there are lessons that can be learned from the tireless grassroots efforts of these families and community activists. They have shown us that collective efficacy is the most effective way for the Black community to hold police accountable and demand that they seriously examine lethal violence against Black women. Criminologist Brent Turvey's contention that police and politicians ignore the families of Black murder victims because of their supposed voter apathy and the nihilism in poor Black communities is refuted by the stories of loved ones demanding action from police and being rebuffed time and time again.

After all, if these murdered women are not seen as fully human by law enforcement, neither are their families.

Since the enslavement of Black women in the US, their bodies have been commodified as wealth-generating property. Their ability to bear children was paramount to producing children to counter the end of the transatlantic slave trade. After slavery ended, Jim Crow policies, reinforced through white domestic terrorism and brutal police practices, perpetuated the idea that Black women's bodies were violable by any willing white man, including law enforcement officers who turned a blind eye and, at times, participated in the sexual violence as well. Instead of being served and protected like their white female counterparts, the virtuous damsels in distress, Black women were dismissed and ignored, and such treatment continues into the present. Thus, their humanity has been asserted forcefully and relentlessly through community activism and coordinated solidarity that has effectuated Black liberation movements since the end of enslavement.

But this work has been exhausting and retraumatizing. It puts the onus on victims' families and the larger Black community to fight for justice for murdered Black women and girls, when it is the role of law enforcement to serve and protect these residents who pay taxes with the expectation that they do so. In short, Black communities should not have to beg or fight so hard to be seen, heard, and protected. As long as Black women and girls are "neglected, disrespected, and unprotected," as Malcolm X so profoundly pointed out, men who view them as disposable will take advantage of their invisibility.

And this is not simply an issue for the Black community to address and solve. It is a societal issue with ramifications extending to victims of other races, including white women who have been victimized by men who first targeted Black women, as Black Panther Party member Eldridge Cleaver shamelessly boasted about in his book *Soul on Ice*.

Without question, Black women have been a formidable force in US society and have contributed to building this nation, while ensuring that it upheld its promise of democracy for all of its citizens. Black women were the initiators of social justice movements such as of Black Lives Matter, the Black Youth Project, the Black Alliance of Just Immigration, Say Her Name (to bring attention to police violence against Black women and girls), Black Girls Vote, and the MeToo movement (which was essentially co-opted by white women from the community activist Tarana Burke) to name a few.[22] This does not include their participation in historical civil rights organizing such as Ida B. Wells's fight for anti-lynching legislation, Jo Ann Robinson's initial organizing of the 1955 Montgomery Bus Boycott, their role in the creation of the NAACP, and a myriad of grassroots social movements focused on environmental justice and racism.

Increasingly, Black women comprise the majority of Black college-degree-earners as a group in the US, holding 66 percent of bachelor's degrees, 70 percent of master's degrees, and 60 percent and higher of doctorate degrees, as well as making up the vast majority of Black law school and medical/dental school admissions.[23] In 2022, as members of the military, 193 of the 416 women ranked as sergeants major (the highest of all US Army enlisted rank) were Black women, despite being only 36 percent of the total number of women serving in the army.[24] Not to be overlooked, Black women and girls have made substantial contributions to science, the arts, and athletics and have had an inimitable impact on pop culture and music.

Moreover, the cumulative regard for lives of Black women and girls has beneficial consequences for the whole of this nation. As Keeanga-Yamahtta Taylor, the brilliant scholar and author of *How We Get Free: Black Feminism and the Combahee River Collective*, has profoundly articulated, "Until the Black woman is free, no one is free."[25] Her liberation signals an end to all systemic tentacles of oppression along the lines of race, class, sex, gender, and sexuality. Since Black women endure multiple systems of oppression at once, based on her intersectional identity, to free her from these shackles means that others who encounter the same constraints will also be absolved of them.

And this is why, as victims of violence, they deserve the same level of commitment and resources from law enforcement to ensure their safety.

As a final note, one surprising platform that has emerged in recent years to obtain justice for homicide victims are true crime podcasts and online citizen sleuth pages. The vast majority of these podcasts, however, focus on white women and girls. Black women are using social media platforms and blogs to promote information about missing and murdered Black women and girls, and true crime podcasts such as *Marginalized Murder* (May–July 2022); *The Fall Line* (June 2017–); and *Freeway Phantom* (May–July 2023) have also begun to focus on cold case murders of Black women and girls.[26] Not to be dismissed as salacious forums that simply provide grisly details of brutal murders, some podcasts have been credited for renewed murder investigations that resulted in arrests and convictions of perpetrators.

When *Your Own Backyard* podcast host Chris Lambert meticulously examined the details of the 1996 murder of nineteen-year-old Kristin Smart, a white California Polytechnic State University student from Stockton, California, in an episode of his podcast, a listener who was also a Stockton homicide detective reopened the case, leading to the arrest and first-degree murder conviction of Paul Flores in October 2022.[27] The podcast generated more than twenty-four million downloads.

Another thirty-year-old cold case in Starkville, Mississippi, was solved as the result of a podcast: the brutal 1990 Labor Day stabbing death of Betty Jones, sixty-five, and the rape of her eighty-one-year-old friend, Kathryn Crigler, an amputee who died two months later from her injuries. In August 2018, Betty Jones's step-grandson, Jason Jones, launched his seven-episode *Knock Knock* podcast, which detailed the murders of the two white elderly women and the impact of Betty's death on his family and the small community of Starkville.[28] The podcast sparked a new examination of the case and a *48 Hours* news broadcast. Cold case investigators used cutting-edge Parabon Nanolabs technology, which allows a physical description of a suspect to be created from DNA left at a crime scene or found on a victim's body, and solved the murders of Betty Jones and Kathryn Crigler.[29] In November 2020, fifty-three-year-old Michael Devaughn pled guilty to capital murder and was sentenced to life in prison.[30] I am hopeful that podcasts focused on the murders of Black women and girls will serve as another useful tool in a growing arsenal of approaches used to find the perpetrators responsible for their deaths.

It was my intention in writing this book to show that some of these Black women and girls with histories of sex work and/or drug addiction were more than their problems or the disdain with which some in society viewed them. To their families, they were the funniest person in the room; the girl with the generous heart who would share her last dollar with you; the daughter who appreciated her mother's efforts to rescue her from the streets and apologized profusely when the pull of addiction made it hard to stay sober; the mother who lost custody of her children and planned to seek help to win them back; the cousin who made the best peanut butter and jelly sandwiches and called you her brother . . . the list is infinite. Unfortunately, for Black women and girls, these endearing qualities and personal histories are not captured in news stories about their deaths, if they are written about at all. Finding personal details about their lives proved to be an almost impossible feat. I apologize for not being able to provide more complete portraits of these women as human beings.

Though I never met them or knew these women and girls personally, I sought to love them with my pen, with my words—to counter a dismissive, cruel, and frightening narrative by police officers who have said with both words and actions that they are victims of homicides "with no human involved."

EPILOGUE

L AST NIGHT I dreamt of Michelle . . .
of a solo walk down a cold, dark street . . .
of distant stars dotting the black sky and clouds of breath
escaping from her mouth as she buried her face in the collar of her
winter jacket in search of warmth . . .

I saw her in my mind's eye standing at the bus stop, finally making it to her destination, still shivering against the sharp cut of a frigid
wind, casting furtive glances down Fenkell Avenue in search of bright
lights that would signal an approaching bus.

Maybe she saw him standing across the avenue under a streetlamp,
attempting to look inconspicuous, yet watching her intently. Maybe
she thought, perhaps fleetingly, she should make her way back to
Jodie's house, a safe space, home. But missing her first class during
finals week would be too much of a risk for an honor student with
hopes of college in her immediate future. Her grade point average
must be protected, so her uneasiness must be quelled.

The bus would come soon enough.

Did she see him cross the street and approach her, menacingly?
Or was he stealthy like a shadow, suddenly upon her with a knife
pressed to her neck, commanding in a harsh whisper that she stifle
her scream? Either way, there he was with a knife . . .

and a plan.

The garage he chose for his attack, to obscure his barbarity from
public view, must have been considered in advance. He forced her
to walk with him, holding the knife to the side of her neck, fervidly

glancing from one direction to another to ascertain if he had an audience. The woman, who only moments before noticed Michelle and then the man watching her from across the street, was gone now. She would provide a description of him to the police within the week. Once he spotted the vacant cement garage just one block north of the bus stop, he hurried toward it, pushing Michelle forward. When he got to the door, he pressed his body against it, expecting to be allowed entry, but it was blocked from the other side. With the next attempt, he used his body weight to force the door open and quickly dragged my friend, his prey, into its dark cavern.

This is where he sexually violated her, terrorized her, brutalized her. It was within these walls that her screams of pain, screams for help, went unanswered. It was in this cold, dismal, space, filled with litter, that he would channel his anger, his hatred of women, his desire to destroy a target of his deepest and most savage insecurities, upon the body of an innocent and frightened teenage girl.

Were her last thoughts centered on survival and finding her way home? Did she think about her plans with her best friend, Charlotte, or her cousin Jodie waiting for her before leaving for night classes? Or was she thinking of her mother, Carlotta, whom she would never see again? A woman who would give her own life in protection of her only daughter and stop what was happening to Michelle's body?

Once arrested, he would describe what he had done to detectives as a "blind sexual rage," trying to hurry past the details that lay bare in the medical examiner's report. Why, then, the humiliation with the bottle? My dream could not assure me that this last violation was postmortem . . . it was my desperate prayer that it was.

But, in the end, darkness would enclose her. The abyss on the other side of what we know as life would prematurely welcome her. Part of the wardrobe she selected that morning was used by this monster in human form to wrap around her neck and strangle her cries, depriving her of the life she was meant to live.

And then it was over. He would leave, probably not looking back to observe what he had done, the evidence of the savagery just beneath the surface of his skin. My friend lay there, lifeless, broken, and sprawled out, with her eyes open but seeing nothing, surrounded by books and homework that her teachers would never grade.

The remnants of a shattered dream.

ACKNOWLEDGMENTS

THERE IS A SAYING that no man is an island. Neither is a writer. It takes a village of support to write a book, especially one focused on such a difficult subject. There are a number of people I want to thank for providing immeasurable support to me during the four years that it took to complete this book.

Thank you first and foremost, Kali Gross, who made the first pitch of this book to Gayatri Patnaik, the director of Beacon Press, who spoke with me personally and encouraged me to submit a book proposal for consideration.

Thank you, Maya Fernandez, my editor and champion who meticulously read drafts of the chapters and offered insight, encouragement, respect, and praise.

Thank you, Jodie Kenney, Charlotte Grant, and Dee Sumpter, for sharing your memories and experiences with me as loved ones of beautiful young women whose lives were cut short too soon by violent predators. I'll never forget our tearful conversations and the pain that haunts you still. Michelle and Shawna will live on in the pages of this book and hearts of those touched by the stories you told of their lives.

Thank you to those who provided pertinent details needed to examine murder cases covered in this book—Barry Scheck of the Innocence Project, Wayne County Prosecutor Victoria Shackelford, Wayne County Detective Sharon Little, and Isaac Tabb, retired homicide detective with the Detroit Police.

Thank you, Thomas Hargrove, founder of the Murder Accountability Project (MAP) for your invaluable knowledge, insight, and commitment to drawing attention to unsolved serial homicides, particularly those of marginalized victims. Your organization's determination to compile the most accurate data on homicides in the country is indispensable in holding law enforcement accountable to find the perpetrators responsible and secure justice for murder victims.

Thank you, John Fountain of Roosevelt University and Samantha Latson, for being advocates of murdered Black women and girls through the Unforgotten 51 project and did something that mainstream media often fails to do: humanize and make visible the lives and love that preceded these victims before their senseless murders.

To my village of family and friends who read chapters of the book and offered me advice, critique, and praise—my loving, supportive, and erudite husband, Carlespie McKinney, who never ceases to cheer me on, believe in me, and push me to pursue my dreams; my sister Cassandra Bell, who has (without fail) eagerly read anything I've written since we were kids in my attic bedroom; my big sis Kimberly Neely, who is endlessly excited by every accomplishment no matter how big or small, and remains my lifelong North Star; Neely Allen, my "gold star," my brilliant and beautiful niece, who never ceases to make me proud and is destined to be a great writer and thinker; my selfless and loving sister-in-law Tracey Neely, who always showers me with love and cheers me on and was excited to read chapters for me; my friend and sister-in-arms, Lashawn Harris, a brilliant scholar and writer who has been a wonderful sounding board and whose new book I can't wait to read; Rosalind Reaves, my colleague, friend, and sis, who is unwavering in her support, praise, and friendship; my friend for close to twenty years, Bernice Eppes, who, despite finding the subject depressing, read chapters from the book and offered helpful critique; and, last but not least, my amazing gift of a daughter, Jewell Bell, my best friend and figurative heartbeat who lives outside of my body—you named my first book, and always reminded me that a PhD means more than being addressed as Dr.; it means scholarship and leaving your mark on the world with your impassioned research and advocacy for issues that matter.

NOTES

PROLOGUE

1. Data is based on the FBI's 2018 Uniform Crime Report (UCR). It must be noted that since police precincts voluntarily report crime data to the FBI, some statistics may not be an accurate accounting for all deaths from homicidal violence; in some cases, manner of death cannot be determined, despite police suspicion of foul play. *Crime in the U.S. 2018*, US Department of Justice, FBI, Criminal Justice Information Services Division, https://ucr.fbi.gov/crime-in-the-u.s.-2018.

2. Sean Gardiner, "NYPD Inaction over a Missing Black Woman Found Dead Sparks a Historic Racial-Bias Lawsuit," *Village Voice*, May 6, 2008, https://www.villagevoice.com/nypd-inaction-over-a-missing-black-woman-found-dead-sparks-a-historic-racial-bias-lawsuit/; Garth Johnston, "Two Guilty Verdicts in Moore Murder Case," *Gothamist*, Mar. 24, 2006, https://gothamist.com/news/two-guilty-verdicts-in-moore-murder-case; Michael Brick, "College Student's Killers Are Sentenced to Life in Prison," *New York Times*, Apr. 12, 2006, https://www.nytimes.com/2006/04/12/nyregion/college-students-killers-are-sentenced-to-life-in-prison.html. Justice Albert Tomei, who presided over the case and sentenced Troy Hendrix and Kayson Pearson to life in prison, referred to the killers during sentencing as "lower than animals" in their torture, sodomy, and rape of Romona Moore. He also referenced Troy Hendrix's attempt to stab his lawyer during court proceedings with a plastic shank he had fashioned from a plastic knife while in jail.

3. Gardiner, "NYPD Inaction."

4. Carol M. Liebler, Wasim Ahmad, and Gina Gayle, "Not at Risk? News, Gatekeeping, and Missing Teens," *Journalism Practice* 15, no. 10 (2021): 1597–612.

5. Cheryl L. Neely, *You're Dead—So What? Media, Police, and the Invisibility of Black Women as Victims of Homicide* (East Lansing: Michigan State University Press, 2015).

INTRODUCTION

1. Manning Marable, *Malcolm X: A Life of Reinvention* (New York: Penguin Press, 2011), 208.

2. Malcolm X made this statement as part of a eulogy he delivered at the funeral of Ronald Stokes, an NOI officer who was killed by Los Angeles police in April 1962. A recording of the speech can be found here: https://speakola .com/political/malcolm-x-speech-to-black-women-1962.

3. Richard A. Oppel, "What We Know About Breonna Taylor's Case and Death," *New York Times*, May 30, 2020, https://www.nytimes.com/article /breonna-taylor-police.html.

4. Associated Press, "Grand Jury Was Never Asked to Mull Homicide Charges in Breonna Taylor Case," *Politico*, Sept. 29, 2020, https://www .politico.com/news/2020/09/29/kentucky-grand-jury-tapes-breonna-taylor -422864.

5. Will Wright, Nicolas Bogel-Burroughs, and John Eligon, "Breonna Taylor Grand Jury Audio Reveals Conflicting Accounts of Fatal Raid: The 15 Hours of Recordings Include Interviews with Witnesses, Audio of 911 Calls and Other Evidence—but Few Statements from Prosecutors," *New York Times*, Oct. 2, 2020, https://www.nytimes.com/2020/10/02/us/breonna-taylor -grand-jury-audio-recording.html.

6. Andrea J. Ritchie, *Invisible No More: Police Violence Against Black Women and Women of Color* (Boston: Beacon Press, 2017), 84. Ritchie describes a police brutality case from 2011 of a young teenage girl described as a "tomboy" being accosted by police while sitting on her grandmother's porch. Police threw her to the ground, kicked her, and jammed a gun in her mouth, threatening her that reporting the violence would result in her "having her brains blown out" or being kidnapped by police, raped, and then killed without anyone ever discovering her body.

7. Cheryl L. Neely, *You're Dead—So What? Media, Police, and the Invisibility of Black Women as Victims of Homicide* (East Lansing: Michigan State University Press, 2015).

8. Zachary Wigon, "The L.A.P.D. Didn't Catch an Alleged Serial Killer for 30 Years. Is It Because the Victims Were Black?" *Vanity Fair*, Dec. 18, 2014, https://www.vanityfair.com/hollywood/2014/12/tales-of-the-grim-sleeper-nick -broomfield.

9. Patrisse Khan-Cullors and Asha Bandele, *When They Call You a Terrorist: A Black Lives Matter Memoir* (New York: St. Martin's Press, 2018).

10. Candice A. Skrapec, "Defining Serial Murder: A Call for a Return to the Original Lustmörd," *Journal of Police and Criminal Psychology* 16, no. 2 (2001): 10–24.

11. Eldridge Cleaver and Maxwell Geismar, *Soul on Ice* (New York: Dell Press, 1968), 33.

12. Robert Gilman's book review for the *Negro American Literature Forum* 3 (Winter 1969) hailed Cleaver's book, as among other things, "unsparing, unaccommodating, tough and lyrical . . . a book for which we have to make room—but not on the shelves we (white America) have already built." Floyd McKissick commented in his 1969 review of Cleaver's writing in the *California Law Review* 57 (Apr. 1969) that in the book Cleaver "chronicles with more clarity and intensity than any other contemporary American writer I know the terrible psychological toll taken by the American attitude toward

sex and race" which in the end "distinguishes him from more ordinary men and reserves for him a special place among modern writers."

13. Madeleine Roberts, "HRC Mourns Jaida Peterson, Black Transwoman Killed in North Carolina," Human Rights Campaign, Apr. 13, 2021, https//www.hrc.org/news/hrc-mourns-jaida-peterson-black-transgender-woman-killed-in-north-carolina.

14. Deadnaming is the act of referring to a transgender person by a name different from the name by which the person prefers to be called. It is insulting and disrespects the person's preferred gender identity.

15. Roberts, "HRC Mourns Jaida Peterson."

16. Devin-Norelle, "Six Black Transwomen Were Found Dead in Nine Days," *Them*, July 14, 2020, https://www.them.us/story/six-black-trans-women-were-found-dead-in-nine-days, accessed May 28, 2021.

17. National Coalition of Anti-Violence Programs (NCAVP), *Lesbian, Gay, Bisexual, Transgender, Queer, and HIV-Affected Hate Violence in 2016: A 20th Anniversary Report from the National Coalition of Anti-Violence Programs*, 2017, http://avp.org/wp-content/uploads/2017/06/NCAVP_2016Hate Violence_REPORT.pdf.

18. "Unerased: Counting Transgender Lives: A Comprehensive Look at Transgender Since 2010," *Mic*, https://unerased.mic.com/unerased. The website based their number of Black trans female murders on reports generated by NCAVP and Mic's reporting staff's deep dive into this data and social media posts about murdered trans women whose deaths were categorized according to their biological sex.

19. German Lopez, "Anti-Gender Bathroom Hysteria, Explained," *Vox*, Feb. 22, 2017, https://www.vox.com/2016/5/5/11592908/transgender-bathroom-laws-rights.

20. Dan Levin, "North Carolina Reaches Settlement on 'Bathroom Bill,'" *New York Times*, July 23, 2019, https://www.nytimes.com/2019/07/23/us/north-carolina-transgender-bathrooms.html.

21. Stephen Gruber-Miller, "Iowa State 'Bathroom Bill' Would Ban Transgender People from Using School Restrooms Matching Gender Identity," *Des Moines Register*, Feb. 10, 2021, https://www.desmoinesregister.com/story/news/politics/2021/02/10/iowa-senate-bathroom-bill-targeting-transgender-people-advances-legislature/4460035001.

22. Daniel Trotta, "U.S. Transgender People Harassed in Public Restrooms: Landmark Survey," Reuters, Dec. 8, 2016, https://www.reuters.com/article/us-usa-lgbt-survey/u-s-transgender-people-harassed-in-public-restrooms-landmark-survey-idUSKBN13X0BK.

CHAPTER 1: BUT FIRST, MICHELLE

1. Mitchell L. Eggers and Douglas S. Massey, "A Longitudinal Analysis of Urban Poverty: Black People in US Metropolitan Areas Between 1970 and 1980," *Social Science Research* 21, no. 2 (1992): 175–203.

2. "Uprising of 1967," *Encyclopedia of Detroit*, https://detroithistorical.org/learn/encyclopedia-of-detroit/uprising-1967. The "1967 rebellion" is an alternative categorization of what is generally referred to in media as the

"1967 Detroit riots." More recent literature frames the riot as the "uprising of 1967" or the "rebellion of 1967"; both terms are used to describe the violent upheaval as a protest by Detroiters against unrelenting police brutality, poverty, racial discrimination, and systemic oppression. In July 1967, over the span of 5 days, 43 people were killed, hundreds more were injured, 1,700 fires were set, and at least 7,000 people were arrested.

3. W. Kim Heron, "Epidemic 'Created by Media': Hart Raps Rape Coverage," *Detroit Free Press*, Feb. 14, 1984.

4. Heron, "Epidemic 'Created by Media.'"

5. Jodie Kenney, interview, July 14, 2020.

6. Jodie Kenney, interview.

7. Joshua Bloom and Waldo E. Martin, *Black Against Empire: The History and Politics of the Black Panther Party* (Berkeley: University of California Press, 2016), 58.

8. Jodie Kenney, interview.

9. Charlotte Grant, interview, Dec. 8, 2020.

10. US District Court, Eastern District of Michigan Southern Division, "In The Matter of the Estate of Eddie Joe Lloyd, Deceased by his Duly Appointed Personal Representative, Ruth Harlin and Tia Terese Glenn," May 10, 2005, 15.

11. Ruth Harlin (sister of Eddie Joe Lloyd) interview from documentary *Defending Gideon: Defending the Right to Counsel in the United States*, July 18, 2013, https://www.youtube.com/watch?v=MkgcD2UkNdY.

12. The actual name of the detective was changed to protect identity.

13. Isaac Tabb, Detroit Police homicide detective, interview, Apr. 27, 2021.

14. Victoria Shackelford, interview, Oct. 28, 2020.

15. Issac Tabb, interview.

16. Oralander Brand-Williams, "Suspect to Be Tried in 1984 Rape, Murder of Detroit Girl," *Detroit News*, Nov. 14, 2019, https://www.detroitnews.com/story/news/local/detroit-city/2019/11/14/kennith-dupree-rape-slaying-detroit-school-girl-35-years-ago/4194817002.

17. Tabb, interview.

18. Kaylee Osowski, "Investigating a Serial Killer: The Development of the FBI's Role Told Through Public Documents," DttP: Documents to the People, https://journals.ala.org/index.php/dttp/article/view/6892/9271.

CHAPTER 2: PANIC IN ROXBURY

1. Howard Husock, "Boston: The Problem That Won't Go Away," *New York Times*, Nov. 25, 1979, https://www.nytimes.com/1979/11/25/archive/boston-the-problem-that-wont-go-away-boston.html.

2. Commonwealth v. Dennis Porter, 384 Mass. 647, Sept. 16, 1981–Dec. 8, 1981, Suffolk County.

3. *Commonwealth v. Dennis Porter*.

4. Nelson O. O. Zounlome, Y. Joel Wong, Elyssa M. Klann, Jessica L. David, and Nat J. Stephens, "'No One . . . Saves Black Girls': Black University Women's Understanding of Sexual Violence," *Counseling Psychologist* 47, no. 6 (2019): 873–908.

5. Tashina L. Khabbaz, Ariel Otruba, and Heather Evans, "Black Bodies and the Role of Schools in Sex Trafficking Prevention," in *The Palgrave Handbook of Educational Leadership and Management Discourse* (2020): 1–19.

6. "South End Man Gets Life Terms in Murders," *Boston Globe*, Apr. 17, 1980; Khabbaz, Otruba, and Evans, "Black Bodies and the Role of Schools in Sex Trafficking Prevention."

7. Gibran Rivera, "The Estuary Projects Installation: Andrea Foye & Christine Ricketts," https://www.gibranrivera.com/new-events/estuaryproject1.

8. Rivera, "The Estuary Projects Installation."

9. Michel D. McQueen, "As Different as Night and Day," *Harvard Crimson*, Mar. 17, 1979, https://www.thecrimson.com/article/1979/3/17/as-different-as-night-and-day.

10. Gayle Pollard, Carmen Fields, and Viola Osgood, "Six Slain Women, and Those Who Loved Them," *Boston Globe*, Apr. 1, 1979.

11. Bettye Collier-Thomas and Vincent P. Franklin, eds., *Sisters in the Struggle: African American Women in the Civil Rights–Black Power Movement* (New York: New York University Press, 2001).

12. Information on Hargett was found on an Instagram page created by Kendra Hicks, a young Black community organizer and activist from Boston who commemorated the deaths of the murdered Roxbury women through an arts project called the Estuary Projects in 2011. See https://www.instagram.com/theestuaryprojects.

13. Terrion L. Williamson, "Why Did They Die? On Combahee and the Serialization of Black Death," *Souls* 19, no. 3 (2017): 328–41.

14. I was unable to find the date of the acquittal despite an extensive search of Massachusetts court records.

15. Commonwealth v. Delrue Lafayette Anderson, 404 Mass. 467, Feb. 7, 1989–May 1, 1989.

16. John E. Yang, Joan Vennochi, and Barbara Stevens, "Back Bay Murder Task Force Is Formed," *Boston Globe*, Mar. 16, 1979.

17. Matthew F. Delmont, *Why Busing Failed: Race, Media, and the National Resistance to School Desegregation* (Oakland: University of California Press, 2016).

18. Boston Planning & Development Agency/Imagine Boston 2040, "Boston's Population (1900–2015)," *Boston by the Numbers*, October 26, 2016, https://www.boston.gov/sites/default/files/embed/file/2018-06/boston-by-the-numbers-population-past-and-future_roxbury_presentation.pdf.

19. Akilah Johnson, "The Forgotten Riot That Sparked Boston's Racial Unrest," *Boston Globe*, June 1, 2017, https://www.bostonglobe.com/metro/2017/06/01/the-forgotten-protest-that-sparked-city-racial-unrest/0ry39I37z87TwdBfrqUnTP/story.html.

20. Jonathan Fuerbringer and Marvin E. Mibauer, "Roxbury, Quiet in the Past, Finally Breaks into Riot; Why Did Violence Occur?" *Harvard Crimson*, June 15, 1967, https://www.thecrimson.com/article/1967/6/15/roxbury-quiet-in-past-finally-breaks.

21. Fuerbringer and Mibauer, "Roxbury, Quiet in the Past, Finally Breaks into Riot."

22. "Roxbury Residents Brutalized," *Bay State Banner*, June 10, 1967.

23. Johnson, "The Forgotten Riot That Sparked Boston's Racial Unrest."

24. Jordan Lebeau, "When This Group of Black Mothers Locked Themselves in a Government Office, Boston Erupted in Riots," Timeline, June 2, 2017, https://medium.com/timeline.

25. Patricia Wen, Akilah Johnson, Liz Kowalczyk, Todd Wallack, Nicole Dungca, Adrian Walker, and Andrew Ryan, "Boston. Racism. Image. Reality," *Boston Globe*, Dec. 10, 2017, https://apps.bostonglobe.com/spotlight/boston -racism-image-reality.

26. "Commission's Report: Reactions of Boston's Leaders," *Bay State Banner*, Mar. 7, 1968.

27. Janel E. Benson, "Exploring the Racial Identities of Black Immigrants in the United States," *Sociological Forum* 21, no. 2 (2006): 219–47.

28. Johnson, "The Forgotten Riot That Sparked Boston's Racial Unrest."

29. "Sundown" towns and areas in a city are places where African Americans faced hostility and violence from the largely white occupants who warned them to "leave town before the sun goes down." See James W. Loewen, *Sundown Towns: A Hidden Dimension of American Racism* (New York: The New Press, 2005).

30. Charles Kenney, "The Politics of Turmoil: The Campaign to Make Greater Roxbury a Separate City Named Mandela Failed at the Ballot Box. But It Revealed an Absence of Political Cohesion Within the Black Community and Highlighted the Harsh Realities of Life in Boston's Minority Neighborhoods," *Boston Globe*, Apr. 19, 1987.

31. Kenney, "The Politics of Turmoil."

32. Allison Manning, "The Story of Boston's All-Black, Short-Lived, Very Successful Tactical Police Unit," Boston.com, May 26, 2015, https://www .boston.com/news/local-news/2015/05/26/the-story-of-bostons-all-black-short -lived-very-successful-tactical-police-unit.

33. Ken O. Botwright, "All-Black Police Unit Opposed," *Boston Globe*, Nov. 20, 1971.

34. Allyson Collins, *Shielded from Justice: Police Brutality and Accountability in the United States*, Human Rights Watch, 1998, http://www.hrw.org /legacy/reports98/police/index.htm.

35. McQueen, "As Different as Night and Day."

36. McQueen, "As Different as Night and Day."

37. Cheryl Devall, "Women March in Boston, Protest Roxbury Killings," *Harvard Crimson*, Apr. 30, 1979, https://www.thecrimson.com/article/1979 /4/30/women-march-in-boston-protest-roxbury.

38. Cheryl Devall, "Community Gathers to Honor the Lives of Six Black Women," *Bay State Banner*, Apr. 5, 1979.

39. Keeanga-Yamahtta Taylor, ed., *How We Get Free: Black Feminism and the Combahee River Collective* (Chicago: Haymarket Books, 2017).

40. Duchess Harris, *Black Feminist Politics from Kennedy to Trump* (Cham: Springer, 2018).

41. Cheryl Devall and Margaret Tarter, "Multiple Murders Provoke Shock, Fear in Community," *Bay State Banner*, Feb. 8, 1979.

42. Cheryl L. Neely, *You're Dead—So What? Media, Police, and the Invisibility of Black Women as Victims of Homicide* (East Lansing: Michigan State University Press, 2015).

43. Williamson, "Why Did They Die?" 328–41.

44. Linda Mishkin, *Legendary Locals of Allston-Brighton* (Charleston, SC: Arcadia, 2013).

45. McQueen, "As Different as Night and Day."

46. McQueen, "As Different as Night and Day."

47. "Suspect Held in Brighton Rape," *Boston Globe*, Feb. 2, 1979.

48. McQueen, "As Different as Night and Day."

49. Mac Margolis, "Defense Mounts New Evidence as Brighton Rape Trial Nears," *Bay State Banner*, Oct. 4, 1979.

50. Margolis, "Defense Mounts New Evidence as Brighton Rape Trial Nears."

51. Mac Margolis, "Willie Sanders 'Not Guilty,'" *Bay State Banner*, Nov. 29, 1979.

52. Devall, "Women March in Boston, Protest Roxbury Killings."

53. Cheryl Devall, "500 March in Anger over Recent Slayings," *Bay State Banner*, May 3, 1979.

54. Kay Bourne, "Columbia Pt. Women: 'Murders Breed Fear,'" *Bay State Banner*, May 5, 1979.

55. Bourne, "Columbia Pt. Women."

56. Patricia Hill Collins, "Learning from the Outsider Within: The Sociological Significance of Black Feminist Thought," *Social Problems* 33, no. 6 (1986): S14–S32.

57. David Ward, "Black Women Are Scared, Ask More Lights, Police," *Boston Globe*, May 8, 1979.

58. Kay Bourne, "Law Put D.A. in Charge, Will It Aid in Solving Murders?" *Bay State Banner*, Feb. 8, 1979.

59. Bourne, "Law Put D.A. in Charge."

60. Devall and Tarter, "Multiple Murders Provoke Shock, Fear in Community."

61. Ward, "Black Women Are Scared, Ask More Lights, Police."

62. "Roxbury Man Charged in Slaying," *Boston Globe*, May 7, 1979.

63. Ward, "Black Women Are Scared, Ask More Lights, Police."

64. "Youth Slain in Charles St. Jail," *Bay State Banner*, July 6, 1972.

65. Thomas Hargrove, interview, founder of the Murder Accountability Project, July 7, 2020.

CHAPTER 3: TACO BELL TERROR

1. German Lopez, "Charlotte Police Officer Who Shot and Killed Keith Lamont Scott Will Not Face Charges," *Vox*, Sept. 21, 2016, https://www.vox.com/2016/9/21/12999366/keith-lamont-scott-north-carolina-police-shooting.

2. Richard Fausset and Yamiche Alcindor, "Video by Wife of Keith Scott Shows Her Pleas to Police," *New York Times,* Sept. 23, 2016, https://www.nytimes.com/2016/09/24/us/charlotte-keith-scott-shooting-video.html.

3. Jim Ware, "Can I Carry a Handgun Openly in North Carolina?" *Wilmington StarNews*, May 11, 2021, https://www.starnewsonline.com/story/news/2021/05/11/legal-carry-handgun-openly-north-carolina/4993516001.

4. Elizabeth Chuck, "No Charges in Killing of Keith Lamont Scott, Whose Police Encounter Was Videotaped by Wife," NBCNews.com, Nov. 30, 2016, https://www.nbcnews.com/news/us-news/no-charges-killing-keith-lamont-scott-whose-police-encounter-was-n690126

5. Cleve R. Wootson and Derek Hawkins, "The Charlotte Police Shooting That Hasn't Gone Away," *Washington Post*, Oct. 26, 2021.

6. WCNC Staff, "Woman Shot, Killed by CMPD Officer During Altercation," WCNC.com, Feb. 20, 2015, https://www.wcnc.com/article/news/crime/woman-shot-killed-by-cmpd-officer-during-altercation/275-213286182.

7. Staff, "The Seconds Before the Shots," *Charlotte Observer*, Mar. 22, 2015, https://www.wbtv.com, https://www.wbtv.com/story/28584188/the-seconds-before-the-shots.

8. Sam Levin, "'We Shouldn't Have to Feel Like This': Girl, Nine, Gives Tearful Speech in Charlotte," *The Guardian,* Sept. 28, 2016, https://www.theguardian.com/us-news/2016/sep/27/keith-scott-killing-charlotte-little-girl-speech-viral.

9. "Queen Charlotte," *Daily Gardener*, June 21, 2021, https://thedailygardener.org/bs20201117; "Why Is Charlotte Called the Queen City?" Charlotte Mecklenburg Library, n.d, https://www.cmlibrary.org/blog/why-charlotte-called-queen-city; Stuart Jeffries, "Was This Britain's First Black Queen?" *The Guardian*, Mar. 12, 2009, https://www.theguardian.com/world/2009/mar/12/race-monarchy. Several historians have also alleged that the monarch descended from a racially diverse background with African and Portuguese ancestry, which appears prominently in facial features of the queen in portraits painted of her during the eighteenth century (although she was described derisively as having the face of a "true mulatto" and "famously ugly").

10. Steve Harrison, "As Black Leaders Rise, Change in Mecklenburg County Governing Follows," *Charlotte Post*, Mar. 26, 2022, https://www.thecharlottepost.com/news/2022/03/26/local-state/as-black-leaders-rise-change-in-mecklenburg-county-governing-follows.

11. Jose Luis Magana, "Charlotte Remembers 1963 Desegregation 'Eat-In,'" *USA Today*, May 20, 2013, https://www.usatoday.com/story/news/nation/2013/05/19/charlotte-1963-desegregation/2325241.

12. Clint Smith and Jelani Cobb, "The Desegregation and Resegregation of Charlotte's Schools," *New Yorker*, Oct. 3, 2016, https://www.newyorker.com/news/news-desk/the-desegregation-and-resegregation-of-charlottes-schools.

13. Smith and Cobb, "The Desegregation and Resegregation of Charlotte's Schools."

14. 1990 Census of Population General Population Characteristics North Carolina, US Department of Commerce, Apr. 17, 1992, https://www2.census.gov/library/publications/decennial/1990/cp-1/cp-1-35.pdf.

15. Greg Lacour, "Breaking Down the Wedge in Charlotte," *Charlotte Magazine*, Sept. 30, 2019, https://www.charlottemagazine.com/breaking-down-the-wedge-in-charlotte.

16. Lacour, "Breaking Down the Wedge in Charlotte"; Jane Monreal, "'There Are Actually What We Call Two Charlottes': Systemic Racism Report Shows History of Disparities in Charlotte," WCNC.com, Feb. 11, 2022, https://www.wcnc.com/article/news/local/systemic-racism-report-history-disparities-charlotte/275-c4c83235-bdec-485a-bff7-898aa8b3fa3d; Jawed Kaleem and Jenny Jarvie, "Charlotte, N.C., Has Prospered in Recent Years, but Many Black Residents Have Been Left Behind," *Los Angeles Times*, Sept. 22, 2016, https://www.latimes.com/nation/la-na-charlotte-racial-tensions-20160922-snap-story.html.

17. Douglas Houck, *Historic Charlotte County: An Illustrated History* (San Antonio, TX: Historical Publishing Network, 2011), 17. Houck describes restrictions on Black people that included not being allowed out in public after 9:30 p.m.; restrictions on the use or purchase of alcohol and smoking; not being allowed to leave the plantation without a written pass; being forced to attend white churches and the forbidding of Blacks holding their own worship services; and white town guards being allowed entry into any "suspected negro houses" whether Black people were enslaved or free.

18. Donovan X. Ramsey, "Before Keith Scott, a Long History of Racist Policing in Charlotte," *Complex*, Apr. 21, 2020, https://www.complex.com/life/2016/09/charlotte-riot-protest-uprising-explainer.

19. C. Vann Woodward, *Reunion and Reaction: The Compromise of 1877 and the End of Reconstruction* (New York: Oxford University Press, 1991).

20. Ramsey, "Before Keith Scott, a Long History of Racist Policing in Charlotte."

21. Ryan L. Sumner, *Charlotte and Mecklenburg County Police* (Charleston, SC: Arcadia Publishing, 2010). Black civic leaders, led by J. S. Nathaniel Tross, felt compelled to form a security force called the "Community Crusaders" to protect the Black community as well as address crime in their neighborhoods; later the group pressured city leaders to hire Black police officers. By 1941, A. M. "Bub" Houston became the first African American police officer in the city of Charlotte. Along with James Ross, another Black officer hired several months after Officer Houston, the two men received the title of "special peace officers," but with no weapon nor civil service protection by the city or police union. It took seven years for the men to be promoted to full officers after Black World War II veterans pressured Charlotte city leaders to do so.

22. Emma Korynta, "Highlighting Rodney Monroe: CMPD's First Black Police Chief," WCNC.com, Feb. 15, 2021, https://www.wcnc.com/article/life/holidays/black-history-month/rodney-monroe/275-ed0d256c-25d9-4d3d-b06b-63501534f094.

23. US Court of Appeals for the 4th Circuit, no. 08–10: Henry Louis Wallace v. Gerald J. Branker, Warden, Central Prison, Raleigh, NC; Supreme Court of North Carolina v. Henry Louis Wallace, no. 241A97, decided May 2, 2000. The majority of the details of the killings were retrieved from court records in the appeal case of Henry Louis Wallace, who was convicted in January 1997 of the murders of nine of the ten rape-homicides to which he confessed in graphic detail. Again, little information exists in Charlotte newspapers of the murders as they occurred in real time, and most of the stories regarding the killings occurred after the arrest of Henry Wallace in March 1994. Many

Black residents of Charlotte expressed anger that not only were police slow to investigate the murders of the victims but the media also provided little coverage of the killings during the time in which the killings took place.

24. I found personal information about Sharon Nance in a brief article on the site Find a Grave (a public site owned by Ancestry.com), which provides the location of a person's grave and their birth and death dates. In addition, the article noted the date of Nance's funeral, her occupation as a domestic worker, and reported that she was the mother of a son, Rasheed Nance, as well as other surviving relatives. I was unable to locate contemporaneous newspaper articles about her murder after her body was discovered.

25. Charles Montaldo, "Profile of Serial Killer Henry Louis Wallace," ThoughtCo, May 24, 2019, https://www.thoughtco.com/serial-killer-henry -louis-wallace-973140.

26. Joseph Geringer, "Henry Louis Wallace: A Calamity Waiting to Happen—Overview," University of North Carolina, Aug. 2011, https://pages .charlotte.edu/ccoston/wp-content/uploads/sites/10/2011/08/Henry-Louis -Wallace-ccrime-library1.pdf.

27. Geringer, "Henry Louis Wallace."

28. Monica Davey, "A Serial Killer Strikes, but No One Sees," *Tampa Bay Times*, May 25, 1994, https://www.tampabay.com/archive/1994/05/25/a-serial -killer-strikes-but-no-one-sees.

29. Eric W. Hickey, *Serial Murderers and Their Victims* (Boston: Cengage Learning, 2015), 252. In several of the murders, Henry Wallace attempted to make detection by police difficult by interfering with the crime scene, wiping surfaces of fingerprints, dressing victims after sexual assaults to hide his rape of victims, submerging them in water, and, in one case, attempting to set a victim's body and apartment on fire. Police would later defend their actions against accusations of indifference by arguing that Wallace's destruction of evidence made it harder to apprehend him.

30. Davey, "A Serial Killer Strikes, but No One Sees."

31. Information about Audrey Spain's life outside of a blog post (*Journal de la Reyna*, June 25, 2019) was unavailable through an online search. Like many Black female homicide victims, their deaths are not readily covered by media and, when they are, the stories often neglect to provide background information on victims' lives. The mission of *Journal de la Reyna* is to spotlight the deaths of Black women when the media ignores them as victims of violence. These details about Audrey were retrieved from a blog post titled "My Post on Miss Audrey, 1968–1993." The blogger attributed the information she reported about Audrey to two articles she claimed to have found online, but I was unable to locate her sources, which she reported as Jeannine F. Hunter, "Family Seeks Closure" (Sept. 1996), and Anonymous, "Sentence Brings Family a Measure of Peace" (Feb. 1997).

32. Montaldo, "Profile of Serial Killer Henry Louis Wallace."

33. Paul Holes and Brian Jensen, "The Taco Bell Strangler, Henry Louis Wallace: Does He Have More Victims?" *The Murder Squad*, audio blog, Aug. 24, 2020, http://themurdersquad.com/episodes/the-taco-bell-strangler-henry -louis-wallace-does-he-have-more-victims.

34. During Wallace's confession to homicide detectives, he shared graphic details of the killings, including quoting victims whom, he disclosed, at times pleaded for their lives.

35. Montaldo, "Profile of Serial Killer Henry Louis Wallace."

36. Supreme Court of North Carolina v. Henry Louis Wallace, No. 241A97, 528 S.E. 2d 326, May 5, 2000.

37. Jason Lapeyre, "The Serial Killer the Cops Ignored: The Henry Louis Wallace Murders," *Crime Magazine*, Oct. 14, 2009, http://www.crimemagazine.com/serial-killer-cops-ignored-henry-louis-wallace-murders.

38. "In Black and White," Opinion/Letters, *Winston-Salem Chronicle*, Mar. 31, 1994.

39. Mary Beth Oliver, "African American Men as 'Criminal and Dangerous': Implications of Media Portrayals of Crime on the 'Criminalization' of African American Men," *Journal of African American Studies* (2003): 3–18; Paul Butler, *Chokehold: Policing Black Men* (New York: New Press, 2018); Douglas A. Smith, Christy A. Visher, and Laura A. Davidson, "Equity and Discretionary Justice: The Influence of Race on Police Arrest Decisions," *Journal of Criminal Law & Criminology* 75 (1984): 234.

40. Peter Applebome, "2 Years, 10 Murders and 1 Question," *New York Times*, Mar. 24, 1994, https://www.nytimes.com/1994/03/24/us/2-years-10-murders-and-1-question.html.

41. Applebome, "2 Years, 10 Murders and 1 Question."

42. "Lock the Door Behind You," *20/20*, season 45, episode 24, ABC, May 13, 2022.

43. Viswa Vanapalli, "Where Is Dee Sumpter Now?" *The Cinemaholic*, May 13, 2022, https://thecinemaholic.com/where-is-dee-sumpter-now.

44. Applebome, "2 Years, 10 Murders, and 1 Question"; Susan Welsh, Joseph Diaz, Andrew Paparella, and Haley Yamada, "Families of Victims of Serial Killer Henry Wallace Remember Loved Ones, Challenges with Investigation," ABC News, May 13, 2022, https://abcnews.go.com/2020/families-victims-serial-killer-henry-wallace-remember-loved/story?id=84543063.

45. Dee Sumpter, interview via Zoom, June 2022.

46. Dee Sumpter, interview.

47. Dee Sumpter, interview.

48. Dee Sumpter, interview.

49. Dee Sumpter, interview.

50. Davey, "A Serial Killer Strikes, but No One Sees."

51. Larry J. Siegel, *Criminology: The Core* (Belmont, CA: Wadsworth 2011).

52. Evan Stark, "Rethinking Homicide: Violence, Race, and the Politics of Gender," *International Journal of Health Services* 20, no. 1 (1990): 3–26; also Terry Allen, Sonia Salari, and Glen Buckner, "Homicide Illustrated Across the Ages: Graphic Depictions of Victim and Offender Age, Sex, and Relationship," *Journal of Aging and Health* 32, nos. 3–4 (2020): 162–74; John A. Humphrey and Stuart Palmer, "Race, Sex, and Criminal Homicide Offender-Victim Relationships," *Journal of Black Studies* 18, no. 1 (1987): 45–57. Humphrey and Palmer concluded in their study that Black males are more likely to murder a female who is either a friend or romantic partner compared with male killers who are white.

53. Humphrey and Palmer, "Race, Sex, and Criminal Homicide Offender-Victim Relationships," 45–57.

54. Cara L. Frankenfeld and Timothy F. Leslie, "Descriptive Epidemiology of Homicides with Victim and Suspect Race or Hispanic Ethnicity Discordance in the United States: Analysis of National Violent Death Reporting System (NVDRS) 2005–2015," *Journal of Interpersonal Violence* 36, nos. 17–18 (2021): NP9693–NP9713.

55. Mark Pettigrew, "The Preference for Strangulation in a Sexually Motivated Serial Killer," *International Journal of Offender Therapy and Comparative Criminology* 63, no. 5 (Apr. 2019): 781–96.

56. Chuck McShane, "1993: Charlotte's Deadliest Year," *Charlotte Magazine*, Nov. 21, 2013, https://www.charlottemagazine.com/1993-charlottes-deadliest-year.

57. McShane, "1993: Charlotte's Deadliest Year."

58. Supreme Court of North Carolina v. Henry Louis Wallace, No. 241A97, 528 S.E. 2d 326, May 5, 2000.

59. Eric W. Hickey, *Serial Murderers and Their Victims* (Boston: Cengage Learning, 2015).

60. Joby Warrick, "Drifter Confesses to 1990 Slaying," *News and Observer*, Mar. 16, 1994.

61. Davey, "A Serial Killer Strikes, but No One Sees."

62. Geringer, "Henry Louis Wallace."

63. Davey, "A Serial Killer Strikes, but No One Sees."

64. McShane, "1993: Charlotte's Deadliest Year."

65. US Census Bureau, Bureau of Justice Statistics, *Special Report: Police Departments in Large Cities, 1990–2000* and *Bureau of Criminal Justice Statistics Sourcebook of Criminal Justice Statistics, 1992–1993*, https://bjs.ojp.gov/library/publications/police-departments-large-cities-1990-2000; McShane, "1993: Charlotte's Deadliest Year."

66. *20/20* producers reached out to the CMPD for comment; the department issued a letter detailing how they improved homicide investigations in the aftermath of the Henry Wallace homicide investigation.

67. Dee Sumpter, interview.

68. Dee Sumpter, interview.

69. In "Lock the Door Behind You," George Burrell disclosed during his interviews with producers that his quest is to get a petition signed to pressure the state to set a date for Wallace's execution.

CHAPTER 4: "NO HUMANS INVOLVED"

1. Stephen Ceasar, "Tales of Loss in Grim Sleeper's Penalty Phase," *Los Angeles Times*, May 13, 2016. Samara Herard, Princess Berthomieux's older foster sister, testified that she assisted her mother in changing the three-year-old toddler's diapers and witnessed Princess' genitals being "severely injured" and the child having cigarette burns all over her body.

2. "Youngest Victim of 'Grim Sleeper' Was Found Dumped in an Alley, Jurors Hear," *Los Angeles Times*, Mar. 3, 2016, https://www.latimes.com/local/lanow/la-me-ln-grim-sleeper-20160302-story.html.

3. "Grim Sleeper's Victims Were Vulnerable, Young and at Times Ignored," *Los Angeles Times*, May 5, 2016, https://www.latimes.com/local/lanow/la-me -ln-grim-sleeper-victims-snap-htmlstory.html.

4. "The Homicide Report—Grim Sleeper Killings, Princess Berthomieux, 15, in 2002," *Los Angeles Times*, Mar. 19, 2002, https://homicide.latimes.com /post/princess-berthomieux/#:~:text=Princess%20Berthomieux%2C%20a %2015%2Dyear,shrubs%2C%20according%20to%20coroner's%20records.

5. Claudia Koerner, "'Grim Sleeper' Serial Killer Had More Victims, Prosecutor Says," *BuzzFeed News*, May 12, 2016, https://www.buzzfeednews.com /article/claudiakoerner/grim-sleeper-serial-killer-had-more-victims-prosecutor -says.

6. Zachary Wigon, "The L.A.P.D. Didn't Catch an Alleged Serial Killer for 30 Years. Is It Because the Victims Were Black?" *Vanity Fair*, Dec. 18, 2014, https://www.vanityfair.com/hollywood/2014/12/tales-of-the-grim-sleeper-nick -broomfield.

7. The People History, https://www.thepeoplehistory.com/1985.html (accessed July 7, 2023); Laura McCrystal, "Investigation into MOVE Remains Will Go 'As Deep as We Can' Kenney Says, Vowing to Reform Medical Examiner's Office," *Philadelphia Inquirer*, May 18, 2021, https://www.inquirer.com /news/move-bombing-remains-kenney-investigation-farley-20210518.html.

8. "Grim Sleeper Killings: Debra Jackson, 29, in 1985—The Homicide Report," *Los Angeles Times*, July 7, 2010, https://homicide.latimes.com/post /debra-jackson.

9. "Victims of the Grim Sleeper," CNN.com, Feb. 15, 2016, https://www .cnn.com/2016/02/15/us/gallery/grim-sleeper-victims/index.html.

10. "Grim Sleeper Verdicts Bring Justice to Forgotten Victims of Serial Killer, Families Say," *Los Angeles Times*, May 6, 2016, https://www.latimes .com/local/lanow/la-me-ln-grim-sleeper-verdict-20160504-story.html.

11. Marisa Gerber and James Queally, "'Grim Sleeper' Is Sentenced to Die; Penalty for Serial Killer in the Murders of 9 Women and a Girl Is Not Vengeance but Justice, Judge Says," *Los Angeles Times*, Aug. 11, 2016.

12. Stephen Ceasar, "Kin of 'Sleeper' Victims Testify; Prosecution Rests After Relatives Identify Slain Women in Lonnie Franklin Jr.'s Trial," *Los Angeles Times*, Mar. 17, 2016.

13. "Only 'Good Victims' Need Apply: 'Tales of the Grim Sleeper' and Poor Black Women in Crack Culture," *Penn Law*, May 27, 2016, https:// www.law.upenn.edu/live/news/6203-only-good-victims-need-apply-tales-of -the-grim.

14. Crowd Captures 'Night Stalker,'" *Los Angeles Times*, Aug. 31, 2006, https://www.latimes.com/archives/la-xpm-2006-aug-31-me-a2anniversary31 -story.html.

15. "Crowd Captures 'Night Stalker.'"

16. Gerber and Queally, "'Grim Sleeper' Is Sentenced to Die." Reporters Gerber and Queally noted in their article that Franklin's victims (young Black females) were ignored by the press and police and "failed to raise alarms the way other famous serial slayings by killers such as the 'Hillside Strangler' or 'the Night Stalker' did." Each of the victims in both of those cases were white.

17. Christine Pelisek, "The Grim Sleeper's Trial Is Moving at Snail's Pace, and Victims' Families Are Furious: Notorious Serial Killer the Grim Sleeper Was on the Lam for Decades. Now There's a Suspect, but His Lawyers Are Dragging Their Feet," *The Daily Beast*, Mar. 21, 2013, https://www.thedaily beast.com/articles/2013/03/21/the-grim-sleeper-s-trial-is-moving-at-snail-s -pace-and-victims-families-are-furious.

18. Maura Dolan, Joel Rubin, and Mitchell Landsberg, "DNA Leads to Arrest in Serial Case; Painstaking Work Turns Up a Match in Grim Sleeper Killings that Began in 1985," *Los Angeles Times*, July 8, 2010, https://www .latimes.com/archives/la-xpm-2010-jul-08-la-me-grim-sleeper-20100708 -story.html.

19. Juliet Bennett Rylah, "Police Still Working to Identify 33 Women from Photos Found in Grim Sleeper's Home," *LAist*, July 25, 2018, https://laist.com /news/grim-sleeper-unidentified-33-women.

20. Scott Gold and Andrew Blankstein, "'It was a terrifying time'; More Than 100 Women Died in a 10-Year Span When Multiple Serial Killers Roamed South L.A.," *Los Angeles Times*, Aug. 4, 2020, https://www.latimes.com /archives/la-xpm-2010-aug-04-la-me-serial-killers-20100804-story.html.

21. John Spano, "Killer Is Sentenced to Death; Chester Turner's Guilt in Slaying 10 Women Was Established 'Beyond All Doubt,' Judge Says," *Los Angeles Times*, July 11, 2007, https://www.latimes.com/archives/la-xpm-2007 -jul-11-me-turner11-story.html.

22. Gold and Blankstein, "'It was a terrifying time.'"

23. City News Service, "California Supreme Court to Hear Case of LA Serial Killer Convicted of Slaying 10 Women," NBC Los Angeles, Aug. 14, 2020, https://www.nbclosangeles.com/news/local/los-angeles-serial-killer-chester -dewayne-turner/2412571.

24. Mathis Chazanoy, "Prime Suspect in Slaying of 4 Prostitutes Identified: Crime: Police Are Searching for Paroled Convict Michael Hubert Hughes, Who They Say Has a History of Violence and Sexual Offenses," *Los Angeles Times*, Dec. 10, 1993, https://www.latimes.com/archives/la-xpm-1993-12-10 -me-508-story.html.

25. Melissa Leu, "California; South L.A. Serial Killer Gets Death Sentence," *Los Angeles Times,* June 23, 2012, https://www.latimes.com/archives /la-xpm-2012-jun-23-la-me-0623-serial-killer-20120623-story.html.

26. "Police Discount Serial Murder Reports," UPI, June 30, 1993, https:// www.upi.com/Archives/1993/06/30/Police-discount-serial-murder-reports /6813741412800.

27. "Man Accused of Killing 9 Women, 1 Teen over 22 Years," ABC7 Chicago, WLS-TV, Feb. 17, 2016, https://abc7chicago.com/grim-sleeper-trial-case -monique-alexander-porter/1204125.

28. Richard A. Serrano, "Little Support for Gates' Comment: Drugs: Police Chief's Statement That Casual Users Should Be Shot Draws Much Criticism in Crime-Ridden Rampart Section of Los Angeles," *Los Angeles Times*, Sept. 7, 1990, https://www.latimes.com/archives/la-xpm-1990-09-07-me-681-story.html.

29. Ailsa Chang, "Looking Back on President George H. W. Bush's Controversial Criminal Justice Legacy," *All Things Considered*, NPR, Dec. 3, 2018,

https://www.npr.org/2018/12/03/673022642/looking-back-on-president-george
-h-w-bushs-controversial-criminal-justice-legacy.

30. "The Warrior Chief; Ever Combative, Daryl Gates Did Things His Way at the LAPD, with Sometimes Tragic Results," *Los Angeles Times*, Apr. 17, 2010, https://www.latimes.com/archives/la-xpm-2010-apr-17-la-ed-gates17-2010apr17-story.html.

31. Eric Slater and Sue Fox, "Ex-LAPD Chief Gate's Son Arrested," *Los Angeles Times*, Oct. 11, 2004, https://www.latimes.com/archives/la-xpm-2004-oct-11-me-gates11-story.html.

32. Russel S. Falck, Jichuan Wang, and Robert G. Carlson, "Among Long-Term Crack Smokers, Who Avoids and Who Succumbs to Cocaine Addiction?" *Drug and Alcohol Dependence* 98, nos. 1–2 (2008): 24–29.

33. Tiffany R. Simmons, "The Effects of the War on Drugs on Black Women: From Early Legislation to Incarceration," *American University Journal of Gender, Social Policy & the Law* 26 (2017): 719.

34. Patricia Klein, "Battering Ram Nets 2 Women, 3 Children, Criticism," *Los Angeles Times*, Feb. 8, 1985, https://www.latimes.com/archives/la-xpm-1985-02-08-me-4746-story.html.

35. Klein, "Battering Ram Nets 2 Women, 3 Children, Criticism."

36. Klein, "Battering Ram Nets 2 Women, 3 Children, Criticism."

37. John L. Mitchell, "The Raid That Still Haunts L.A.," *Los Angeles Times*, Mar. 14, 2001, https://www.latimes.com/archives/la-xpm-2001-mar-14-mn-37553-story.html.

38. Mitchell, "The Raid That Still Haunts L.A."

39. Mitchell, "The Raid That Still Haunts L.A."

40. Michael Levine and Laura Kavanau-Levine, *The Big White Lie: The CIA and the Cocaine/Crack Epidemic: An Undercover Odyssey* (Emeryville, CA: Thunder's Mouth Press, 1993).

41. Tonya Mosely, "Why the Crack Cocaine Epidemic Hit Black Communities 'First and Worst,'" author interview with Donovan X. Ramsey, *Fresh Air*, NPR, July 13, 2023, https://www.npr.org/2023/07/13/1186778651/crack-cocaine-epidemic-when-crack-was-king-donovan-x-ramsey.

42. Norm Stamper, *Breaking Rank: A Top Cop's Exposé of the Dark Side of American Policing* (New York: Bold Type Books, 2009), 47.

43. Stamper, *Breaking Rank*.

44. Tanya Telfair LeBlanc and Barbara C. Wallace, "Sex for Crack Cocaine Exchange: The Continuing Impact of Crack Cocaine on Poor Black Women and Their Families," *Journal of Equity in Health* 3, no. 1 (2014): 55–65.

45. Wigon, "The L.A.P.D. Didn't Catch an Alleged Serial Killer for 30 Years."

46. Kathleen Hendrix, "Passionate Pursuer's Crusade Against the South Side Slayer: Margaret Prescod Trying to Raise Community Awareness on the Streets of South-Central L.A. . . . and Beverly Hills," *Los Angeles Times*, Oct. 16, 1986, https://www.latimes.com/archives/la-xpm-1986-10-16-vw-5852-story.html. The article described Prescod and members of Black Coalition Fighting Back Serial Murders going to Beverly Hills, a very affluent community, and distributing flyers about the murders of Black women in South

Central Los Angeles to raise awareness throughout the city and mount a public pressure campaign on the LAPD to investigate the homicides. This bold move raised the ire of LAPD police chief Daryl Gates, who attacked Prescod's actions as "asinine" and the members of her organization making accusations of police indifference as "dummies."

47. According to the Uniform Crime Reporting for 1980, 1985, and 1990, there were 1,011 in 1980, declined in 1985 to 778 homicides, and began to increase again to 987 by 1990, https://cde.ucr.cjis.gov/LATEST/webapp/#/pages/explorer/crime/crime-trend.

48. Nick Broomfield, dir. *Tales of the Grim Sleeper*. 2015; HBO.

49. Broomfield, *Tales of the Grim Sleeper*, interview with Tony, friend of Lonnie Franklin.

50. Broomfield, *Tales of the Grim Sleeper*.

51. Broomfield, *Tales of the Grim Sleeper*, interview with Nana Gyamfi.

52. Broomfield, *Tales of the Grim Sleeper*, interview with Margaret Prescod.

53. Broomfield, *Tales of the Grim Sleeper*, interview with Nana Gyamfi.

54. Murder Accountability Project (MAP), "Police Departments Failed to Report Nearly 3,000 Homicides in 2018," May 10, 2020, www.murderdata.org.

55. MAP, "Police Departments Failed to Report Nearly 3,000 Homicides in 2018."

56. Meleiza Figueroa and Alan Minskey, "Where Black Lives Don't Matter: Serial Murder and Silence in South L.A.," *Truthdig*, Apr. 15, 2015, https://www.truthdig.com/articles/where-black-lives-dont-matter-serial-murder-and-silence-in-south-l-a.

57. Gold and Blankstein, "'It was a terrifying time.'"

58. Christine Pelisek, "The Grim Sleeper Returns: He's Murdering Los Angelenos, as Cops Hunt His DNA," *L.A. Weekly*, Aug. 27, 2008, https://www.laweekly.com/grim-sleeper-returns-hes-murdering-angelenos-as-cops-hunt-his-dna.

59. Wigon, "The L.A.P.D. Didn't Catch an Alleged Serial Killer for 30 Years."

60. Paresh Dave, "Grim Sleeper: Judge Allows DNA Evidence Gathered at Restaurant," *Baltimore Sun*, June 18, 2018, https://www.baltimoresun.com/la-me-ln-grim-sleeper-dna-evidence-20140107-story.html.

61. "Community Member Takes Mic from LAPD Chief," YouTube video, 3:00, July 15, 2010, https://www.youtube.com/watch?v=MTDXClISINU.

62. Dolan, Rubin, and Landsberg, "DNA Leads to Arrest in Serial Case."

63. Pelisek, "The Grim Sleeper Returns."

64. Andrew Blankstein and Molly Hennessy-Fiske, "Man Is Charged in Westside Home-Invasion Heists; 'Silverware Bandit' Suspect Is Accused of Robbery and Assault," *Los Angeles Times*, Aug. 27, 2008, https://www.latimes.com/archives/la-xpm-2008-aug-27-me-homeinvasion27-story.html.

65. Pelisek, "The Grim Sleeper Returns." Porter Alexander, the father of victim Monique Alexander, and Laverne Peters, mother of Janecia Peters, divulged that they learned from investigative reporting conducted by *L.A. Weekly* reporter Pelisek that their daughters' deaths were suspected to be the work of a serial killer. According to the article, the paper was the first media source to inform families that police were linking the cases to a single offender.

66. Christine Pelisek, "Grim Sleeper Sleuth Christine Pelisek Tells Daily Beast: 'How I Tracked Lonnie David Franklin,'" *L.A. Weekly*, July 9, 2010, available at http://www.lacp.org/2010-Articles-Main/082010-GrimSleeper SleuthChristinePelisek-familialDNA.htm.

67. Pelisek, "The Grim Sleeper Returns."

68. Christopher Weber, "Grim Sleeper Case Rattles Jail System," *Winnipeg Free Press*, July 11, 2010.

69. "LAPD Works to Tie 8 More Homicides to the 'Grim Sleeper,'" *Daily Breeze*, Apr. 5, 2011, https://www.dailybreeze.com/general-news/20110405 /lapd-works-to-tie-8-more-homicides-to-the-grim-sleeper.

70. Stephen Ceasar, "The Grim Sleeper Victim Testifies; the Serial Killer's Lone Survivor Was Shot and Left for Dead in 1989," *Los Angeles Times*, Feb. 26, 2016, https://www.latimes.com/local/lanow/la-me-ln-grim-sleeper-survivor -testifies-20160225-story.html.

71. Associated Press, "LA Grim Sleeper Suspect Had 4-Decade Arrest Record," *Deseret News*, July 10, 2010, https://www.deseret.com/2010/7/10 /20127067/la-grim-sleeper-suspect-had-4-decade-arrest-record/#los-angeles -police-investigators-collect-evidence-in-bags-during-a-search-at-the-home-of -suspect-lonnie-david-franklin-jr-on-friday-july-9–2010-in-los-angeles.

72. Ceasar, "Tales of Loss in Grim Sleeper's Penalty Phase."

73. Ceasar, "Tales of Loss in Grim Sleeper's Penalty Phase."

74. Sarah Charman, "Making Sense of Policing Identities: The 'Deserving' and the 'Undeserving' in Policing Accounts of Victimisation," *Policing and Society* (2019): 81–97; police often refer to individuals they view as blameless and "true" victims that deserve protection as "deserving" of the label of "victim."

75. "After 5 Prostitutes Are Killed, Police Crack Down on Clients: A Killer Is Put Away, but Women Are Still Dying in Rochester," *New York Times*, Dec. 22, 1991, https://www.nytimes.com/1991/12/22/nyregion/after-5-prostitutes -are-killed-police-crack-down-on-clients.html.

76. Robert Hanley, "Rochester Slaying Suspect Is Called Kind but Violent," *New York Times*, Jan. 13, 1990, https://www.nytimes.com/1990/01/13 /nyregion/rochester-slaying-suspect-is-called-kind-but-violent.html.

77. "After 5 Prostitutes Are Killed, Police Crack Down on Clients."

78. "After 5 Prostitutes Are Killed, Police Crack Down on Clients."

CHAPTER 5: CLEVELAND IS DANGEROUS FOR BLACK WOMEN

1. Michael Rotman, "Forest Hill," Cleveland Historical, https://cleveland historical.org/items/show/83.

2. US Census Bureau QuickFacts, "East Cleveland City, Ohio," www .census.gov/quickfacts.

3. Kate Warren, "Cleveland Neighborhood Profiles: Highlights from the Data," Center for Community Solutions, Feb. 16, 2018, https://community solutions.com/cleveland-neighborhood-profile.

4. "Blockbusting," *Encyclopedia of Chicago*, Encyclopedia.chicagohistory .org. "Blockbusting" refers to the act of real estate agents using whites' fear of declining home values in an integrated neighborhood to scare white homeowners

into selling their homes quickly for a cheaper price and then moving Black families in at a higher price than the home was actually purchased for. Some of the tactics included having a Black mother with her child in a stroller walk through a white neighborhood and knock on the doors of residents, looking for a friend with a name like "Johnnie Mae." This would give the appearance that Black families had moved into the community, and that more would join in quick succession.

5. "Cuyahoga River," *Encyclopedia of Cleveland History*, Case Western Reserve University, Nov. 11, 2020, https://case.edu/ech/articles/c/cuyahoga-river.

6. Evan Comen, "East Cleveland Ranked America's 4th Poorest City, Study Says," WKYC.com, June 18, 2018, https://www.wkyc.com/article/money /economy/east-cleveland-ranked-americas-4th-poorest-city-study-says/95-565 279641#:~:text=East%20Cleveland%20was%20ranked%20fourth,to%20see %20the%20full%20list; Juhohn Lee, "37.9 Million Americans Are Living in Poverty, According to the U.S. Census. But the Problem Could Be Far Worse," CNBC, Mar. 7, 2023, https://www.cnbc.com/2023/03/07/why-poverty-might -be-far-worse-in-the-us-than-its-reported.html; US Census Bureau QuickFacts, "East Cleveland City, Ohio."

7. Warren, "Cleveland Neighborhood Profiles."

8. Morgan Trau, "East Cleveland Mayor Barely Keeps Seat; Councilman Ousted Following Recall Election," News 5 Cleveland WEWS, Nov. 29, 2022, https://www.news5cleveland.com/news/politics/ohio-politics/east-cleveland -mayor-barely-keeps-seat-councilman-ousted-following-recall-election. Brandon King survived a recall vote by only 19 votes, while city councilman Ernest Smith was removed from office by 150 votes after being accused of inappropriate behavior involving teenage girls and selling alcohol to minors at a party.

9. "East Cleveland Fire Department Without an Ambulance," News 5 Cleveland WEWS, Oct. 3, 2016, https://www.news5cleveland.com/news/local -news/oh-cuyahoga/east-cleveland-fire-department-without-an-ambulance.

10. "Woman Dies After Struck by Vehicle in East Cleveland Where Traffic Light Was Removed," WKYC.com, Jan. 2, 2020, https://www.wkyc.com /article/news/local/cuyahoga-county/woman-dies-after-struck-by-vehicle-in -east-cleveland-where-traffic-light-was-removed.

11. Melissa Reid, "ODOT Working to Replace Traffic Signals After Community Members Protest in Wake of Woman's Death," Fox 8 Cleveland WJW, Jan. 3, 2020, https://fox8.com/news/community-members-hold-protest-candle light-vigil-after-36-year-old-mother-struck-killed-while-crossing-east -cleveland-road.

12. Daniel McGraw, "Cleveland Officer Not Guilty over Deaths of Two People Shot at 137 Times by Police," *The Guardian*, May 23, 2015, https:// www.theguardian.com/us-news/2015/may/23/cleveland-officer-not-guilty -shot-137-times-police.

13. McGraw, "Cleveland Officer Not Guilty over Deaths of Two People Shot at 137 Times by Police."

14. Michelle Dean, "'Black Women Unnamed': How Tanisha Anderson's Bad Day Turned into Her Last," *The Guardian*, June 5, 2015, https://www.the guardian.com/us-news/2015/jun/05/black-women-police-killing-tanisha-anderson.

15. C. Shardae Jobson, "'They Killed My Sister': Police Slam Black Woman's Head into the Concrete in Front of Her Family," 97.9: The Beat, Nov. 18, 2014, https://thebeatdfw.com/2751193/they-killed-my-sister-police-slam-black-womans-head-into-the-concrete-in-front-of-her-family.

16. Dean, "'Black Women Unnamed.'"

17. Dean, "'Black Women Unnamed.'"

18. Dean, "'Black Women Unnamed.'" The writer noted that Tanisha Anderson's death initially received local and national media attention; however, after the death of Tamir Rice, stories about her killing quickly faded from view. The tendency to downplay Black women's deaths from police violence has led to the rallying cry of "Say Her Name" among social justice activists.

19. Jamiel Lynch, Christina Carrega, and Steve Almasy, "Justice Department Won't Pursue Charges Against Officers in Tamir Rice Shooting," CNN.com, Dec. 30, 2020, https://www.cnn.com/2020/12/29/us/tamir-rice-shooting-no-federal-charges/index.html. Officer Loehmann told investigators that he thought Tamir's toy was an actual gun, and that the prepubescent child was a twenty-year-old adult male. This, despite the 911 operator relaying to officers that the person who called police about a Black male pointing a gun was probably a child and the gun was "probably fake." Both officers, Loehmann and his partner, Frank Garmback, were not charged in the killing since federal prosecutors claimed they could not prove that "Rice's constitutional rights were violated or the officers obstructed justice."

20. Eliott McLaughlin, "Tamir Rice's Teen Sister 'Tackled,' Handcuffed After His Shooting, Mom Says," CNN, Dec. 9, 2014, https://www.cnn.com/2014/12/08/us/cleveland-tamir-rice-mother/index.html. An FBI agent in the neighborhood saw what occurred and hurried to Tamir and began to provide aid, while officers called for EMS.

21. Mike Creef, "FBI's Cleveland Division Indicts 16 East Cleveland Officers on Civil Rights Violations," The Black Wall Street Times, Mar. 13, 2023, https://theblackwallsttimes.com/2023/03/13/fbis-cleveland-division-indicts-16-east-cleveland-officers. During a news conference, Cuyahoga County prosecutor Michael O'Malley stated that "the real victim here was the entire city, all the citizens of East Cleveland, who had to live in a city with fear" and described the actions of the indicted officers as a "cancer growing in the East Cleveland Police Department."

22. Creef, "FBI's Cleveland Division Indicts 16 East Cleveland Officers on Civil Rights Violations"; John H. Tucker, "11 East Cleveland Police Officers Indicted on Civil Rights Violations After Video Captures Shocking Brutality," Cleveland.com, Mar. 10, 2023, https://www.cleveland.com/crime/2023/03/11/east-cleveland-police-officers-indicted-on-civil-rights-violations-after-video-captures-shocking-brutality.html.

23. Christopher Hooton, "Cleveland Police Promise to Stop Pistol-Whipping People," The Independent, May 27, 2015, https://www.independent.co.uk/news/world/americas/cleveland-police-promise-to-stop-pistol-whipping-people-10278172.html.

24. Numerous studies have been conducted that confirm incidents of police violence toward Black women that are on par with rates committed

toward Black men and are substantially higher than known incidents of violence toward white women. See Andrea J. Ritchie, *Invisible No More: Police Violence Against Black Women and Women of Color* (Boston: Beacon Press, 2017); Michelle R. Decker, Charvonne N. Holliday, Zaynab Hameeduddin, Roma Shah, Janice Miller, Joyce Dantzler, and Leigh Goodmark, "'You Do Not Think of Me as a Human Being': Race and Gender Inequities Intersect to Discourage Police Reporting of Violence Against Women," *Journal of Urban Health* 96 (2019): 772–83; and Ceylin H. Ucok, "An Intersectional Analysis of Structural Racism and Police Violence Against Black Women" (senior thesis, University of South Carolina, Columbia, 2020). See also Michelle S. Jacobs, "The Violent State: Black Women's Invisible Struggle Against Police Violence," *William & Mary Journal of Women and the Law* 24 (2017): 39.

25. Tyler Carey, "Ohio Supreme Court Upholds Death Sentence for Alianna DeFreeze's Killer," WKYC.com, Aug. 23, 2022, https://www.wkyc.com/article/news/crime/ohio-supreme-court-upholds-death-sentence-alianna-defreeze-killer.

26. Charlie O'Brien, "The Tragic Murder of Alianna DeFreeze," *Medium*, July 24, 2022, https://medium.com/@Charlie_OBrien/the-tragic-murder-of-alianna-defreeze-9edd9dbb6a97.

27. Brie Stimson, "Cleveland Parents of Alianna DeFreeze, 14, Receive $1M Settlement After Her 2017 Murder," Fox News, Jan. 14, 2022, https://www.foxnews.com/us/cleveland-parents-alianna-defreeze-settlement-2017-murder.

28. Staff, "Cleveland Police Charge Man in Alianna DeFreeze Murder Case," News 5 Cleveland WEWS, Feb. 3, 2017, https://www.news5cleveland.com/news/local-news/cleveland-metro/cleveland-division-of-police-to-hold-press-conference-on-alianna-defreeze.

29. Thomas Hargrove, interview, July 7, 2020.

30. Rachel Dissell, "Patterns Persist in the Unsolved Murders of Cleveland Women: Update," *Plain Dealer*, Feb. 27, 2018, https://www.cleveland.com/metro/2018/02/patterns_persist_in_the_unsolv.html.

31. Tracy Carloss and Justin Madden, "Body Found Near East 93rd Street Is One of Several Discovered in That Area Since 2013," News 5 Cleveland WEWS, Jan. 31, 2017, https://www.news5cleveland.com/news/local-news/oh-cuyahoga/body-found-in-cleveland-fuels-questions.

32. Sara Goldenberg, "Authorities Not Ruling Out Serial Killer After Latest Body Found on E. 93rd," Cleveland19.com, Feb. 2, 2017, https://www.cleveland19.com.

33. Kelly Kennedy, "Families of 4 Women Murdered a Decade Ago Continue to Push for Justice," Cleveland19.com, Mar. 29, 2023, https://www.cleveland19.com/2023/03/29/families-4-women-murdered-decade-ago-continue-push-justice.

34. "Cleveland Official Questions Handling of Complaints About Death House," CNN, Nov. 5, 2009, http://www.cnn.com/2009/CRIME/11/05/cleveland.bodies.identified.

35. John Horton, "Would the Imperial Avenue Killings Have Been Prevented If Extra Steps Were Taken?" *Plain Dealer*, Nov. 22, 2009, https://www.cleveland.com/metro/2009/11/would_the_imperial_avenue_kill.html.

36. Lan Urbina and Christopher Maag, "After Gruesome Find, Anger at Cleveland Police," *New York Times*, Nov. 6, 2009, https://www.nytimes.com /2009/11/06/us/06cleveland.html.

37. Urbina and Maag, "After Gruesome Find, Anger at Cleveland Police."

38. Urbina and Maag, "After Gruesome Find, Anger at Cleveland Police."

39. Urbina and Maag, "After Gruesome Find, Anger at Cleveland Police." Journalists described the home as a "cream colored duplex" that was one of a few "better maintained homes" in the community. The house was torn down December 6, 2011.

40. Associated Press, "More Bodies Found at Cleveland Home," *New York Times*, Nov. 4, 2009, https://www.nytimes.com/2009/11/04/us/04rape .html.

41. Horton, "Would the Imperial Avenue Killings Have Been Prevented If Extra Steps Were Taken?"

42. Cheryl L. Neely, *You're Dead—So What? Media, Police, and the Invisibility of Black Women as Victims of Homicide* (East Lansing: Michigan State University Press, 2015); Cheryl Lynn Neely, "News Reflects Views: An Analysis of Media and the Perpetuation of the Invisibility of Black Women as Victims of Homicide in Three Major City Newspapers" (PhD diss., Wayne State University, 2009).

43. Margaret Bernstein, "Crystal Dozier Was a Responsible Child: The Women of Imperial Avenue," *Plain Dealer*, Mar. 14, 2011, https://www .cleveland.com/metro/2011/03/the_women_of_imperial_avenue_c.html.

44. Stan Donaldson, "Tishana Culver Never Lost Her Kindness: The Women of Imperial Avenue," *Plain Dealer*, Mar. 13, 2011, https://www .cleveland.com/metro/2011/03/the_women_of_imperial_avenue_t.html.

45. Stan Donaldson, "Leshanda Long Had a Chance for a Normal Life: The Women of Imperial Avenue," *Plain Dealer*, Mar. 15, 2011, https://www .cleveland.com/metro/2011/03/the_women_of_imperial_avenue_l.html.

46. Stan Donaldson, "Tonia Carmichael Came from Humble Beginnings: The Women of Imperial Avenue," *Plain Dealer*, Mar. 16, 2011, https://www .cleveland.com/metro/2011/03/the_women_of_imperial_avenue_t_1.html.

47. Margaret Bernstein, "Michelle Mason Wanted a Better Life: The Women of Imperial Avenue," *Plain Dealer*, Mar. 17, 2011, https://www .cleveland.com/metro/2011/03/the_women_of_imperial_avenue_m.html.

48. Stan Donaldson, "Kim Smith and Her Father Made a Pact: The Women of Imperial Avenue," *Plain Dealer*, Mar. 18, 2011, https://www .cleveland.com/metro/2011/03/the_women_of_imperial_avenue_k.html.

49. Stan Donaldson, "Nancy Cobbs Doted on Her Grandchildren: The Women of Imperial Avenue," *Plain Dealer*, Mar. 13, 2011, https://www .cleveland.com/metro/2011/03/the_women_of_imperial_avenue_n.html.

50. Margaret Bernstein, "Amelda 'Amy' Hunter Loved Reading the Classics: The Women of Imperial Avenue," *Plain Dealer*, Mar. 20, 2011, https:// www.cleveland.com/metro/2011/03/the_women_of_imeperial_avenue.html.

51. Stan Donaldson, "Janice Webb Didn't Like Being Away from Family: The Women of Imperial Avenue," *Plain Dealer*, Mar. 13, 2011, https://www .cleveland.com/metro/2011/03/the_women_of_imperial_avenue_j.html.

52. Margaret Bernstein, "Telacia Fortson Wanted a Family: The Women of Imperial Avenue," *Plain Dealer*, Mar. 13, 2011, https://www.cleveland.com /metro/2011/03/the_women_of_imperial_avenue_t_2.html.

53. Margaret Bernstein, "Diane Turner Was Poised for a Comeback: The Women of Imperial Avenue," *Plain Dealer*, Mar. 23, 2011, https://www .cleveland.com/metro/2011/03/the_women_of_imperial_avenue_d.html.

54. Leila Atassi, "Sowell's Role as Childhood Rapist Recounted in Niece's Testimony," *Plain Dealer*, Aug. 3, 2011, "Serial Killer's Niece Paints Picture of Horrific Childhood Abuse," Cleveland19.com, Aug. 3, 2011, https://www .cleveland19.com/story/15192687/sowell.

55. Horton, "Would the Imperial Avenue Killings Have Been Prevented If Extra Steps Were Taken?"

56. State v. Sowell, Supreme Court of Ohio, https://www.supremecourt .ohio.gov/rod/docs/pdf/0/2016/2016-Ohio-8025.pdf.

57. Olivia Mitchell, "'There's Life After Trauma': Anthony Sowell Survivor Opens Up About the Struggles of Being a Victim the System Brushed Aside," Cleveland.com, Feb. 17, 2021, https://www.cleveland.com/news/2021/02 /theres-life-after-trauma-anthony-sowell-survivor-opens-up-about-the-struggles -of-being-a-victim-the-system-brushed-aside.html.

58. Laura Paglin, dir. *Unseen*. 2016, Creative Filmmakers Association; Mitchell, "There's Life After Trauma."

59. Paglin, *Unseen*.

60. Leila Atassi, "Pleasant Conversations with Anthony Sowell Turned Violent Without Warning, 3 Women Testify," Cleveland.com, July 1, 2011, https:// www.cleveland.com/anthony-sowell/2011/06/pleasant_conversations_with _anthony_sowell_turned_violent_without_warning_three_women_testify.html.

61. Atassi, "Pleasant Conversations with Anthony Sowell Turned Violent Without Warning."

62. Thomas J. Sheeran, "Judge Drops Remaining Cases Against Ohio Killer," *San Diego Union Tribune*, Sept. 13, 2011, https://www.sandiegouniontribune .com/sdut-judge-drops-remaining-cases-against-ohio-killer-2011sep12-.

63. Eric Heisig, "Cleveland Settles Lawsuit with Living Victims of Serial Killer Anthony Sowell, Refuses to Disclose Amount," Cleveland.com, June 18, 2019, https://www.cleveland.com/court-justice/2019/06/cleveland-settles -lawsuit-with-living-victims-of-serial-killer-anthony-sowell-refuses-to-disclose -amount.html.

64. Mitchell, "'There's Life After Trauma.'"

65. Atassi, "Pleasant Conversations with Anthony Sowell Turned Violent Without Warning."

66. Heisig, "Cleveland Settles Lawsuit with Living Victims of Serial Killer Anthony Sowell."

67. Kim Palmer, "Woman Used Window to Escape Alleged Serial Killer," Reuters, July 6, 2011, https://www.reuters.com/article/us-crime-sowell-id USTRE76562V20110706.

68. Palmer, "Woman Used Window to Escape Alleged Serial Killer."

69. Palmer, "Woman Used Window to Escape Alleged Serial Killer."

70. Kim Palmer, "Father of Alleged Serial Killer Victim Waited for Call," Reuters, July 6, 2011, https://www.reuters.com/article/us-crime-sowell/father-of-alleged-serial-killer-victim-waited-for-call-idUSTRE76508720110706.

71. Adam Ferrise, "City Pays $300,000 Settlement to Two Surviving Victims of Cleveland Serial Killer Anthony Sowell," Cleveland.com, July 25, 2019, https://www.cleveland.com/metro/2019/07/city-pays-300000-settlement-to-two-surviving-victims-of-cleveland-serial-killer-anthony-sowell.html.

72. Cory Shaffer, "Families of Six Anthony Sowell Victims Reach $1 Million Settlement with Cleveland over Detective's Botched Investigation," Cleveland.com, Sept. 17, 2018.

73. Urbina and Maag, "After Gruesome Find, Anger at Cleveland Police."

74. Urbina and Maag, "After Gruesome Find, Anger at Cleveland Police."

75. Associated Press, "Women Still Unaccounted for in Ohio Neighborhood," *Las Vegas Review-Journal*, Feb. 23, 2017, https://www.reviewjournal.com/news/nation-and-world/women-still-unaccounted-for-in-ohio-neighborhood.

76. Ian Urbina, "Neighbor Says Police Did Little About Reports of Violence at a Rapist's House," *New York Times*, Nov. 3, 2009, https://www.nytimes.com/2009/11/03/us/03rape.html.

77. Urbina, "Neighbor Says Police Did Little About Reports of Violence at a Rapist's House."

78. Urbina, "Neighbor Says Police Did Little About Reports of Violence at a Rapist's House."

79. Urbina, "Neighbor Says Police Did Little About Reports of Violence at a Rapist's House."

80. Associated Press, "More Bodies Found at Cleveland Home."

81. Urbina, "Neighbor Says Police Did Little About Reports of Violence at a Rapist's House."

82. Urbina and Maag, "After Gruesome Find, Anger at Cleveland Police."

83. Atassi, "Pleasant Conversations with Anthony Sowell Turned Violent Without Warning"; Tanya Doss, Latundra Billips, and Vanessa Gay testified in court and were interviewed in the *Unseen* documentary about their encounters with Sowell, stating that he told each of them that they were going to die, called them bitches, and reminded them that, as cracked-addicted women, no one would care if he killed them.

84. Kim Palmer, "Ohio Man Charged with Kidnap, Murder of Three Women Found in Plastic Bags," Reuters, July 22, 2013, https://www.reuters.com/article/us-usa-crime-cleveland/ohio-man-charged-with-kidnap-murder-of-three-women-found-in-plastic-bags-idUSBRE96L02J20130722.

85. Associated Press, "Registered Sex Offender Arrested After Police Find Three Bodies Wrapped in Plastic Bags," *National Post*, July 21, 2013, https://nationalpost.com/news/canada/three-bodies-found-wrapped-in-bags-ohio-police-chief-says-one-or-two-victims-likely-as-search-continues.

86. K. Querry, "'You Caused My Baby Great Pain,' Father of Murder Victim Says Serial Killer Taunted Him While in Court," KFOR.com, June 3, 2016, https://kfor.com/news/you-caused-my-baby-great-pain-father-of-murder-victim-says-serial-killer-taunted-him-while-in-court.

87. Emma G. Fitzsimmons, "Discovery of 3 Bodies Wrapped in Bags Fuels a Search in Ohio," *New York Times*, July 22, 2013, https://www.nytimes.com /2013/07/22/us/discovery-of-3-bodies-wrapped-in-bags-fuels-a-search-in -ohio.html.

88. Regina Garcia Cano and Thomas J. Sheeran, "Teen Victim of Alleged Cleveland Serial Killer Was 'a Good Girl,'" NBCNews.com, July 24, 2013, https://www.nbcnews.com/news/us-news/teen-victim-alleged-cleveland-serial -killer-was-good-girl-flna6c10729705.

89. Querry, "'You Caused My Baby Great Pain.'"

90. Cano and Sheeran, "Teen Victim of Alleged Cleveland Serial Killer Was 'a Good Girl.'"

91. "In Cleveland, Killings Show Social Costs of Deterioration," *New York Times*, July 24, 2013, https://www.nytimes.com/2013/07/25/us/in-cleveland -killings-show-social-costs-of-deterioration.html.

92. Ed Pilkington and Thomas McCarthy, "Cleveland Police Criticized as City Asks: Why Were Women Not Found Sooner?" *The Guardian*, May 7, 2013, https://www.theguardian.com/world/2013/may/07/cleveland-police -questions-women-held-missing; Justin Peters, "Did the Cleveland Cops Botch the Search for the Missing Women?" *Slate*, May 9, 2013, https://slate.com/news -and-politics/2013/05/cleveland-kidnapping-the-police-did-everything-they -could-and-it-still-wasnt-enough-to-find-the-missing-women-heres-why.html.

93. Sara Brookbank, "Study: 5 Ohio Cities Among the 50 Worst Cities to Live In," *Cincinnati Enquirer*, June 14, 2018, https://www.cincinnati.com /story/news/2018/06/13/study-5-ohio-cities-among-50-worst-cities-live /697647002.

94. "In Cleveland, Killings Show Social Costs of Deterioration."

95. "In Cleveland, Killings Show Social Costs of Deterioration."

96. "In Cleveland, Killings Show Social Costs of Deterioration."

97. "In Cleveland, Killings Show Social Costs of Deterioration."

98. Spectrum News Staff, "Disappearance of 2 Black Women Raises Questions about Investigations," SpectrumNews1, Nov. 19, 2021, https://spectrum news1.com/oh/columbus/news/2021/11/16/search-for-missing-women-of -color-raise-questions-about-who-is-looked-for.

99. Spectrum News Staff, "Disappearance of 2 Black Women Raises Questions about Investigations."

100. A 2016 study conducted by researchers at Northwestern University School of Law analyzed the amount and frequency of news coverage of missing persons according to race and gender in articles published in four news outlets— the *Minneapolis Star Tribune*, the *Atlanta Journal-Constitution*, CNN, and the *Chicago Tribune*—and found that white women disproportionately accounted for victims in these articles. I found the same patterns of biased coverage in my research and wrote about it in a subsequent book, *You're Dead—So What? Media, Police, and the Invisibility of Black Women as Victims of Homicide*, in 2015. I also included the *Atlanta Journal-Constitution* as a data source.

101. Thomas Hargrove, interview, July 7, 2020.

102. Thomas K. Hargrove, "Black Homicide Victims Accounted for All of America's Declining Clearance Rate," Murder Accountability Project (MAP),

Feb. 18, 2019, https://www.murderdata.org. Data used in figure 1 was re-trieved from this report, and numbers were rounded to the nearest percentage point. The chart reflects the earliest decade that data was collected (1976–79) and the latest and most recent data collected by MAP researchers (2010–17).

103. Rachel Dissell, "Could an Algorithm Help Detect Serial Killers in Cleveland?" *Plain Dealer*, Feb. 19, 2017, https://www.cleveland.com/metro /2017/02/could_an_algorithm_help_detect.html.

104. Dissell, "Could an Algorithm Help Detect Serial Killers in Cleveland?"

105. Dissell, "Could an Algorithm Help Detect Serial Killers in Cleveland?"

106. Mark Pettigrew, "The Preference for Strangulation in a Sexually Mo-tivated Serial Killer," *International Journal of Offender Therapy and Compara-tive Criminology* 63, no. 5 (Apr. 2019): 781–96.

107. Dissell, "Could an Algorithm Help Detect Serial Killers in Cleveland?"

108. Dissell, "Could an Algorithm Help Detect Serial Killers in Cleveland?"

109. Thomas Hargrove, interview.

110. "What's in the Cleveland Police Budget?" Policy Matters Ohio, https: //www.policymattersohio.org/research-policy/quality-ohio/justice-reform/whats -in-the-cleveland-police-budget.

111. Jordan Heller, "Down but Not Out in East Cleveland," Eye on Ohio, Oct. 6, 2019, https://eyeonohio.com/down-but-not-out-in-east-cleveland.

112. Leila Atassi, "Cleveland Council President Rejects East Cleveland Merger Proposal, Says Demands Are 'Non-Starter,'" Cleveland.com, Aug. 26, 2016, https://www.cleveland.com/metro/2016/08/cleveland_council_president _re.html.

113. Jennifer K. Wesely and Susan Dewey, "'I Want That Money Saved for 'Real' Victims: Homicide Detectives' Perceptions of Victims and Impacts on Advocacy and Services for Loss Survivors," *Homicide Studies* (2022), https:// journals.sagepub.com/doi/abs/10.1177/10887679221108327.

114. Wesely and Dewey, "'I Want That Money Saved for "Real" Victims,'" 10.

115. Wesely and Dewey, "'I Want That Money Saved for "Real" Victims,'" 11.

CHAPTER 6: "SAY THEIR NAMES—ALL FIFTY-ONE OF THEM"

1. Maudlyne Ihejireka, "Judge Yanks Bond, Calls Man 'Real and Pres-ent Danger' After Disabled Man Killed," *Chicago Sun-Times*, Sept. 28, 2018, https://chicago.suntimes.com/2018/9/28/18431898/judge-yanks-bond-calls -man-real-and-present-danger-after-disabled-man-killed.

2. Alice Yin and Megan Crepeau, "Top Cop Says DNA Tests Delayed Charges in Woman's Slaying 3 Years Ago: As Ex-Boyfriend Charged, Her Fam-ily Calls for Change," *Chicago Tribune*, Jan. 31, 2020, https://www.chicago tribune.com/2020/01/30/chicagos-top-cop-says-dna-tests-delayed-charges-in -womans-slaying-3-years-ago-family-replies-hurry-up-and-get-a-better-system.

3. Deanese Williams-Harris, "Mother of Slain Woman Found in Garbage Bin: 'It Was Total Disrespect,'" *Chicago Tribune*, Apr. 28, 2017, https://www .chicagotribune.com/2017/04/28/mother-of-slain-woman-found-in-garbage -bin-it-was-total-disrespect.

4. Yin and Crepeau, "Top Cop Says DNA Tests Delayed Charges in Wom-an's Slaying 3 Years Ago."

5. Charlie Goudie, Ross Weidner, and Diane Pathieu, "Man Charged in 2017 Murder of Diamond Turner Accused in Stabbing Death of 2 Others: Police," ABC 7 Chicago, Jan. 30, 2020, https://abc7chicago.com/chicago-news-breaking-police-department/5890890/.

6. Goudie, Weidner, and Pathieu, "Man Charged in 2017 Murder of Diamond Turner Accused in Stabbing Death of 2 Others."

7. "Diamond Turner's Family Grateful but Have Questions After Alleged Killer Arrested," NBC Chicago, Jan. 30, 2020, https://www.nbcchicago.com/news/local/diamond-turners-family-grateful-but-have-questions-after-alleged-killer-arrested/2210628.

8. "Diamond Turner's Family Grateful but Have Questions After Alleged Killer Arrested."

9. Chuck Goudie, Ross Weidner, and Barb Markoff, "Punishment for Concealing a Killing in Chicago? 150 Days," ABC 7 News Chicago, Jan. 29, 2019, https://abc7chicago.com/arthur-hilliard-cook-county-jail-body-in-shopping-card-man-hides-death/5111935.

10. Bob Chiarito, "Man Suspected in at Least 3 Murders Charged—Years After Woman's Body Found Behind His Home," *Block Club Chicago*, Jan. 31, 2020, https://blockclubchicago.org/2020/01/31/man-suspected-in-at-least-3-murders-charged-years-after-womans-body-found-behind-his-home.

11. Chiarito, "Man Suspected in at Least 3 Murders Charged."

12. Goudie, Weidner, and Pathieu, "Man Charged in 2017 Murder of Diamond Turner Accused in Stabbing Death of 2 Others."

13. Ihejireka, "Judge Yanks Bond."

14. Chiarito, "Man Suspected in at Least 3 Murders Charged."

15. Annie Sweeney, "Unsolved Slayings Get New Scrutiny: CPD Checking for Connections in at Least 55 Strangulation Cases," *Chicago Tribune*, May 14, 2019, https://www.chicagotribune.com/2019/05/14/chicago-police-are-taking-a-new-look-at-the-unsolved-slayings-of-55-women-and-the-possibility-a-serial-killer-is-involved.

16. "The Great Migration (1910–1970)," National Archives and Records Administration, https://www.archives.gov/research/african-americans/migrations/great-migration.

17. Dahleen Glanton, "Returning South: A Family Revisits a Double Lynching That Forced them to Flee to Chicago 100 Years Ago," *Chicago Tribune*, July 13, 2020.

18. Glanton, "Returning South."

19. Glanton, "Returning South."

20. Priscilla A. Ocen, "The New Racially Restrictive Covenant: Race, Welfare, and the Policing of Black Women in Subsidized Housing," *UCLA Law Review* 59 (2011): 1540.

21. Madeline Parrish and Chima Ikoro, "Chicago Public Schools and Segregation," *Southside Weekly*, Feb. 24, 2022, https://southsideweekly.com/chicago-public-schools-and-segregation.

22. Sheryll Cashin, *White Space, Black Hood: Opportunity Hoarding and Segregation in the Age of Inequality* (Boston: Beacon Press, 2021), 50.

23. Richard Wright, *Twelve Million Black Voices* (New York: Basic Books Reprint Edition, [1941] 2002), 104.

24. Cashin, *White Space, Black Hood*, 50.

25. Michelle Obama, *Becoming* (New York: Crown, 2018), 32.

26. Obama, *Becoming*, 32.

27. Obama, *Becoming*, 35.

28. Isabel Wilkerson, *The Warmth of Other Suns: The Epic Story of America's Great Migration* (New York: Random House, 2010), 218.

29. Daniel Hautzinger, "The Horrific Violence and Continuing Legacy of Chicago's 1919 Race Riot," WTTW Chicago, Sept. 25, 2020, https://interactive.wttw.com/playlist/2019/07/26/chicago-1919-race-riot.

30. Hautzinger, "The Horrific Violence and Continuing Legacy of Chicago's 1919 Race Riot."

31. Bill Jones, "Headstone Shares Story of Teen Whose Killing Sparked 1919 Chicago Race Riot: Unveiled in Blue Island's Lincoln Cemetery Saturday," *Chicago Tribune*, July 26, 2021.

32. Hautzinger, "The Horrific Violence and Continuing Legacy of Chicago's 1919 Race Riot."

33. Simon Balto, *Occupied Territory: Policing Black Chicago from Red Summer to Black Power* (Chapel Hill: University of North Carolina Press, 2019).

34. Jill Lepore, "The History of the 'Riot' Report," *New Yorker*, June 15, 2020, https://www.newyorker.com/magazine/2020/06/22/the-history-of-the-riot-report.

35. Cashin, *White Space, Black Hood*. Cashin describes Black migrants being "quarantined behind the color line" in slum conditions in Chicago during the Great Migration as whites reacted to the increasing Black population with anger and hostility, using zoning as a method to create ghettos and forbidding homeownership through redlining and restrictive covenants (51). Additionally, the author references interviews conducted by famed Black psychologist Kenneth Clark with Blacks living in Chicago who referred to police as "overseers" who utilized violence and brutality to control the movements of Black people within their racially confined communities (62).

36. Christy Gutowski, "'This Kid Had an Impact on People': The Troubled Life and Fleeting Potential of Laquan McDonald," *Chicago Tribune*, Sept. 14, 2018, https://www.chicagotribune.com/news/laquan-mcdonald/ct-met-laquan-mcdonald-20180904-story.html

37. Gutowski, "'This Kid Had an Impact on People.'"

38. Paige Fry and Madeline Buckley, "Seven Years After Slaying, CPD Seen as Slow to Change: Critics Say Police Reform Efforts Coming Up Short in the Wake of Laquan McDonald's Killing," *Chicago Tribune*, Jan. 31, 2022, https://www.chicagotribune.com/2022/01/31/chicago-police-department-slow-to-make-reform-progress-since-the-shooting-of-laquan-mcdonald-and-still-in-need-of-a-cultural-change-experts-say.

39. Fry and Buckley, "Seven Years After Slaying."

40. Fry and Buckley, "Seven Years After Slaying."

41. Damien Cave, "Officer Darren Wilson's Grand Jury Testimony in Ferguson, Mo., Shooting," *New York Times*, Nov. 25, 2014, https://www.nytimes .com/interactive/2014/11/25/us/darren-wilson-testimony-ferguson-shooting.html.

42. US Department of Justice Civil Rights Division and US Attorney's Office, Northern District of Illinois, *Executive Summary*, Investigation of the Chicago Police Department, Jan. 13, 2017, https://www.justice.gov/d9/chicago _police_department_findings.pdf, p. 4.

43. Fry and Buckley, "Seven Years After Slaying."

44. Emmanuel Camarillo, "In Botched Anjanette Young Raid, Chicago Police Board Votes to Fire Sergeant in Charge," *Chicago Sun-Times*, June 15, 2023, https://chicago.suntimes.com/crime/2023/6/15/23763033/anjanette -young-chicago-police-board-alex-wolinski-botched-raid.

45. John Byrne, "Anjanette Young Botched Raid Settlement: 'No Amount of Money Could Erase What Ms. Young Has Suffered,'" *Chicago Tribune*, Dec. 15, 2021, https://www.chicagotribune.com/2021/12/15/anjanette-young -botched-raid-settlement-no-amount-of-money-could-erase-what-ms-young -has-suffered.

46. Camarillo, "In Botched Anjanette Young Raid."

47. Camarillo, "In Botched Anjanette Young Raid."

48. Anita Padilla, "Angela Ford: Family of Chicago Woman Murdered over 2 Decades Ago Awaits Justice," Fox 32 Chicago, Dec. 8, 2022, https://www.fox 32chicago.com/news/angela-ford-family-of-chicago-woman-murdered -over-2-decades-ago-awaits-justice.

49. Cheryl L. Neely, *You're Dead—So What? Media, Police, and the Invisibility of Black Women as Victims of Homicide* (East Lansing: Michigan State University Press, 2015), 12.

50. James Nesbitt Golden, "'Unforgotten 51' Project Has Roosevelt University Students Telling the Stories of Dozens of Murdered and Missing Chicago Women," *Block Club Chicago*, Apr. 21, 2021, https://blockclubchicago .org/2021/04/21/with-unforgotten-51-roosevelt-university-students-tell-the -stories-of-dozens-of-murdered-and-missing-chicago-women.

51. John W. Fountain and Samantha Latson, "Gwendolyn Williams and Other Murdered Women Whose Lives Mattered," *Chicago Sun-Times*, Jan. 9, 2021, https://chicago.suntimes.com/columnists/2021/1/9/22221431/gwendolyn -williams-chicago-serial-killer-murder-accountability-project-john-fountain -samantha-latson.

52. To compile a complete list of the names of the fifty-one unsolved homicides, I used newspaper articles and other media sources. The most comprehensive article was written by Anne Sweeney and Ariana Figueroa, "Murder on the Margins: 75 Women, Many At-Risk, Have Been Strangled or Smothered in Chicago Since 2001," *Chicago Tribune*, Jan. 14, 2018, https://www .chicagotribune.com/2018/01/16/75-women-have-been-strangled-or-smothered -in-chicago-since-2001-most-of-their-killers-got-away. The reporters listed seventy-five victims; twenty-four of the cases have been solved, but fifty-one remain open, with no arrests or identification of the perpetrator.

53. Don Babwin, "'It Screams Serial Killer': Algorithm Helps Reopen Chicago Cold Cases," *Las Vegas Review-Journal*, May 30, 2019, https://www

.reviewjournal.com/news/nation-and-world/it-screams-serial-killer-algorithm
-helps-reopen-chicago-cold-cases-1675532.

54. John W. Fountain, "'Say Their Names. Say All 51 of Their Names,'"
Chicago Sun-Times, Feb. 21, 2020, https://chicago.suntimes.com/columnists
/2020/2/21/21147953/murder-accountability-project-unsolved-murder
-homicide-john-w-fountain.

55. John W. Fountain, "Portraits of Life: Say Her Name; Say All Their
Names: Reo Renee Holyfield," Unforgotten 51, Dec. 30, 2020, https://www
.unforgotten51.com/2020/12/portraits-say-her-name-say-all-their.html.

56. Jamie Nesbitt Golden, "What's Being Done to Solve the Murders of
Black Women on the South and West Sides? 'Don't Dismiss This,' Families Im-
plore," *Block Club Chicago*, June 7, 2019, https://blockclubchicago.org/2019
/06/07/whats-being-done-to-solve-the-murders-of-black-women-on-the-south
-and-west-sides-dont-dismiss-this-families-implore.

57. Golden, "What's Being Done to Solve the Murders of Black Women on
the South and West Sides?"

58. Jamie Nesbitt Golden, "Serial Killer Task Force Offers Some Hope
to Families of Slain Chicago Women—But Others Ask, 'What Took Them So
Long?'" *Block Club Chicago*, Apr. 16, 2019, https://blockclubchicago.org
/2019/04/16/serial-killer-task-force-offers-some-hope-to-families-of-slain
-chicago-women-but-others-ask-what-took-them-so-long.

59. Golden, "Serial Killer Task Force Offers Some Hope to Families of
Slain Chicago Women."

60. Sweeney and Figueroa, "Murder on the Margins."

61. Sweeney and Figueroa, "Murder on the Margins."

62. Sweeney and Figueroa, "Murder on the Margins."

63. Samantha Latson, "One Brother's Search for a Sister; One Family's
Lingering Quest for Answers," *The Crusader*, Sept. 5, 2023, https://chicago
crusader.com/one-brothers-search-for-a-sister-one-familys-lingering-quest
-for-answers.

64. Latson, "One Brother's Search for a Sister."

65. Latson, "One Brother's Search for a Sister."

66. Latson, "One Brother's Search for a Sister."

67. Latson, "One Brother's Search for a Sister."

68. Pascal Sabino, "After Years of Unsolved Murders, West Side Women
Launch Stop Taking Our Girls Campaign," *Block Club Chicago*, Mar. 2, 2020,
https://blockclubchicago.org/2020/03/02/after-years-of-unsolved-murders
-west-side-women-launch-stop-taking-our-girls-campaign.

69. Sabino, "After Years of Unsolved Murders."

70. Sabino, "After Years of Unsolved Murders."

71. Matt O'Connor and Ray Gibson, "Operation Silver Shovel," *Chicago
Tribune*, Jan. 12, 1996; Pascal Sabino, "Westsiders Were Promised a Say in Silver Shovel Redevelopment. But Decisions Were 'Made Behind Closed Doors,'
Residents Say," *Block Club Chicago*, Feb. 2, 2022, https://blockclubchicago
.org/2022/02/02/silver-shovel-redevelopment-decisions-were-made-behind
-closed-doors-residents-say. Operation Silver Shovel was a 1990s federal investigation into corruption, money laundering, and bribery between construction

companies and city officials that coalesced in contracts to haul construction debris and hazardous waste. Construction companies used an illegal dumping area in the West Side Lawndale neighborhood that was as high as six stories and led to a proliferation of disease, rats, and crime. The bodies of homicide victims were found among the detritus in the dump.

72. Daniel Tucker, "Activists Have Said There's a Chicago Serial Killer Since 2007," WBEZ Chicago, Apr. 17, 2019, https://www.wbez.org/stories/activists-have-said-theres-a-chicago-serial-killer-since-2007/fc06aaa9-1b79-40fc-9ab5-3fc5be263c80.

73. Tucker, "Activists Have Said There's a Chicago Serial Killer Since 2007."

74. Tucker, "Activists Have Said There's a Chicago Serial Killer Since 2007."

75. Neely, *You're Dead—So What?*, chapter 3.

76. Tucker, "Activists Have Said There's a Chicago Serial Killer Since 2007."

77. Matthew Hendrickson, "Video Shows Man Hauling Bulging Suitcase with Woman's Body Inside: Prosecutors," *Chicago Sun-Times*, Nov. 1, 2018, https://chicago.suntimes.com/2018/11/1/18439337/video-shows-man-hauling-bulging-suitcase-with-woman-s-body-inside-prosecutors.

78. Jamie Nesbitt Golden, "Family of Slain Woman Say Her Body Is in an Indiana Landfill—But No One Will Help Them Get Her Out," *Block Club Chicago*, Oct. 28, 2019, https://blockclubchicago.org/2019/10/28/family-of-slain-woman-say-her-body-is-in-an-indiana-landfill-but-no-one-will-help-them-get-her-out.

79. Stephanie Wade, "Family Furious After Man Charged with Killing Chicago Mother Goes Free: 'The Judge Failed Me,'" ABC 7 Chicago, Apr. 23, 2022, https://abc7chicago.com/missing-woman-chicago-crime-murder-trial-security-cameras/11783738.

80. Golden, "Family of Slain Woman Say Her Body Is in an Indiana Landfill."

81. Golden, "Family of Slain Woman Say Her Body Is in an Indiana Landfill."

82. Golden, "Family of Slain Woman Say Her Body Is in an Indiana Landfill."

83. Associated Press, "During Search for Missouri Woman Missing 13 Years Authorities Discover Human Remains," FOX 4 News, Sept. 19, 2019, https://fox4kc.com/news/during-search-for-missouri-woman-missing-for-13-years-authorities-discover-human-remains.

84. Steve Levine, "Woman Whose Body Was Discovered in Southern Ohio Landfill Remembered as a Loving Friend," ABC 6 News, Mar. 15, 2023, https://abc6onyourside.com/news/local/woman-whose-body-was-discovered-in-southern-ohio-landfill-remembered-as-loving-friend-renee-benedetti-rumpke-waste-and-recycling-gene-scott-brown-county.

85. Mary Mitchell, "Why Won't Cops Search Indiana Landfill for Remains of Missing Chicago Senior?" *Chicago Sun-Times*, Oct. 19, 2018, https://chicago.suntimes.com/2018/10/19/18432186/why-won-t-cops-search-indiana-landfill-for-remains-of-missing-chicago-senior.

86. Carlos Sadovi, "Autopsy: Woman Found Strangled in West Side Alley," *Chicago Tribune*, Feb. 24, 2014, https://www.chicagotribune.com/news/ct

-xpm-2014-02-24-chi-autopsy-woman-found-strangled-in-west-side-alley
-20140224-story.html.

87. Sweeney and Figueroa, "Murder on the Margins."

88. Sweeney and Figueroa, "Murder on the Margins."

89. Sweeney and Figueroa, "Murder on the Margins."

90. Sweeney and Figueroa, "Murder on the Margins."

91. Sweeney and Figueroa, "Murder on the Margins."

92. Sweeney and Figueroa, "Murder on the Margins."

93. Thomas Hargrove with Ben Kuebrich, "Afrikka Didn't Need to Die,"
Algorithm, episode 1, June 15, 2021, https://podcasts.apple.com/us/podcast
/afrikka-didnt-need-to-die/id1570192032?i=1000525558184.

94. "Suspected Serial Killer/Rapist Gets Another 100 Years in Prison," Fox
32 Chicago, Sept. 21, 2015, https://www.fox32chicago.com/news/suspected
-serial-killer-rapist-gets-another-100-years-in-prison.

95. Fox 32 Chicago, "Suspected Serial Killer/Rapist Gets Another 100
Years in Prison."

96. Ben Austen, "Have You Seen These 51 Women?" *Chicago Reader*, Feb. 18,
2021, https://chicagoreader.com/news-politics-have-you-seen-these-51-women.

97. Austen, "Have You Seen These 51 Women?"

98. "Dozens of Unsolved Murders in Chicago Prompt Outrage Over DNA
Testing Backlog," CBS News Chicago, Mar. 25, 2019, https://www.cbsnews
.com/chicago/news/pam-zekman-serial-killer-dna-testing-backlog/#:~:text
=At%20the%20March%2025%20hearing,assaults%20and%20658%20
murder%20cases.

99. Golden, "Serial Killer Task Force Offers Some Hope to Families of
Slain Chicago Women."

100. Golden, "Serial Killer Task Force Offers Some Hope to Families of
Slain Chicago Women."

101. Austen, "Have You Seen These 51 Women?"

102. *Mind of a Serial Killer, Nova*, PBS, 1992.

103. Sabino, "After Years of Unsolved Murders."

104. Steve Hendershot, "Chicago's Violence Spike Spurs Ideological Debate," *Crain's Chicago*, Oct. 24, 2022, https://www.chicagobusiness.com/crains
-forum-safer-chicago/chicago-violence-problem-debate-safety-inequality. Hendershot's article points out that despite the high homicide rate in the city of
Chicago, it is lower than New York and Los Angeles, with the majority of
murders concentrated in the South and West Side neighborhoods in the city.

105. A. D. Quig, "What's the Full Cost of the Chicago Police Department?
CPD Budget Doesn't Give the Whole Picture, Former City Analyst Says," *Chicago Tribune*, Nov. 3, 2022, https://www.chicagotribune.com/2022/11/03
/whats-the-full-cost-of-the-chicago-police-department-cpd-budget-doesnt-give
-the-whole-picture-former-city-analyst-says/#:~:text=The%20mayor's%20
%2416.4%20billion%20spending,cost%20is%20over%20%243%20billion.

106. Quig, "What's the Full Cost of the Chicago Police Department?"

107. Quig, "What's the Full Cost of the Chicago Police Department?"

108. Data is retrieved from FBI, *Crime in the U.S. 2019*, July 20, 2020,
https://ucr.fbi.gov/crime-in-the-us/2019/crime-in-the-u.s.-2019. Each year

eighteen thousand police precincts across the US report crime data to the FBI. This information is from the National Incident-Based Reporting System (NIBRIS), known as the Uniform Crime Report (UCR) for the year 2019, and is the most complete data available.

109. Jesse Howe and Andy Boyle, "Homicides in Chicago: A List of Every Victim," *Chicago Sun-Times Graphics*, Oct. 16, 2023, https://graphics.suntimes.com/homicides.

110. Babwin, "'It Screams Serial Killer.'"

111. Austen, "Have You Seen These 51 Women?"

112. Tucker, "Activists Have Said There's a Chicago Serial Killer Since 2007."

113. Babwin, "'It Screams Serial Killer.'"

114. Anne Branigin, "Samuel Little Is the Most Prolific Serial Killer in U.S. History. Most of His Victims Were Black Women," *The Root*, Oct. 8, 2019, https://www.theroot.com/samuel-little-is-the-most-prolific-serial-killer-in-u-s-1838874325.

115. Rachel Sharp, "First Victim of America's Most Prolific Serial Killer Samuel Little Is Finally Identified After 46 Years," *The Independent*, May 19, 2023, https://www.the-independent.com/news/world/americas/crime/samuel-little-serial-killer-victim-yvonne-pless-b2342307.html.

116. Mark Berman and Wesley Lowery, "How America's Deadliest Serial Killer Was Caught, Charged and Tried—but Never Stopped," *Washington Post*, Dec. 2, 2020, https://www.washingtonpost.com/graphics/2020/national/samuel-little-serial-killer/part-two.

117. Karen Zraick, "F.B.I. Hopes Samuel Little's Drawings Will Help Identify His Murder Victims," *New York Times*, Feb. 13, 2019, https://www.nytimes.com/2019/02/13/us/samuel-little-serial-killer.html.

118. Zraick, "F.B.I. Hopes Samuel Little's Drawings Will Help Identify His Murder Victims."

119. US Department of Justice, FBI, "2019: Crime in the United States," https://ucr.fbi.gov/crime-in-the-u.s/2019/crime-in-the-u.s.-2019/tables/expanded-homicide-data-table-6.xls.)

120. Thomas Hargrove, interview, July 2020.

121. Hargrove, interview.

122. Sabino, "After Years of Unsolved Murders."

123. US Department of Justice Civil Rights Division and US Attorney's Office Northern District of Illinois, "Executive Summary," *Investigation of the Chicago Police Department*, Jan. 13, 2017, https://www.justice.gov/d9/chicago_police_department_findings.pdf, p. 4.

124. US Department of Justice Civil Rights Division and US Attorney's Office Northern District of Illinois, "Executive Summary," p. 4.

125. Becky Jacobs, "Plea Deal for Serial Killer Darren Vann, Who Murdered 7, a Long Process Solidified in Final Minutes: Attorneys," *Chicago Tribune*, June 2, 2018, https://www.chicagotribune.com/2018/06/02/plea-deal-for-serial-killer-darren-vann-who-murdered-7-a-long-process-solidified-in-final-minutes-attorneys.

126. Becky Jacobs, "'Done and Over with': Families Find Closure After Darren Vann, Who Killed 7 in Gary Area Sentenced to Life," *Chicago Tribune*,

May 25, 2018, https://www.chicagotribune.com/2018/05/25/done-and-over
-with-families-find-closure-after-darren-vann-who-killed-7-in-gary-area-sentenced
-to-life.

127. Thomas Hargrove and his staff at MAP obtained fifteen hours of interrogation interviews with Vann through a Freedom of Information request
and shared them on the *Algorithm* podcast with host Ben Kuebrich in 2022;
see note 130.

128. "Indiana Serial Killer Claims 'Way More' Victims in Illinois," *Murder
Accountability Project Blog*, Aug. 24, 2021, https://www.murderdata.org
/2021/08/indiana-serial-killer-claims.html.

129. *Murder Accountability Project Blog*, "Indiana Serial Killer Claims
'Way More' Victims in Illinois."

130. Austen, "Have You Seen These 51 Women?"

131. Thomas Hargrove with Ben Kuebrich, "The Algorithm," ep. 1, *Algorithm*, June 15, 2021, https://www.iheart.com/podcast/1119-algorithm
-83051915.

132. Hargrove with Kuebrich, "The Algorithm."

133. Hargrove with Kuebrich, "The Algorithm."

134. Rob Stafford and Lisa Capitanini, "Taped Interviews with Indiana
Serial Killer Darren Vann Reveal More Potential Victims," 5 Chicago, Aug. 25,
2021, https://www.nbcchicago.com/investigations/taped-interviews-with
-indiana-serial-killer-darren-vann-reveal-more-potential-victims/2598499/.

135. "Brent Turvey," Forensic Institute, https://www.forensic-institute.com
/instructors/Brent Turvey.

136. Brent Turvey with Paul Ciolino and Lupe Aguirre, "51 Murders:
Making the Case for a Serial Killer in Chicago," *The Chicago PoPo Report*, ep.
72, Mar. 1, 2020. Comments made by Brent Turvey were in response to questions asked by podcast hosts Paul Ciolino, Lupe Aguirre, John Fountain, and
Samantha Latson. These statements were transcribed by me and used as narrative data for this chapter.

137. Turvey with Ciolino and Aguirre, "51 Murders."

138. Associated Press, "Critical Mass: Volunteer 'Detroit 300' Hit the
Streets in Search of Serial Rapist," *MLive News*, Jan. 14, 2011, https://www
.mlive.com/news/detroit/2011/01/volunteer_detroit_300_hit_the.html.

139. Amy Lange and Fox 2 News Staff, "Detroit Serial Killer Deangelo
Martin Gets 45 to 70 Years in Prison for Murders of 4 Women," Fox 2 News
Detroit, Oct. 6, 2022, https://www.fox2detroit.com/news/detroit-serial-killer
-deangelo-martin-sentenced-thursday-for-murders-of-6-women.

140. Turvey with Ciolino and Aguirre, "51 Murders."

141. Yin and Crepeau, "Top Cop Says DNA Tests Delayed Charges in
Woman's Slaying 3 Years Ago."

142. Mary Stroka, "How Chicago Is Trying to Solve 51 Strangulation Homicides of Women," *A&E True Crime Blog and News*, May 21, 2020, https://
www.aetv.com/real-crime/chicago-female-homicides-police; Murder Accountability Project, "Chicago Police Make First Arrest Among 51 Female Strangulations," Feb. 1, 2020, https://www.murderdata.org/2020/02/chicago-police
-make-first-arrest-in-51.html.

CONCLUSION

1. Kathryn Mannie, "Black Woman Who Escaped Basement Dungeon Says 2 Others Killed by Missouri Abductor," *Global News*, Oct. 19, 2022, https://globalnews.ca/news/9210692/serial-killer-black-women-victim-escaped-basement-excelsior-springs-timothyhaslett.

2. Minyvonne Burke, "Body Found in Barrel Identified as Potential Witness in Case of Missouri Man Accused of Holding Woman in Basement," NBC News, Aug. 8, 2023, https://www.nbcnews.com/news/us-news/body-found-barrel-identified-potential-witness-case-missouri-man-accus-rcna98824.

3. Justice and Dignity Center, "Who We Are & What We Do," https://www.justiceanddignitycenter.org/about.

4. Kansas City Defender, https://www.tiktok.com/@kansascitydefender/video/7147343546595413291?_r=1&_t=8Wdok07J33D&is_from_web app=v1.

5. Associated Press, "Kansas City Man Convicted of Killing 6 Women," NBC News, Mar. 27, 2008, https://www.nbcnews.com/id/wbna23833388. Tony Blair's victims—Anna Ewing, 42; Patricia Wilson Butler, 45; Darci Williams, 25; Carmen Hunt, 40; and Claudette Juniel, 31—were sex workers whom he raped, strangled to death, and dumped in areas along Prospect Avenue.

6. Katie Moore, "'Completely Unfounded': Rumor About Serial Killer in Kansas City Is Untrue, Police Say," *Kansas City Star*, Mar. 2, 2023, https://www.kansascity.com/news/local/article266366851.html.

7. KCTV5 Staff, "KCPD: Social Media Post Claiming Serial Killer on Loose in KC 'Completely Unfounded,'" KCTV5 News, Sept. 26, 2022, https://www.kctv5.com/2022/09/26/kcpd-social-media-post-claiming-serial-killer-loose-kc-completely-unfounded.

8. Weihua Li, "What Can FBI Data Say About Crime in 2021? It's Too Unreliable to Tell," Marshall Project Analysis, June 14, 2022, https://www.themarshallproject.org/2022/06/14/what-did-fbi-data-say-about-crime-in-2021-it-s-too-unreliable-to-tell.

9. Troy Meyers, "University of Florida Removes Years of Campus Crime Data Online," WUFT, NPR News, Apr. 18, 2023, https://www.wuft.org/news/2023/04/18/university-of-florida-removes-years-of-campus-crime-data-online. The University of Florida removed eight years of crime data at the same time that the college was experiencing the highest rates of rape and sexual battery. Without this data, parents and students found it difficult to ascertain the level of campus safety and which areas on campus were the most unsafe.

10. Beth Schwartzapfel, "When Does Murder Make the News? It Depends on the Victim's Race," Marshall Project Justice Lab, Oct. 28, 2020, https://www.themarshallproject.org/2020/10/28/when-does-murder-make-the-news-it-depends-on-the-victim-s-race.

11. Murder Accountability Project, "Why We Exist," https://www.murderdata.org/p/about.html.

12. KC Defender Staff, "New Victim." in KC 'Serial Killer' Case Found in Missouri River, Clay County Prosecutor Admits Greater Public Safety Threat

Than Initially Stated," Aug. 1, 2023, https://kansascitydefender.com/justice
/breaking-remains-of-2nd-victim-in-kc-serial-killer-case-discovered-in-barrel
-floating-in-missouri-river-jaynie-crosdale/.

13. Peggy Lowe, "Jaynie Crosdale, Slain Women Connected to Timothy
Haslett Case, Was 'Full of Energy and Life,'" KCUR 89.3, NPR, Aug. 28, 2023,
https://www.kcur.org/news/2023-08-28/jaynie-crosdale-slain-woman-connected
-to-timothy-haslett-case-was-full-of-energy-and-life.

14. Lowe, "Jaynie Crosdale."

15. KC Defender Staff, "New Victim."

16. Lowe, "Jaynie Crosdale."

17. Julia Jacobo, "Cops Allegedly Dismissed Claims About Abducted
Black Women Weeks Before Woman Escaped," ABC 7 Chicago, Oct. 18, 2022,
https://abc7chicago.com/cops-allegedly-dismissed-claims-about-abducted-black
-women-weeks-be/12340354.

18. "The Myth of Cassandra," Greek Myths & Greek Mythology, https://
www.greekmyths-greekmythology.com/the-myth-of-cassandra. According to
Greek myth, Cassandra of Troy was cursed by the god Apollo for rejecting his
advances so that her prophetic warnings of impending doom would be disbelieved by others, leading to a Trojan horse being used by the Greeks to bring
down the city of Troy. The term "Cassandra syndrome" is used in modern-day
vernacular to refer to valid warnings or alarms about impending disaster being
dismissed by others.

19. Ed White, "A Serial Killer Set Detroit on Edge. Police Missteps over 15
Years Allowed Him to Roam Free," Associated Press, Dec. 21, 2023, https://
sentinelcolorado.com/uncategorized/a-serial-killer-set-detroit-on-edge-police
-missteps-over-15-years-allowed-him-to-roam-free.

20. White, "A Serial Killer Set Detroit on Edge."

21. White, "A Serial Killer Set Detroit on Edge." Family members of two
of Martin's victims blamed police failure to pursue leads, DNA hits, and rape
victim reports for the murders that followed Annetta Nelson's death in particular. Anthony Ellis, the brother of Trevesene Ellis, one of Martin's four victims,
told the press, "My sister would be alive today if police had done their jobs."

22. Briana Z. Ross, William DeShields, Christopher Edwards, and Jonathan N. Livingston, "Behind Black Women's Passion: An Examination of Activism Among Black Women in America," Journal of Black Psychology 48, nos.
3–4 (2022): 428–47.

23. Robert B. Slater, "Black Women Students Far Outnumber Black Men
at the Nation's Highest-Ranked Universities," Journal of Blacks in Higher Education (2006), https://jbhe.com/news_views/51_gendergap_universities.html.

24. Eden Stratton and Anne Marshall-Chalmers, "Sergeants Major Built
a Culture of Camaraderie, as Soldiers and as Black Women," The War Horse,
Oct. 5, 2023, https://thewarhorse.org/half-of-us-army-women-command
-sergeants-major-are-black.

25. Keeanga-Yamahtta Taylor, ed., How We Get Free: Black Feminism and
the Combahee River Collective (Chicago: Haymarket Books, 2017).

26. In 2015, I wrote about blogs such as What About Our Daughters by
Gina McCauley and Journal De La Reyna in You're Dead—So What? Media,

Police, and the Invisibility of Black Women as Victims of Homicide (72–80) as platforms to raise awareness of homicides of Black women and girls and demand effective homicide investigations from police.

27. Kate Storey, "The Podcast That Helped Solve a Murder," *Vanity Fair*, Jan. 9, 2023, https://www.vanityfair.com/hollywood/2023/01/the-podcast-that-helped-solve-a-murder-chris-lambert; Joshua Correa, "These 10 Unsolved Cases Were Reopened Because of Their True Crime Podcasts and Their Supporters," *BuzzFeed*, Mar. 30, 2023, https://www.buzzfeed.com/joshcorrea/true-crime-podcasts-that-helped-reopen-unsolved-cases.

28. Jason Jones, *Knock Knock: The Unsolved Murders of Betty Jones and Kathryn Crigler*, podcast, season 1, Sept. 2017, https://podcasts.apple.com/us/podcast/knock-knock/id1240535421.

29. Richard Schlesinger, "Podcast Spotlights Mississippi Double Murder—Can New DNA Technology Solve the Cold Case?" *48 Hours*, June 29, 2019, https://www.cbsnews.com/news/podcast-spotlights-starkville-mississippi-double-murder-can-new-dna-technology-solve-the-case.

30. Isabelle Altman, "Rienzi Man to Serve Life for 30-Year-Old Starkville Murder," *The Dispatch*, Nov. 18, 2020, https://cdispatch.com/news/rienzi-man-to-serve-life-for-30-year-old-starkville-murder.

SELECTED BIBLIOGRAPHY

The following served as sources for my research.

Eldridge Cleaver and Maxwell Geismar, *Soul on Ice* (New York: Dell Press, 1968)

Eric W. Hickey, *Serial Murderers and Their Victims* (Boston: Cengage Learning, 2015)

Patrisse Khan-Cullors and Asha Bandele, *When They Call You a Terrorist: A Black Lives Matter Memoir* (New York: St. Martin's Press, 2018)

Manning Marable, *Malcolm X: A Life of Reinvention* (New York: Penguin Press, 2011)

Cheryl L. Neely, *You're Dead—So What? Media, Police, and the Invisibility of Black Women as Victims of Homicide* (East Lansing: Michigan State University Press, 2015)

Andrea J. Ritchie, *Invisible No More: Police Violence Against Black Women and Women of Color* (Boston: Beacon Press, 2017)

INDEX

248 • INDEX

Taylor, Keeanga-Yamahtta, 191
Terry, Shirellda Helen (murder victim), 134
Terry, Van, 134–35
Thomas, Lucyset (Mary, cold case murder victim), 158, 160
Thomas, Mary (murder victim), 125
T.J. (kidnapping and rape victim), 183–84, 186
Tomei, Albert, 199n2
Torres, Denise V. (cold case murder victim), 159
town guards (slave patrols), 52
transgender violence, 6–8, 201n18
Tripplett, Andrea (murder victim), 85
Tross, J. S. Nathaniel, 207n21
Trotter, Jazmine (murder victim), 118
true crime podcasts, 191, 192
Tubman, Harriet, 34
Turner, Chester, 85–86, 109
Turner, Diamond (cold case murder victim), 144–46, 159, 164, 171, 182
Turner, Diane (murder victim), 124
Turner, Latonya, 146
Turvey, Brent, 179–80, 181–82, 189, 231n136
20/20 (ABC news show), program on Charlotte murders, 60–61, 65, 69, 73, 74, 77

"Unforgotten 51: The Untold Story of Murdered Chicago Women" (student journalism project), 143, 156–57
Uniform Crime Report (UCR, FBI), 43, 98, 138, 175, 185, 230n108
United States, attitudes toward Black people in, 5
University of Florida, removal of crime data, 232n9
Unseen (documentary), 125, 128, 141
unsolved crimes, impact of, 137–38
uprising of 1967, 202n2
Upshaw, Cheryl (murder victim), 45

Vance, Paula (murder victim), 85–86
Van Dyke, Jason, 154
Vann, Darren, 177–78
Van Pelt, Patricia, 170
victimology, 67
victims of violent crimes, detectives' classification of, 141
Villaraigosa, Antonio, 93, 102

Wade, Gladys (Sowell attack victim), 127–28, 130, 131
Walker, Gloria (murder victim), 131
Walker, Kenneth, 2
Walker, Nancy (cold case murder victim), 158
Wallace, Barbara C., 91–92
Wallace, Henry Louis: arrest of, 59; destruction of evidence by, 208n29; jewelry worn by, 70; murders by, 53, 54, 55–57, 60–61; on police inaction, 70; in prison, 77; sources of information on, 207–8n23; victims' connections to, 71–72, 71f
Ware, Barbara (murder victim), 83, 98, 103
war on drugs, 87–92
Washington, Enietra (murder attempt survivor), 99, 102, 103, 106
Washington, Regina (murder victim), 85
Washington Park, Boston, Massachusetts, 27
Webb, Janice (murder victim), 123
Wells, Ida B., 191
Wesely, Jennifer K., 141
Westside Health Authority, 164
When They Call You a Terrorist (Khan-Cullors), 5
Whitaker, Christopher, 116–17
White, Herbert L., 74
White, Kevin, 33, 39
whites: police response to murders of white women, 108, 170–71; rapes of and police responses to white women in Boston, 36–39;